Global Economy in Transition

The European Union and beyond

Linda A. Winkler
Wilkes University

Harold Codrington
Central Bank of Barbados

(Editors)

Vernon Series in Economics

VERNON PRESS

www.vernonpress.com

In the Americas:
Vernon Press
1000 N West Street,
Suite 1200, Wilmington,
Delaware 19801
United States

In the rest of the world:
Vernon Press
C/Sancti Espiritu 17,
Malaga, 29006
Spain

Vernon Series in Economics

Library of Congress Control Number: 2017943288

ISBN: 978-1-62273-276-0

Table of Contents

Biographies of Contributors

Jakub Bis earned his PhD from Polytechnika Lubelska in Poland. He is a faculty member at Lublin University of Technology, Poland, in the Department of Economics and Management Economics. He is an author or co-author of 34 scientific articles and chapters in monographs including several papers and monographs on Poland and the Ukraine. His PhD thesis is entitled *Role of foreign direct investments in economic development of poorly-developed areas of Poland and Ukraine (Lubelskie and Podkarpackie Voivodships and Lviv Oblast).* His research is concentrated mainly on foreign direct investments and special economic zones. He is a member of Scientific Society for Organization and Management (TNOiK). He is involved as a subsidiary expert in a union project, with the purpose of creating a strategy for cluster "Organic Food Valley" in the Lubelskie Voievodship. He is a member of a science team project entitled *Foreign Direct Investments (FDI) in poorly developed regions – Comparative studies Poland and Ireland, Effects and Threats.*

Ewa Bojar is a specialist in the field of business management and a professor of economics at the Lublin University of Technology. She serves as the Dean of the Faculty of Management, Head of the Department of Economics and Management Economics, Head of Postgraduate Management Studies, and as a guardian of the student scientific movement. Professor Bojar is a member of the Committee on Organization and Management Sciences of the Polish Academy of Sciences, the chairwoman of the Main Scientific Board of the Warsaw-based Scientific Society for Organization and Management, a member of the Editorial Board of the Russian Journal of Management, and a member of the Scientific Board of the International Journal of Contemporary Management (previously Contemporary Management), which is published by the Jagiellonian University. Moreover, she is a member of the Polish Section of the European Regional Science Association and the Congress of Political Economists. The scope of Professor Bojar's scientific and research interests include globalization, foreign direct investments, offshoring and outsourcing, regional policy and regional development, industrial clusters, clustering and cluster-based economic development policy, government-industry-academia relations (triple helix), knowledge management, and corporate social responsibility. Professor Bojar is the author and co-author of more than 200 publications, including 15 books on economics, business management, and regional policy.

Harold Codrington obtained his Master's Degree in Economics from York University, Toronto in 1979. He joined the Central Bank of Barbados in 1979, rising through the ranks to hold the position of Deputy Governor from 2011 to 2016. From 1989 to 1990, he was seconded to the International Monetary Fund as Technical Assistant to the Executive Director for Barbados, Canada, Ireland, and the English-speaking Caribbean. During the summer of 1993, he was a Fulbright Scholar at George Washington University in Washington D.C. He has published papers on the Balance of Payments, Public Transport, Taxation, Monetary Union, Development Issues and Social Partnerships. He was the Editor of the Newsletter of the Barbados Economics Society from 1998 to 2012. He currently serves on the boards of a number of public sector and private sector entities.

Cristanna Cook is a consultant with various international, national, and local organizations. Her specialty is marketing research, and in particular, research into the gem and jewelry industry. She has a PhD in Agricultural Economics with a concentration in Marketing and a diploma as a Graduate Gemologist from the Gemological Institute of America. She is an Associate Professor of Business Administration at Husson University, an Adjunct Professor of Mathematics at the University of Maine, and a Visiting Professor in the MBA program at the University of the South Pacific. Her current research has produced a book on marketing in the South Pacific as well as papers and a case study. She researches supply chains in the gem and jewelry industry. In addition, she studies the economics of animal welfare issues in the South Pacific. One of her interests is the application of macro-marketing to the South Pacific.

Anna Krajewska graduated from the University of Warsaw (Department of Political Economy) in 1964, obtaining a master's degree in Economics. Between 1964 and 2016 she worked in the University of Łódź at the Institute of Economics, attaining the professorship title in 1990. She is currently a professor in the College of Economic and Social Sciences at the Warsaw University of Technology. Her research interests focus on the compensation and motivation of employees, the theory and practice of the operation of enterprises, and tax systems and income differentials. Within the framework of her research activities, she participates in many international programs, including those run by the International Labor Office, World Bank, and International Monetary Fund. She has also prepared reports for a number of government institutions in Poland. She has been awarded four individual awards and several team awards by the Minister of Science and Higher Education, as well as awards from the Rector of the University of Łódź. She is the author of five monographs, co-author of several more, and author of more than 130 scientific articles.

Fyodor I. Kushnirsky has been an Economics Professor at Temple University since 1980. He received his education in the former Soviet Union: a

BA-equivalent degree in Economics, a MS-equivalent degree in Mathematics, and a PhD-equivalent degree in Economics. At Temple, he teaches undergraduate courses in Macroeconomics, Microeconomics, Economics of Development and Growth, Comparative Economic Systems, Introduction to Econometrics, and International Monetary Economics, as well as graduate courses in Theory of Economic Development, Comparative Economic Systems, Mathematics for Economists, and Econometrics. His main areas of research are Transition Economies, Economic Development, and Applied Econometrics. He has served as a consultant for the U.S. government and private corporations and has participated in projects of technical assistance to the former Soviet Union. In the U.S., he has published several books and monographs. His papers appear in the Papers of the Joint Committee of the U.S. Congress and in academic journals such as the *Journal of Policy Modeling*, the *Journal of Regional Studies, Soviet Studies, Problems of Communism, Post-Soviet Geography and Economics, Comparative Economic Studies, Europe-Asia Studies, and the Journal of Economic and Social Measurement.* He also has co-authored four papers with the Nobel Laureate in Economics, Lawrence Klein, and has presented at various national and international conferences.

Walentyna Kwiatkowska is a professor and the head of the Department of Microeconomics at the Institute of Economics, University of Łódź, Poland. She lectures to undergraduate students in economics, as well as to those doing masters theses and doctoral seminars. Her main interests lie in the problems of structural changes in the labor market, income inequalities, and income indexation. In regards to structural changes in the labor market, she researches the sectoral structures of employment, as well as the determinants of economic activity and unemployment. She has particular interests in the labor market in Poland as compared to other EU countries. Her publications include *Income Indexation, The Problems of Theory and Politics* (1993), and *Structural Changes in the Labour Market in Poland* (2007).

Svitlana Maksymenko is a senior lecturer in the Department of Economics at the University of Pittsburgh as well as an affiliated faculty member at the Graduate School for Public and International Affairs and the University Center for International Studies. She has also taught at universities in Argentina, South Africa, and China. She received a PhD in Economics from Temple University in 2006. Dr. Maksymenko's research focuses on policy modeling, economic growth, and reforms in emerging market economies. Her work has been published in *Comparative Economic Studies, the Journal of Economic Development, Macroeconomics and Finance in Emerging Market Economies, the Journal of Policy Modeling, and the International Journal of Educational Development.* She teaches a variety of undergraduate and graduate courses, including Microeconomics, International Economics, and Financial Economics. In addition to teaching at the main campus of the University of Pittsburgh, Dr. Maksymenko directs the Economics summer study abroad program in the Czech Republic and Poland. She has been a recipient of the Senator Edmund Muskie Fellowship, Best Faculty Paper Award of the Northeastern Association of Business, Economics, and Technology, a Hewlett International Grant, and the John Bowman Faculty Grant for expanding the international component of the University of Pittsburgh curriculum.

George Morgan is the SunTrust Professor of Banking at Virginia Tech University where he has been on the faculty since 1984. He currently teaches courses on banking and fixed income securities. Previously, he taught at the University of Texas at Austin and was an economist at the US Treasury's Office of the Comptroller of the Currency. He served as a visiting scholar at the Commodity Futures Trading Commission and at the International Space University. As a member and director of the Center for Wireless Telecommunications, he conducted interdisciplinary research and taught engineers and MBA students. In the last ten years, he developed and now advises the student group that manages $5 million of the University's endowment in bonds, providing an extensive experiential education for dozens of students each year. His research focuses on financial firms' decisions and the effects of regulation. He has published in elite financial journals such as the *Journal of Finance* and the *Journal of Financial and Quantitative Analysis* as well as in *Management Science,* the *Journal of Banking and Finance, and IEEE Communications.*

Andrij Razhyk is associated with Lublin University of Technology and has earned two master's degrees. His Master`s thesis is entitled *Foreign Direct Investment in the Economy of Ukraine.* He is the author or co-author of 6 scientific articles. His research focuses on foreign direct investment in poorly developed regions and their role in regional development. Also his research interests lie in features of accounting and auditing in Ukraine.

Stanislaw Rudolf is a researcher and professor at the University of Łódź, Poland. He is the author of over 250 scientific publications, including several dozen in English. His research interests focus on issues of employee participation and corporate governance. He supervises research on Polish representation in the European Works Councils and the effectiveness of corporate governance. In recent years, his research interests have expanded to cover issues of new institutional economics, particularly transaction cost theory. Professor Rudolf has many duties in scientific and professional organizations including President of the Polish Economic Association (Łódź

Branch) and Vice-President of the Polish Economic Association National Board. Between 2002 and 2006, he was President of COPE.

Katarzyna Skorupińska, PhD in Economics, is a lecturer in the Faculty of Economics and Sociology, University of Łódź, Poland. She is the author of over 30 scientific publications, including over a dozen in English. Her research interests include employee participation, human resource management, as well as labor market and industrial relations in Central and Eastern Europe. She supervises a research project on the role, position, and range functioning of works councils in Polish labor relations. She participated in research projects on Polish representation in the European Works Councils and direct forms of employee participation in Polish companies. She is also a Board member of the Polish Economic Association-Łódź Branch and a subject editor of *Economic Studies of Łódź Region.*

Mark Thorum holds a PhD from the Virginia Polytechnic Institute and State University - School of Public and International Affairs. He received a MA from The Johns Hopkins University – School of Advanced International Studies, and a D.E.A. from the Institut d'études politiques de Paris (Institute of Political Studies) Paris, France. He serves as Assistant Inspector General for Inspections and Evaluations; Office of Inspector General (OIG) with the U.S. Export-Import Bank, where he directs the inspection and policy evaluation functions within the OIG. These roles assess the efficiency and effectiveness of the EXIM Bank programs and develop recommendations for improving program performance. Prior to joining EXIM Bank in 2010, Dr. Thorum worked in senior management positions within two international financial institutions. He has more than 25 years of experience with structured finance, risk mitigation, and capital market advisory. In addition, he has taught courses on international relations and quantitative research methods. His research interests include international political economy with a focus on global finance, financial regulatory reform, and comparative politics.

James P. West is a professor of Economics and Business and a former Chairman of the Department of Economics and Business at Moravian College. He earned a BS from Marquette University, a Master of Commerce at the University of Pune, and a MBA and PhD from Lehigh University. His areas of research and expertise are International and Development Economics, Financial Economics, International Management and Globalization, Development of Economic Thought, and Business and Society. He began his professional career as a developmental economist and rural development project member in Maharashtra, India. His interest in India's economic and political development has led to frequent return trips and projects. He was a Fulbright Professor in Slovakia and won the Lindback Award for Distinguished Teaching at Moravian College as well as a President's award for Faculty

Excellence. Dr. West has served as a consultant and expert witness for various government, business, and non-profit organizations. He served as a co-chair of the Cohen Lecture Series and received a fellowship with the United States Institute of Peace and the Atlantic Council. He also served as an advisory board member for Bridgeworks Business Incubator and for the Great Decision Lectures Series in Bethlehem for many years.

Miron Wolnicki is an Associate Professor of Economics at the Villanova University School of Business. He earned his MA and PhD from University of Łódź, Poland. He is interested in global political economy, international economic policy, and development economics. He has published numerous articles in the areas related to social economics and globalization. He has served as a Fulbright Scholar and has been supported by the German Marshall Fund.

Linda Winkler is currently a Professor of Anthropology at Wilkes University. She earned her PhD in Anthropology from the University of Pittsburgh. Her research interests include global development, international education, global health, and developing broader global partnerships. She has been involved in ongoing international projects in Central America, Africa, and Asia. She received the Chancellor's Outstanding Teaching Award at the University of Pittsburgh (2005), an Incubator Award from the Savings Lives at Birth USAID/ Gates Foundation for her research and partnerships in Tanzania, and awards from Wilkes University, Midland University, and Rotary International for her work in promoting diversity, her international development projects, and career successes. She has published numerous articles and three edited volumes as well as served as an editor for journals on a variety of topics including global development, international education, global health, and anthropology. She has previously served as a co-editor for a conference book for the Congress of Political Economists. One of her favorite endeavors has been developing children's books in Kiswahili for use in East Africa. She is active in professional organizations including as a Board Member for COPE, in the American Anthropological Association, and in Sigma Xi. She serves as a reviewer for several journals, publishers, and grant organizations.

Acronyms within this volume

ARDL: Autoregressive Distributed Lag
BCI: Business Competitiveness Index
BRICS: Brazil, Russia, India, China, and South Africa
BSEC: Black Sea Economic Cooperative
BTI: Bertelsmann Transformation Index
CCC: Cost Conditional on Contagion Events
CPI: Corruptions Perceptions Index
ECB: European Central Bank
EDBI: Ease of Doing Business Index
ES: Exponential Smoothing
EU: European Union
FADECO: Family Alliance for Development and Cooperation
FAO: Food and Agriculture Organization of the United Nations
FDI: Foreign Direct Investment
FSU: Former Soviet Union
G20: Group of Twenty
GCI: Global Competitiveness Index
GDP: Gross Domestic Product
GM: General Motors
GRP: Gross Regional Product
GUAM: GUAM Organization for Democracy and Economic Development
GVA: Gross Value Added
HDI: Human Development Index
IAS: International Accounting Standards
ICE: Information Systems, Communications, and Entertainment
IFC: International Finance Corporation
IIT: Indian Institute of Technology
IMF: International Monetary Fund
IPRI: International Property Rights Index
IR: International Relations
IRA: Independent Regulatory Agency
IT: Information Technology
JNU: Jawaharlal Nehru University
LO: Landsorganisationen i Sverige/Swedish Trade Union Confederation
MB: Machine Building
MC: Monetary Cost
MDG: Millennium Development Goals
MIFID: Markets in Financial Instruments Directive
NACD: National Association of Corporate Directors

NBU: National Bank of Ukraine
NGO: Non-Governmental Organization
NRB: Net Regulatory Burden
OECD: Organization for Economic Cooperation and Development
ONZ: Organizacja Narodów Zjednoczonych/United Nations
PIT: Personal Income Tax
PLN: Polish Zloty
PM: Prime Minister
PRC: People's Republic of China
PSC: Probability of a Systemic Crisis or Contagion
PTK: Swedish Federation of Salaried Employees in Industry and Services
QE: Quantitative Easing
RMSE: Root Mean Square Error
SIDA: Swedish International Development Cooperation Agency
SM: Subsistence Minimum
SOX: Sarbanes-Oxley Act
SSC: Social Security Contribution
STEM: Science, Technology, Engineering, and Mathematics
TCB: Taxes, Corruption, and Bureaucracy
TVC: Temporary workers, vendors, and contract works
UAH: Ukraine hryvni
UI: Unemployment Insurance
UK: United Kingdom
UN: United Nations
UNDP: United Nations Development Program
UNESCO: United Nations Education, Scientific, and Cultural Organization
UNICTAD: United Nations Conference on Trade and Development
UNIDO: United Nations Industrial Development Organization
USAID: United States Agency for International Development
USD: United States Dollars
WHO: World Health Organization
WOMEDA: Women's Emancipation and Development Agency
WTO: World Trade Organization
WWII: World War II

Acknowledgements

We gratefully acknowledge and thank the leadership of the Congress of Political Economists who organized the meetings which led to this book. We thank Ms. Karley Stasko who served as an editorial assistant, spending many hours reviewing and formatting the chapters in this volume, Dr. Marisa Winkler for serving as an outside reviewer and for her manuscript assistance, Ms. Elizabeth Sullivan for formatting tips, and Dr. Paul Riggs for logistical support. Finally, we thank our authors who patiently worked with us in updating and responding to our editing and comments.

Chapter 1

Introduction

Linda A. Winkler and Harold Codrington (Editors)

This volume consists of numerous papers that were presented at the 2015 and 2016 annual meetings of the Congress of Political Economists (COPE). This group, composed of international academics and economic development proponents, has met to present research and discuss economic issues annually since 1990. The papers included in this volume cover various issues in global development and global economic transformation across the world. They address factors affecting economies and development in the member states of the European Union (EU), Ukraine, and select countries in Africa, the Caribbean, the South Pacific, as well as India and the United States. This is a timely and useful volume for several reasons. First, the global economy is in transition, from the 1990s status quo to the "new normal" of heavy reliance on the internet, superfast communications, sophisticated payments systems, the diminishing importance of size and distance, and changing notions of the market. The papers show how this process is affecting economies across the globe and why an appreciation of it will help to underpin efforts by governmental bodies and the private sector to reassess societal relationships - both economic and political. Second, this volume shows that challenges to policy-making and the achievement of social consensus on development issues are often quite similar in all countries, irrespective of size, geographical location, endowment and developmental status. Third, the offerings do not have a singular focus; the research speaks to concerns that touch on a wide cross-section of topical issues which are driving transition and transformation at the national and international levels.

The chapters in this edited volume revolve around international comparisons. As a group, they compare economic factors across transnational economic or political associations (OECD, EU, and G20) or make comparisons across or within emerging markets or small states (Brazil, Russia, India, China and South Africa (BRICS), various African countries, the Caribbean, South Pacific). They include the presentation of a new model for transnational agreements, discussions of policies related to labor compensation and corporate governance, comparisons of nations across the world using indices of economic development and governance, an analysis of gender inequality in employment in the EU, comparisons of tax burdens across the European Union and the USA, discussions of employee representation in corporate governance, and a look at grassroots development and markets in developing economies. As a whole, these contributions make an important scholarly contribution to international economics in their breadth and cross-national analyses.

Harold Codrington (**Does size matter in economic development?**) opens the volume by providing an overview of measures of economic development with his exploration of the relationship between the size (population) of a country and its economic development. His analysis compares performance between states across the globe on five indices that are used to measure economic well-being and good governance: the Human Development Index (HDI), the Index of Economic Freedom, the Ease of Doing Business Index, the Corruption Index, and the Travel and Tourism Competitiveness Index. He identifies various attributes or features associated with small countries and mini-states which can explain their relatively better performance on the indices when compared to large countries.

Several chapters in the volume deal with factors affecting workers including taxation, gender, and governance. For example, Anna Krajewska (**A comparison of the tax burden on labor in Poland and the United States**) discusses and compares the tax burden on workers in different types of households in the 34 OECD countries. She also examines employer tax contributions for social security in the OECD countries. Her analysis provides detailed comparisons of these taxes in Poland and the USA with a discussion of differences. Walentyna Kwiatkowska (**Women and men in the labor market in Poland and other EU Countries**) analyzes the status of women in the labor market relative to men in the EU from 2005 to 2014. Her comparisons look at changes in the activity, employment and unemployment rates. These factors improve for women over the time period included in her analysis, but women continue to lag across the EU relative to their male counterparts. She offers additional insights for these factors in Poland. In examining governance, Stanisław Rudolf and Katarzyna Skorupińska (**The role and position of works councils in the Polish system of labor relations**) look at EU directives and their implementation in labor relations and employee participation in Poland through trade unions and work councils. They conduct a national survey on the activity of the work councils, their position in companies, and the barriers that they face. Work councils in Poland are also compared to those elsewhere in the EU. Stanisław Rudolf (**The efficiency of employee representation in corporate governance in the selected EU countries**) further examines employee representation in corporate governance by comparing German and Swedish employee representation relative to the economic and social performance of the companies involved. He discusses these in relation to corporate governance systems, concentration of capital, the position of institutional investors and the scope of employee representation.

In a continued focus on the EU and transnational relationships, George Morgan and Mark Thorum (**Determinants of transnational regulatory regimes**) develop a model of demand and supply with respect to regulation for transnational agreements. This is explored in relation to the EU. They also discuss conceptual models for the successful establishment of cross-country regulatory regimes and explore the interplay between the private sector, government, and society within these models. Their goal is to provide a baseline economic foundation for discussions of transnational regulation. Miron Wolnicki (**The death of the social contract and the misery of XXI century interventionism**) examines the policies of labor compensation relative to productivity gains. He discusses the relationships between labor and capital in the G20 and OECD and the change in Post-World War 2 growth models as well as policy underlying the development of the EU. He explores the need for fair and economically justified higher wages for labor, suggesting that policy must change to better compensate labor and accommodate new paradigms regarding capital and profit redistribution.

Although not part of the EU, Ukraine is an area of special interest to the Union, particularly after the suggested EU-Ukraine association agreement which proposed free trade and cooperation between the two. Ewa Bojar and her co-authors (**Ukraine in a transformation period: An assessment of Ukraine's investment climate by foreign direct investors**) discuss the reasons why foreign investors might choose to invest, or not to invest, in Ukraine. Weak competition, labor costs, access to cheap raw materials, and opportunities to gain above-average profits are the factors that encourage foreign investment, whereas government policy and corruption are the main barriers. Fyodor Kushnirsky and Svitlana Maksymenko (**Regional growth and poverty in Ukraine**) build an econometric model to forecast and examine regional growth and poverty in Ukraine. They discuss and compare industry, agriculture, construction, and service indicators by region, concluding that mining and the service sector are important to economic growth, while agriculture continues to be important for poverty reduction.

James West (**TCB in India's new ICE age: Lessons for BRICS**) expands the discussion beyond the EU to BRICS. He explores the transition challenges (mainly taxation, corruption and bureaucracy) in emerging markets using the example of India with comparisons to BRICS countries. West highlights India's successes in education and the Information, Communication and Entertainment (ICE) industry relative to cultural values and ongoing challenges. Cristanna Cook (**Western marketing principles in the South Pacific and the decline of communal values)** uses data from the South Pacific to explore the applicability of Western marketing and economic principles in that area relative to traditional values that emphasize communalism. Community values and norms are in decline, but the shift to Western management and marketing concepts has failed to address many of the issues of the small South Pacific states. Harold Codrington (**Barbados at 50: Lessons for other small developing countries**) shifts the focus to two other continents or areas through his examination of economic outcomes and measures of well-being (literacy, life expectancy, and access to technology and infrastructure) in several former British colonies in Africa and the Caribbean, all which emerged from colonialism approximately 50 years ago. The more successful countries of Barbados and Botswana have more stable governments and political environments, are less prone to be overly influenced by ideology, and generally practice prudent economic policies, particularly with regard to exchange rate stability and debt management. Overall, Barbados scores highest on the indicators and reasons for this are discussed. The final contribution in the edited collection is from Linda Winkler (**Grass-roots initiatives driving economic development in rural Tanzania**). She continues the examination of economic development in Africa by discussing the role of grassroots development in rural Eastern Africa and the key components necessary for its success. She provides case studies of several NGOs working in the local community over the last twenty years. Her analysis includes a discussion of key components of grassroots leadership and characteristics important to economic sustainability.

Chapter 2

Does Size Matter in Economic Development?

Harold Codrington[1]

Abstract

This paper addresses the issue of whether small size is a contributor to economic development. The link between size and development is an issue which has been explored by several writers during the last 40 years. These authors use various measures of development and size and their findings show positive as well as negative correlation. However, the use of more recently developed indicators of country performance show that small countries perform better. This paper indicates that it is possible to identify several enabling factors in small countries, which provide a platform for steady or rapid development. These include, but are not limited to, social cohesion or social partnership, stability (lack of security issues), fiscal discipline, high public spending on education and healthcare, less complex governmental structures, and the rule of law.

Introduction

The link between the size of a country, particularly small size, and performance is the subject of this paper. Several writers during the last 40 years have dealt almost exclusively with the implications of size for economic growth and development. However, it has become increasingly evident that size may be a determinant of both economic and non-economic outcomes.

Over time, a number of indices have been developed to measure the performance of countries in several important areas. In this paper, we examine five of them. These are: the Human Development Index (HDI), the Index of Economic Freedom, the Ease of Doing Business Index, the Corruption Index, and the Travel and Tourism Competitiveness Index. These

[1] harev@hotmail.com

cover a cross-section of the attributes that are considered necessary for a country that is doing well: overall economic well-being, an unfettered private sector, good governance, and the country's international appeal in the tourism industry.

An analysis of these indices shows that overall, developed countries do better than developing ones, as expected. However, a more interesting revelation is that, on average, small countries perform better than large ones. There are various indicators of size, but in this paper, we are accepting Paul Streeten's advice that in a choice between population, area and GDP, population is the best measure (1993). For the purposes of this paper, small countries are defined as those with a population of less than 10 million people. Among that group are the mini-states with populations of less than one million people. Large countries are those with populations in excess of 25 million people.

This paper will first briefly list the work of several writers who have addressed the link between country size and economic growth and/or development and specific economic variables. Next, it will explain the methodology underpinning the various indices, show selected country rankings for the most recent year, and comment on their evolution since introduction. Third, the paper will identify a number of attributes or features associated with small countries and mini-states which can explain their relatively better performance on the indices.

The Literature on Size and Development: A Brief Overview

The literature on development is replete with studies about the impact of size on economic performance. Kutznets (1959) and Demas (1965) are among the earliest commentators to promote the issue of country size in economic theorizing by pointing out that the study of development could be enriched if a distinction was made between large and small countries. Halaf, in 1971, analyzed the Lebanese economy from the perspective of size. Other commentators – Farrugia (1993), Armstrong et al (1998) and Ocampo (2002) – were among those who have examined developments in very small economies. Most of the subsequent writing on small countries focuses on the growth of Gross Domestic Product (GDP) or per capita GDP and emphasizes the disadvantages of small size, such as a narrow resource base, the small size of the domestic market, the presence of diseconomies of scale, the specialization in primary exports, and a vulnerability to natural hazards. Khalaf (1974), who examines commodity and geographic concentration, finds that there is no discernible relationship between country size and economic development nor between country size and economic growth, a conclusion

Srinivasan (1988) as well as Milner and Westaway (1993) support. Conversely, Codrington, in 1989, shows that size features prominently in the tax effort of very large and very small developing countries. Alouini and Hubert (2015), using a principal components approach that enables the incorporation of population, GDP, and arable land into one measure, also conclude that country size has a significant negative correlation with economic performance.

Size and Performance - The Global Indices

Notwithstanding the indecisiveness in the literature about the impact of size on economic development, in this section, we examine whether size is a determinant of several economic and non-economic variables. To do this, we analyze whether size affects country ranking on several global indices of performance.

The Human Development Index (HDI)

The UN publishes the HDI, which focuses on 187 countries, every year since 1990. The HDI can be described as a tool to measure and rank countries' levels of social and economic development based on four criteria: life expectancy at birth, mean years of schooling, expected years of schooling, and gross national income per capita. According to its authors, the motivation behind the production of the index is "*to shift the focus of development economics from national income accounting to people-centered policies*" (Mahbub ul Haq, 1995).

With respect to the various criteria, countries' performances are expressed as a value between zero and one, with the higher values denoting better performance. The HDI is therefore, a summary measure of average achievement in key dimensions of human development: a long and healthy life, knowledge, and a decent standard of living. In the HDI, the countries are categorized under Very High (0.8-1.0), High (0.7-0.79), Medium (0.55-0.69), and Low (below 0.55) levels of Human Development.

An analysis of the HDI since 1990 shows that the world's smallest countries are among the most stellar performers. For the 2014 HDI, of the 49 countries listed under Very High Human Development, 21 have populations of less than 10 million; indeed, six have populations of less than 1 million (see Table 2.1).

Table 2.1: Very High Human Development in Small Countries/Mini-states in 2014

Small countries		Mini-states	
Rank	**Country**	**Rank**	**Country**
1	Norway	13	Iceland
3	Switzerland	18	Liechtenstein
7	New Zealand	23	Luxembourg
9	Singapore	30	Brunei
10	Denmark	32	Cyprus
11	Ireland	39	Malta
12	Sweden		
19	Israel		
21	Austria		
24	Finland		
25	Slovenia		
31	Qatar		
33	Estonia		
35	Lithuania		

Source: https://en.wikipedia.org/wiki/Human_Development_Index

Looking at it from another perspective, only 12 countries with populations of 25 million or more are in the Very High Human Development category. Of the five largest countries in the world in terms of population, China, India, United States, Indonesia, and Brazil, only the United States has consistently achieved the Very High Human Development designation since 1990. During that period, China moved from Low to High, Brazil and Indonesia from Medium to High, and India from Low to Medium designations.

The results are the same for the next lower category in the index, which is High Human Development. This includes the rankings from 50 to 102. Thirty-five of the 53 countries listed in this category have a population of less than 10 million; 15 have a population of less than one million (See Table 2.2 for the rankings of the mini-states in this category). Only 12 countries with populations of 25 million or more are listed under High Human Development.

Table 2.2: Mini-states with High Human Development

Population Less Than 1 Million	
Countries	
The Bahamas (51)	Belize (84)
Montenegro (52)	Fiji (88)
Barbados (59)	St. Vincent and the Grenadines (92)

Palau (60)	Dominica (94)
Antigua and Barbuda (61)	St. Lucia (97)
Seychelles (72)	Suriname (100)
St. Kitts and Nevis (73)	Tonga (101)
Grenada (81)	

Source: https://en.wikipedia.org/wiki/Human_Development_Index

In sum, of the 102 countries that are described as having Very High or High Human Development, 55 have populations of less than 10 million (with 21 having populations of less than one million), while only 24 have populations exceeding 25 million (see Figure 2.1).

Figure 2.1: Shares accruing to countries ranked as having Very High or High Human Development

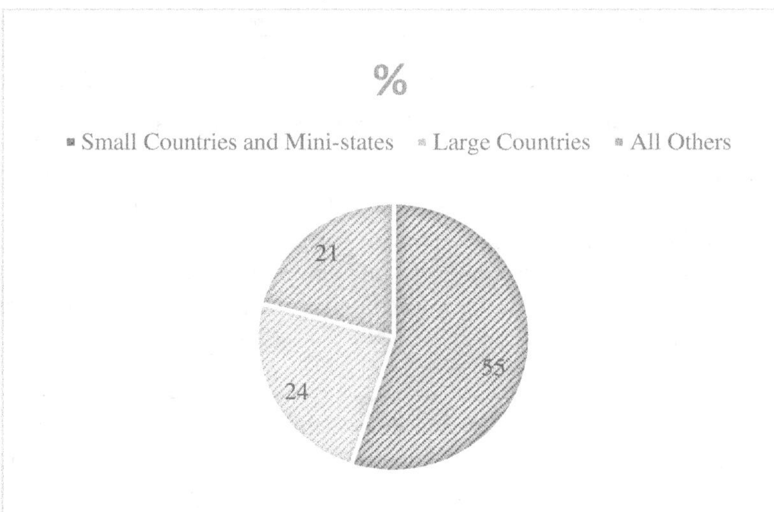

Source: https://en.wikipedia.org/wiki/Human_Development_Index

Another interesting observation is that the smaller countries have continued to perform creditably irrespective of the global economic circumstances. The time period since 1990 provides a good example of the global business cycle at work, with years of steady economic growth interrupted by recession in 1990-93, 1998, 2001-02, and 2008-09. Since 1990, small countries have been consistently high performers. The following small states have been among the top 25 performers during this period: Norway, Switzerland, New Zealand, Denmark, Iceland, Ireland, Sweden, Israel, Austria, Luxembourg, and Finland. Indeed, Norway has held the top position for most of the time since 2000. The mini-states have also largely maintained their relatively good Very High or High HDI rankings throughout the period (See Table 2.3).

Table 2.3: Rankings for Small countries or Mini-states with Very High or High HDI

1990		2000		2008		2013	
Rank	**Country**	**Rank**	**Country**	**Rank**	**Country**	**Rank**	**Country**
12	Iceland	10	Luxembourg	13	Iceland	13	Iceland
15	Luxembourg	14	Iceland	14	Luxembourg	23	Luxembourg
16	Brunei	24	Brunei	30	Cyprus	30	Brunei
34	Malta	31	Cyprus	31	Brunei	32	Cyprus
38	Cyprus	40	Malta	41	Malta	39	Malta
44	Barbados	41	The Bahamas	47	The Bahamas	51	The Bahamas
		46	Barbados	50	Montenegro	59	Barbados
				52	Barbados		

Source: https://en.wikipedia.org/wiki/Human_Development_Index

However, over time there has been some fall in the rankings of those mini-states (like the Bahamas and Barbados) that were very dependent on tourism and financial services. Foreign exchange earnings from those activities have been adversely impacted by the economic downturn which took root in 2008, leading to declining revenue for governments and lower disposable incomes for the populace.

Per Capita Income

When we consider growth of income per capita rather than income levels, again we find small countries among the top performers. In fact, the richest countries in the world in 2013, using various measures of income per capita, are the tiny jurisdictions of Liechtenstein and Monaco, with populations of 37,000 and 36,000, respectively. Ignoring countries with populations of less than 100,000, the picture is the same. Among the 25 leading countries using all methodologies, there are 15 small states including two mini-states. Luxembourg was the best performer across the four methodologies.

Index of Economic Freedom

The Index of Economic Freedom, a creation of the Heritage Foundation and *The Wall Street Journal*, covers 178 countries. This measure speaks to the fundamental right of every human to control his or her own labor and property. When a society is free, individuals can work, produce, consume, and invest in any way they please. Governments allow labor, capital, and goods to move freely, and refrain from coercion or constraint of liberty beyond the extent necessary to protect and maintain liberty itself. The major components of this index are: the Rule of Law (property rights and freedom from corruption), Limited Government (fiscal freedom and government spending), Regulatory Efficiency (business freedom, labor freedom, and monetary freedom), and Open Markets (trade freedom, investment freedom, and financial freedom). Countries are ranked as Free, Mostly Free, Moderately Free, Mostly Unfree and Repressed.

For the 2014 assessment, the dominance of smaller countries is evident.

Table 2.4: Rankings for Top Performing Small Countries in 2014

Rank	Country
1	Hong Kong
2	Singapore
3	Switzerland
4	New Zealand
8	Mauritius
9	Ireland
19	Denmark
11	Estonia

Source: www.heritage.org/index

Table 2.5: Ranking for Top Performing Mini-states in 2014

Rank	Country
16	Luxembourg
23	Iceland
33	St. Lucia
36	The Bahamas
40	Brunei
45	Barbados
46	Cyprus

Source: www.heritage.org/index

Among the 35 countries rated as Free or Mostly Free, 19 are small countries or mini-states and only eight have populations in excess of 25 million (see Figure 2.2).

Figure 2.2: Shares Accruing to Countries Rated Free or Mostly Free

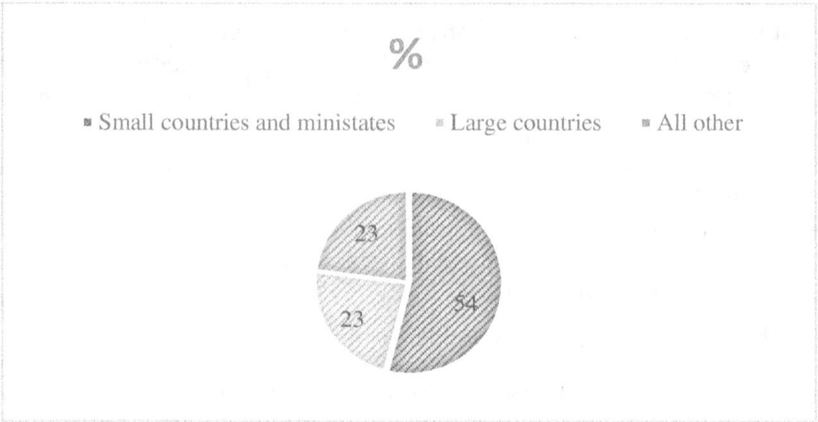

Source: Created with data from www.heritage.org/index

Since 1995, among the countries that are not dependencies or provinces of another state, Singapore is ranked at number one throughout. Ireland, Denmark, Estonia, Mauritius, Botswana, and Finland have all shown significant improvement in their rankings. Iceland and Barbados are the mini-states and Canada the only large country to attain a significantly higher ranking during this period.

The Ease of Doing Business Index

This index is published by the World Bank Group and categorizes 189 countries (Doing Business, 2017). The index relies on economic research and surveys conducted by the World Bank. It speaks to several factors which directly affect how business is conducted: starting a business, dealing with construction permits, getting electricity, registering property, accessing credit, protecting investors, paying taxes, trading across borders, enforcing contracts, and resolving insolvency.

For 2014, small countries featured in this index are shown in Table 2.6.

Table 2.6: Ease of Doing Business Index in 2014 for Small Countries

Rank	Country
1	Singapore
2	New Zealand
4	Denmark
6	Norway

9	Finland
11	Sweden
12	Iceland
13	Ireland
17	Estonia
21	Austria
22	United Arab Emirates
23	Latvia
24	Lithuania
28	Mauritius
30	Macedonia

Source: Doing Business (2016)

Half of the top 30 positions are occupied by small countries or mini-states, but mini-states as a group do not perform as well. Besides Iceland, other mini-states are ranked as follows: Luxembourg (59), Cyprus (64), Samoa (67), Tonga (69), Vanuatu (76), Bahamas (84) Antigua (89), Malta (94), Dominica (97), St. Lucia (100), and Barbados (106). Only seven large countries are in the top 30.

With respect to performance on the various categories of the index, Singapore is first in two (trading across borders and enforcing contracts) and New Zealand is first in three (starting a business, getting credit, and enforcing minority interests). South Korea is the only large country to dominate a category, namely dealing with construction permits.

The Corruption Index

This index, first launched in 1995, has been credited with putting corruption on the front burner. It is a product of Transparency International and ranks 177 countries on a scale ranging from 100 (very clean) to zero (very corrupt) relying on expert assessments and opinion surveys (see: www.transparency.org/research/cpi/overview). It is a composite index, a combination of polls drawing on corruption-related data collected by a variety of reputable institutions, and the views of observers from around the world, including experts living and working in the countries and territories evaluated. One drawback of this index is that it uses a different methodology every year which makes year-to-year comparisons very difficult.

For the 2014 assessment (Table 2.7), 19 of the top 30 countries are small countries and of these five are mini-states. Only six large countries are in the top 30. Since its inception, New Zealand, Denmark, Singapore, Finland,

Sweden, and Switzerland have always been among the top 10. Canada is the only large country to achieve this. With respect to mini-states, Iceland is a top 10 performer early in the rankings, while Barbados is ranked among the top 25 beginning in 2006.

Table 2.7: The Corruption Index 2014: small countries and mini-states

Rank	Country
1	Denmark
2	New Zealand
3	Finland
4	Sweden
5	Norway
6	Switzerland
7	Singapore
9	Luxembourg
12	Iceland
17	Barbados; Ireland
21	Uruguay
23	Austria
24	The Bahamas
25	United Arab Emirates
26	Estonia; Qatar
29	St. Vincent and the Grenadines
30	Bhutan

Source: www.transparency.org

The Travel and Tourism Competitiveness Index

This index, which ranks 139 countries, was first published by the World Economic Forum in 2007. It measures the factors and policies that make a country a viable place in which to invest in the travel and tourism sector. In this regard, it focuses on the regulatory framework, the business environment and infrastructure, and human, cultural, and natural resources.

This is the only index in which the large countries dominated. The 2014 rankings show Spain, France, Germany, the United States, and the United Kingdom holding positions one through five, with Italy, Japan, and Canada at positions eight through 10. The top 30 includes 12 large countries and 13 small countries (including two mini-states). During the last decade, several large countries are consistently top performers and some (Spain and France deserve mention) have improved their rankings. Among the small countries,

Switzerland and Sweden have remained very competitive, but only three mini-states (Iceland, Luxembourg, and Barbados) have been highly-ranked (*see Table 2.8*).

Table 2.8: Travel and Tourism Competitiveness Index 2014: Small Countries and Mini-states

Rank	Country
6	Switzerland
11	Singapore
12	Austria
16	New Zealand
18	Iceland
19	Ireland
20	Norway
22	Finland
23	Sweden
24	United Arab Emirates
26	Luxembourg
27	Denmark
28	Barbados

Source: https:/en.wikipedia.org/wiki/Travel_and_Tourism_Competitiveness_Report

Some Possible Explanations

Overall, there is some evidence that smaller countries take on the characteristics of the states in their geographical region. This would help to explain why Iceland, Malta, and Cyprus perform as well as the large economies of Western Europe on several indices and why, in the Western Hemisphere, the highest per capita incomes outside of the United States and Canada are found in some of the smallest islands. Are there other reasons for the good performance of small countries and mini-states on the global indices?

The HDI

In a 1989 paper, this author demonstrates that mini-state developing countries are better at collecting taxes than large ones. This means that they are more capable of raising the necessary revenues to finance healthcare and education, which promote longevity and literacy, two important planks of the HDI. There is also evidence that some small countries and mini-states spend more per capita on health and education than large developing countries and indeed, some developed ones (For example, see https://en.wikipedia.org/list_of_countries_by_total_health_expenditure_per_capita). In addition, the smaller the country, the more likely it is that remittances from abroad can make a significant difference to disposable income much of which is spent on health and education, and through the circular flow of income, positively impacts per capita GDP. Furthermore, smaller countries receive higher foreign aid per capita and this augments government revenue. Moreover, given the small populations, even modest increases in GDP can translate into high per capita incomes.

Economic Freedom

Societal consensus is important for upholding the rule of law and keeping governments in check as well as preserving aspects of regulatory freedom. Small countries have sociological and political advantages in achieving greater social cohesion. The smallness of the population provides better information for internal partners, thus reducing the possibility of information asymmetries and moral hazard. It favors better social cohesion and facilitates the relationship between state and citizen thereby reducing the "*distance*" between policy-makers and policy-takers. Official social partnership programs that exist mainly in smaller countries like Ireland and Barbados allow dialogue that helps to remove distrust and suspicion, and thus facilitates labor market freedom. In addition, several small countries or mini-states have retained colonial rule longer than other countries and may have absorbed many of the cultural norms of the colonial power. For example, the small countries and mini-states in the Anglophone Caribbean imported the Westminster parliamentary system that brings with it regular, fair elections, respect for the rule of law, and political stability.

Ease of Doing Business

Social consensus is also an important determinant of the investment climate and economic growth since it promotes labor market stability that is attractive to investors. Apart from that, small countries have closely integrated societies containing an intricate network of personal relationships. These factors facilitate communication between private investors and bureaucrats. Accordingly, ideas and requests for information or complaints about difficult processes can be communicated easily, thereby cutting out long delays. Essentially, smaller bureaucracies give rise to fewer difficulties in doing business.

With respect to the poor showing of mini-states on this index, one reason may be a tendency to stave off any criticism that they are not serious about doing business by making many of the associated requirements as difficult as possible. This is quite evident in those mini-states that rely heavily on the international financial sector, which sometimes go overboard in trying to keep out entities that may damage the country's reputation. In addition, to the extent that these countries are emerging economies, there is still some way to go in fully embracing the use of information technology and, thus, some tasks are still done manually thereby delaying the process.

Corruption

Small size, on average, should mean that there are more personal linkages per head of population. Small size can compromise underhand dealings since secret transactions are more difficult to conduct because of the higher likelihood that someone will find out. To the extent that there is a less complex system of economic and financial relations in small countries, the stakes may be somewhat lower. It may also be the case that the high per capita incomes in the smaller countries allow for relatively high salaries and benefits to be paid to public servants, thereby reducing the possibility of corruption. This political stability, which is a feature of most smaller countries, is also beneficial because it prevents the creation of an environment in which there is a weak bureaucracy or vulnerable politicians and civil servants who are susceptible to corruption.

Travel and Tourism Competitiveness

Each country in the world has a tourism industry and is therefore in competition with every other country. Accordingly, they all naturally allocate resources to several of the factors that influence this index. For example, high priority must be given to maintaining the air transport infrastructure, ground and port infrastructure, and tourist service infrastructure. There is also the need to pay attention to environmental sustainability and the management of natural and cultural resources, safety and security, health and hygiene, and information technology (IT) readiness. The highly developed, large democracies are clearly better able than the less-endowed countries to do so and would have a higher degree of societal buy-in for issues like environmental sustainability. These types of considerations are also important for smaller countries that are competing in the upper end of the tourism market, since these factors, in particular IT readiness, would make a country more appealing to the high net worth demographic.

Conclusions

The literature is inconclusive about the role of size in economic development; small countries and mini-states by and large outperform the large country economies on a variety of global economic and non-economic yardsticks. Casual observance seems to suggest there may be a set of factors that facilitate this outcome. These include, but are not limited to, social cohesion or social partnership, political stability (lack of security issues), fiscal discipline, high public spending relative to GDP on education and healthcare, less complex governmental structures, and respect for the rule of law.

The observations in this paper confirm the view long held by some social scientists that size is not necessarily an impediment to performance. There is a set of small states that are in the top 20 places on all the indices. These are Singapore, New Zealand, and Ireland; Switzerland was a top performer in four out the five indices. Iceland has also received a high ranking across the board and other developing mini-states have improved their standing throughout time. One group of mini-states, which deviates from this pattern, is those in the South Pacific, which signifies that remoteness may be an issue in some cases. An examination of the areas in which mini-states are deficient shows that significant improvement can occur if there is the political will on the part of the governments to enact and enforce necessary legislation, forge alliances with the private sector and civil society, and increase public awareness of the issues.

The realization that small size could be an advantage and not a hindrance to achieving excellence is good news for smaller countries. It adds more substance to the call for new models of development that de-emphasize physical endowments in favor of more qualitative attributes. Taken alongside the improvements in IT that continue to narrow the so-called "*digital divide*" and expose small countries, especially those in the developing world, to more modern and efficient banking and payment systems, telecommunications, and distance learning, this could lead to a real leveling of the playing field that augurs well for smaller jurisdictions.

References

Alouini, O., and Hubert, P. (2015). *Country size, economic performance and volatility.* Paper presented at the OFCE Seminar, Paris France.

Armstrong, H., De Kervenoael, R., Li, X., & Read, R. (1998). A comparison of the economic performance of different micro-states and between micro-states and larger countries, *World Development.* 26 (4), 639-656.

Codrington, H. (1989). Country size and taxation in developing countries. *Journal of Development Studies.* 25 (4), 508-520.

Doing Business (2016). Retrieved from http://www.doingbusiness.org/rankings.

Demas. (1965). *The economics of development in small countries with special reference to the Caribbean.* Montreal: McGill.

Farrugia, C. (1993). The special working environment of senior administrators in small states. *World Development.* 21 (2), 221-226.

Halaf. (1971). *Economic implications of the size of nations.* Leyden: Brill.

Human Development Index. Retrieved from https://en.wikipedia.org/wiki/Human_Development_Index.

Index of Economic Freedom (2014). Retrieved from www.heritage.org/index.

Khalaf, N., (1974). Country size and trade concentration. *Journal of Development Studies.* 11 (1), 81-85.

Kutznets, S. (1959). *Six lectures on economic growth.* Illinois: the Free Press of Glencoe.

List of countries by total health expenditure per capita. Retrieved from https://en.wikipedia.org/wiki/List_of_countries_by_total_health_expenditure_per_capita.

Mahbub ul Haq (1995). *Reflections on human development.* Oxford: Oxford University Press.

Milner, C., and Westaway, T. (1993). Country size and the medium-term growth process: some cross-country evidence. *World Development.* 21 (2), 203-211.

Ocampo, J. A., Executive Secretary ECLAC. (2002, May). Small Economies in the Face of Globalization. *3rd William G. Demas Memorial Lecture,* Cayman Islands.

Srinivasan, T. (1988). Population growth and economic development. *Journal of Policy Modeling.* 10 (1), 7-28.

Streeten, P. (1993). The special problems of small countries. *World Development,* 21 (2), 197-202.

Transparency International. Retrieved from http://www.transparency.org/research/cpi/overview.

Travel and Tourism Competitiveness Report (2016) Retrieved from https://reports.weforum.org/travel-and-tourism-competitiveness-report-2015/.

Chapter 3

A Comparison of the Tax Burden on Labor in Poland and the United States

Anna Krajewska[2]

Abstract

Tax wedge consists of three components: personal income tax and the social security contributions paid by the employee and employer. OECD statistical data on tax wedge are a convenient and reliable tool which can be used to show differences in such labor taxation between countries. OECD includes 34 countries that differ economically as well as according to their social state. Therefore, it is not surprising that tax wedge in those countries is significantly diversified. In a comparative analysis of the tax wedge in OECD countries, the focus is on Poland and the United States. Compared to the other OECD members, Poland's and the United States' level of tax wedge can be considered as moderate. Taxes exercise different functions including fiscal, economic stimulation, stabilization, and redistribution. Statistical data (for 2013) is used to compare labor taxation of different household types in Poland, USA and the other OECD countries taking into account non-fiscal functions. Comparative analysis includes the following household types:

1) A single person without children at the different levels of income: 67% of average wage, average wage, 167% of average wage;
2) A single person at 67% of average wage, no child and with two children;
3) A single person at 100% of average wage, no child and one-earner married couple at 100% of average wage, two children;
4) A single person at 167% of average wage, no child and two-earner married couple, one at 100% average wage and the other at 67%, two children;
5) Two-earner married couple, one at 100% of average wage and the other at 33% of average wage – no child and two children.

---

[2] annakraj@uni.lodz.pl

The analysis of this data shows very little progressiveness in the Polish tax wedge, meaning that it does not take under consideration the employee's level of income and his/her family situation. Moreover, the internal structure of the Polish tax wedge is also quite unusual because of the high share of insurance contributions. This article discusses reasons why Polish tax wedge is so different compared to the United States and other countries as well as defining the economic and social consequences of these differences.

Introduction

The economic and financial crisis which began in 2008 led to a drop in budget revenues from taxes. The structure of these revenues has also changed (Eurostat, 2014). Statistical data show that taxes on capital have fallen at the fast rate while the taxes on labor are falling slowly (Krajewska, 2013). At the same time, income inequalities are rapidly increasing, especially property inequality (Piketty, 2015), which leads to negative economic and social consequences.

It therefore seems appropriate to show the tax burden on labor in the OECD member countries, with special focus on two countries: the United States and Poland. The United States is a country with a consistently liberal socio-economic policy. On the other hand, Poland is an example of a country going through systemic transformation, in a clearly liberal direction of changes. Taxes are an important element of income redistribution. Therefore, it is worth comparing labor taxation systems operating in both countries as well as in the context of other OECD countries.

Statistical data used in this paper come from OECD surveys of all 34 member nations on their labor tax burden (OECD, 2014). The OECD calculates this tax burden by adding together the personal income tax (PIT), employees' and employers' social security contributions and other taxes put on labor.

Tax wedge is defined as total taxes put on labor expressed as a percentage of labor costs.

$$tax\ wedge = \frac{PIT + SSC\ of\ employee + SSC\ of\ employer}{labour\ costs} \times 100$$

$$labour\ costs = gross\ wage + SSC\ of\ employer$$

Taxation of labor in the United States

There are two major types of taxes levied on labor in the United States (Pomerleau, 2014):

1) Individual Income Taxes levied by the federal, state, and sometimes, local governments. They fund the general operations of government.
2) Social Security Contributions levied on both the employee and the employer. They fund programs such as Social Security, Medicare and Unemployment Insurance Funds.

Federal Individual Income Tax has a progressive rate structure with marginal rates that range from 10% on the first $ 9,075 of taxable income to as high as 39.6% on income over $ 406,750 (see Table 3.1). According to IRS data from 2011, 50% of all tax payers have adjusted gross income of $ 34,824 or below. On the other hand, 1% of all tax payers have income over $ 388,905 (Pomerleau, 2013).

Table 3.1: Taxable Income Brackets and Rates, in $ (2014)

Rate	Single filers	Married joint filers	Head of household filers
10%	0 to 9,075	0 to 18,150	0 to 12,950
15%	9,076 to 36,900	18,151 to 73,800	12,951 to 49,400
25%	36,901 to 89,350	73,801 to 148,850	49,401 to 127,550
28%	89,351 to 186,350	148, 851 to 226,850	127, 551 to 206,600
33%	186,351 to 405,100	226,851 to 405,100	206,601 to 405,100
35%	405,101 to 406,750	405,101 to 457,600	405,101 to 432,200
39%	406,751+	457,601+	432,201+

Source: OECD (2014)

The United States, similar to most OECD countries, provides some tax reliefs. For example, in 2013, the Child Tax Credit and the personal exemption reduced the tax burden of families with two children (a rate of 20.3%) by 35.1% compared to the tax burden on a single, childless worker (a rate of 31.3%). Lower-income workers with children also benefited more from the Earned Income Tax Credit than lower–income workers without children (OECD, 2014).

Social Security contributions (in 2014) consist of two parts:

1) Social Security – 12.4% is levied from one dollar on individual income up to a cap of $ 117,000. The tax is paid half by employers and half by employees.
2) Tax to fund Medicare has a progressive rate: 2.9% ($ 117,000 – $ 199,000) and 3.8% ($ 200,000 and over). This tax is also split evenly between employers and employees.

Employers are also obliged to pay additional tax to fund Unemployment Insurance (UI). UI is a joint federal-state insurance program that insures workers against an unexpected loss of income due to losing one's job. The federal unemployment tax is 6% on the first $ 7,000 of payroll. States also set UI tax rates and bases which can vary substantially.

Taxation of labor in Poland

The tax burden on labor in Poland consists of three components:

1) Personal Income Tax (PIT),
2) Social Security Contributions (SSC) paid by employees and employers,
3) Other taxes on labor levied on employers, namely:

– Contributions to the Labor Fund (2.45% of aggregate wages) intended, e.g., for financing unemployment benefits, training benefits, and apprenticeship to work or retraining of the unemployed.

– Contributions to the Guaranteed Employee Benefits Fund (0.1% of the aggregate wages) intended for the protection of employees' claims in the event of insolvency of their employer.

– Contributions to the State Fund for Rehabilitation of Disabled Persons imposed on companies employing at least 25 employees. This contribution does not apply to sheltered workshops and factories in which at least 6% of employees are disabled.

The personal income tax (PIT) was introduced in Poland in 1992. Previously, state-owned enterprises paid 20% tax on aggregate wages and the income earned in the private sector was taxed on a separate basis. The tax structure uses Western patterns: progressive rates, the amount of income tax-free, tax reductions and exemptions. Initially (1992-1993), three rates were in force: 20%, 30% and 40%. In subsequent years, they have undergone minor modifications. The highest were in the years 1995-1996: 21%, 33% and 45%. However, between 1998 and 2008, they stabilized at 19%, 30% and 40%. Since 2009, there were two rates: 18% (on income not exceeding PLN 85,528 ($ 26,750)) and 32% on income in excess of this amount. Since 2009, less than 3% of taxpayers achieved income taxed at a higher rate (32%). At the same time, however, the tax paid by them brought more than 20% of budget revenues (*Informacja dotycząca rozliczania podatku dochodowego od osób fizycznych za lata,* 2009-2014).

It is worth noting that since 2009, the income threshold from which a higher PIT rate is calculated has not been indexed. Since 2008, the income tax-free amount PLN 3089 ($ 965) has also not been indexed. Therefore, the level of tax-free amount in relation to the monthly average wage has been steadily declining: from 149.1% in 1992 to 84.4% in 2013, and to 81.8% in 2014 (GUS, 2015; own calculation). It is also worth noting that the amount of income tax-free in Poland (approx. € 750 in 2015) is the lowest among the countries using tax progression. The highest amount (€ 19,500) occurred in Cyprus (*Praca w Unii Europejskiej – podatki i składki...*, 2015).

A gradual reduction of tax reliefs diminishes the redistributive function of PIT. Pro-family relief (for the upbringing of children) was introduced in 2007. For several years, it was deducted from the tax preventing its use for people with many children with low incomes.

Before the transformation, the social security contribution accounted for 38% of the aggregate wages and was entirely covered by the employer. In 1990, it was raised to 43% and in 1992 to 45%. When introducing income tax in 1992, salaries were "*gross-upped*" and the contribution was divided between the employer and the employee. Currently, contributions account for 43.42% and are spread between the employee (22.71%) and the employer (20.71%).

Table 3.2: The Amount of Insurance Contribution (in %)

Specification	Overall contribution	Contribution paid by the employee	Contribution paid by the employer
Old age pension Insurance contribution	19.52	9.76	9.76
Disability insurance contribution	8.0	1.5	6.5
Industrial injury Insurance contribution	1.9	-	1.9
Sickness insurance contribution	2.45	2.45	-
Health insurance contribution	9.0	9.0	-
Labor Fund	2.45	-	2.45
Guaranteed Employee Benefits Fund	0.1	-	0.1
Total	43.42	22.71	20.71

Comparison of tax wedge in the United States and in Poland

Tax wedge of a single, childless US and Polish workers earning the average wage is shown in Figure 3.1. The tax wedge is the difference between what employees take home in earnings (net wages) and what the cost is of employing them.

Figure 3.1: Tax Wedge of a Single, Childless US and Polish Worker Earning the Average Wage, 2013

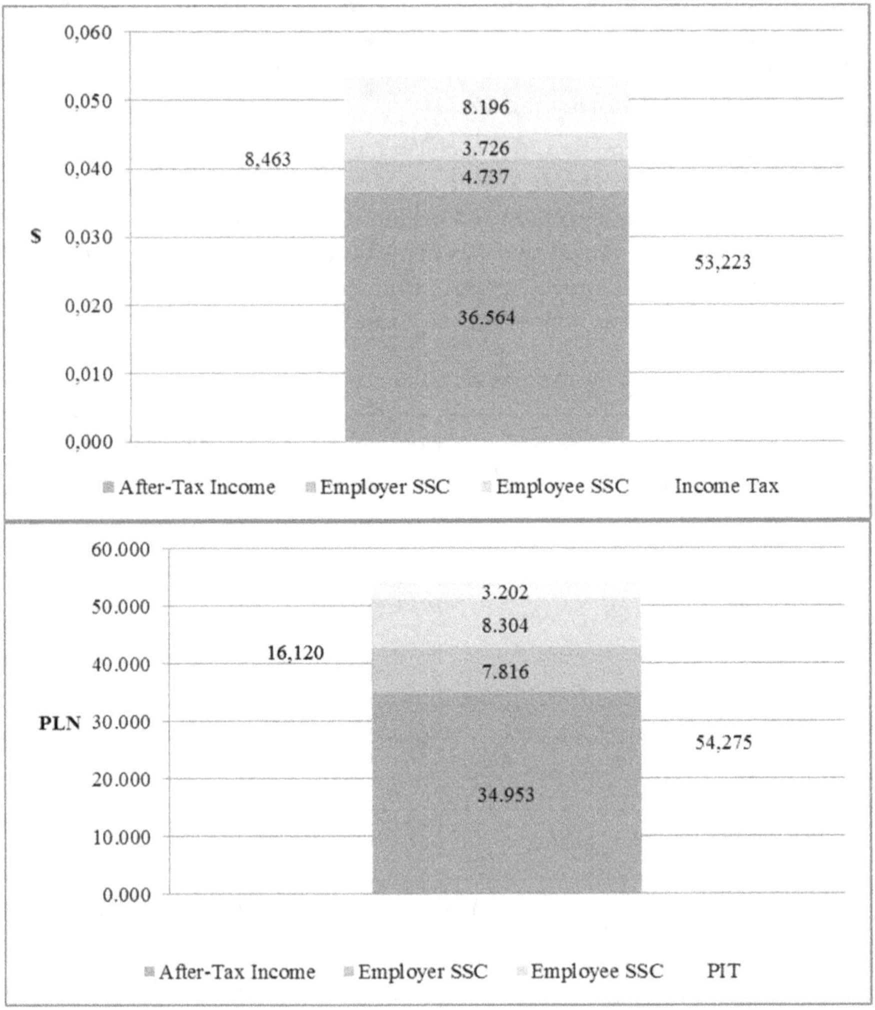

Source: US: OECD (2014)

The average annual gross wage in the United States in 2013 was $ 48,486 (net wage $ 36,564 + income tax $ 8,196 + employee SSC $3,726). Adding up the total average tax rate of income tax (15.4%) and SSC (15.9%), this worker faced an average tax wedge of 31.3% (Figure 3.2). In the absence of these three taxes, the average worker would have taken home $ 53,223, instead of $ 36,564.

Figure 3.2: Tax Wedge of a Single, Childless US and Polish Worker Earning the Average Wage, 2013 in %.

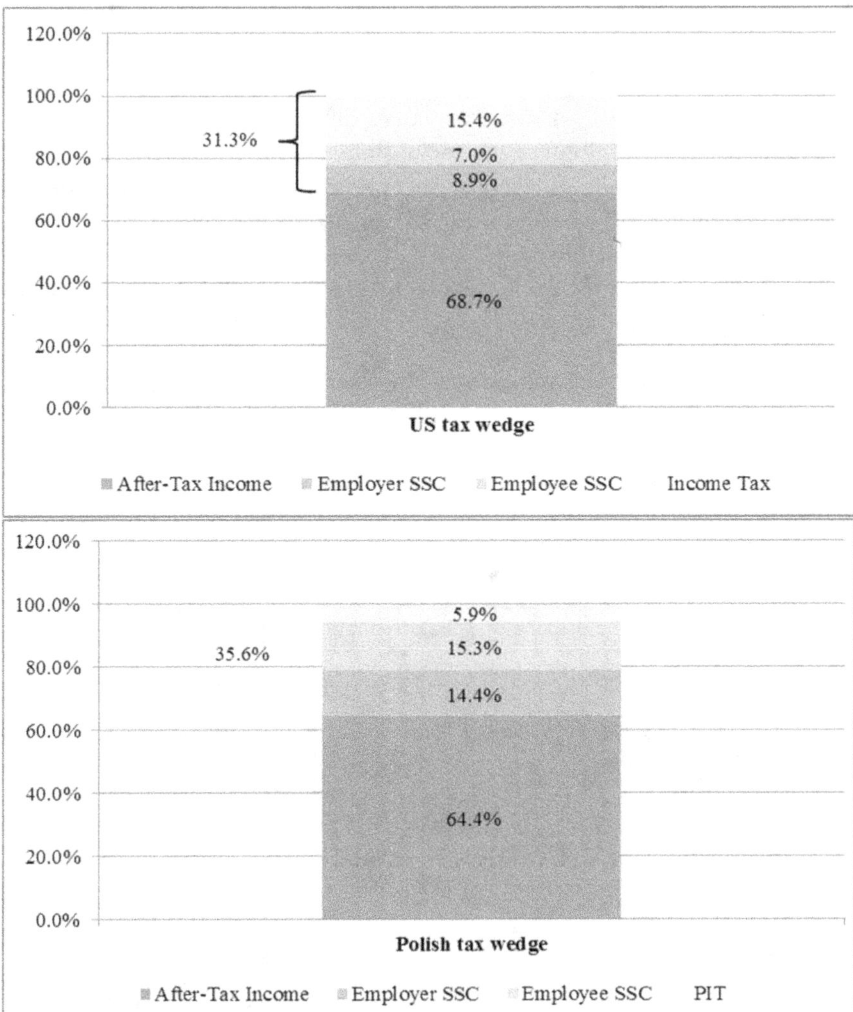

Source: US: OECD (2014)

In Poland in 2013, the average annual gross wedge was PLN 46,459 (net wage PLN 34,953 + income tax PLN 3,202 + employee SSC PLN 8,304). Tax burden put on average wage (single, childless) is shown in Figure 2.1. Summing up the total tax rate of income tax (5.9%) and SSC (29.7%), this worker faced an average tax wedge of 35.6%. In the absence of these three taxes, he would have taken home PLN 54,275 instead of PLN 34,953.

Tax wedge in OECD countries

The level of the tax wedge

OECD is composed of 34 countries that differ economically as well as according to their definition of the social state. Therefore, it is not surprising that the tax wedge of an average income earner in those countries is significantly diversified (see Appendix 3.1). In 2013, it has ranged from 7.0% in Chile to 55.8% in Belgium and 49.0% in Germany, Austria, Hungary and France. OECD average tax wedge stands at 35.8% while it is 31.3% in the US and 35.6% in Poland.

Figure 3.3: Total Tax Wedge of Average Income Earner by OECD Country, 2013, in %.

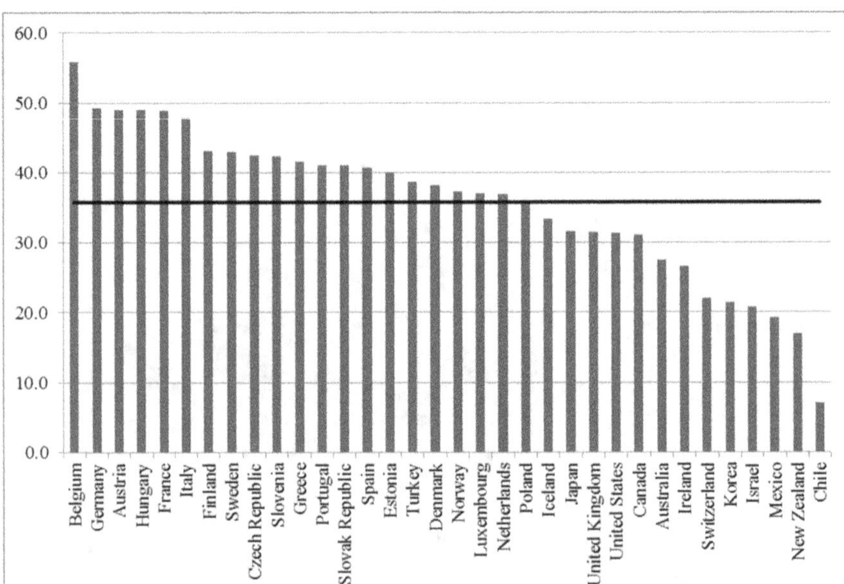

Source: OECD (2014)

Redistributive aspects of the tax wedge

Taxes have different functions in economies including fiscal, economic stimulation, stabilization, and redistribution functions. Statistical data will be used to compare labor taxation of different household types in Poland and the other EU countries taking into account non-fiscal functions.

The tax wedge on low wage workers, which is the tax wedge for a single worker without children at two-thirds of average earnings, is very often recognized as a basis for evaluation of tax burden put on labor (67% of average earnings is very close to median).

Table 3.3: Tax Wedge for a Single Person, No Child, 2013, in %

Country	Tax wedge			Difference between column 4 and 2
	67%	100%	167%	
	of average wage			
1	2	3	4	5
Ireland	21.0	26.6	38.5	17.5
Luxembourg	29.7	37.0	44.3	14.6
Portugal	34.7	41.1	47.4	12.7
Greece	36.9	41.6	49.2	12.3
Finland	37.6	43.1	48.9	11.3
USA	**29.3**	**31.3**	**36.2**	**6.9**
Japan	30.3	31.6	34.5	4.2
Estonia	38.7	39.9	40.8	2.1
Poland	**34.7**	**35.6**	**36.2**	**1.5**
Chile	7.0	7.0	7.8	0.8
Hungary	49.0	49.0	49.0	0
OECD	**32.2**	**35.8**	**40.3**	**8.1**

Source: OECD (2014)

In the most OECD tax systems, particularly in "*old*" UE countries, the financial situation of employees is taken into consideration by the tax system. Employees who earn more are obliged to pay higher taxes (Table 3.3). This rule is not respected in Poland. Those who earn 67% of average wage have almost the same tax wedge as those who earn two and half times more. In the United States, the difference between employees achieving different income is slightly smaller than the average for the OECD.

Because taxes are an important tool for income redistribution, the OECD statistics identify different types of household's diversity in terms of income level and family situation of taxpayers. Tables 3.4-3.7 present four types of households in respect to their economic and social situations, especially the number of dependent children.

Table 3.4: Tax Wedge for a Single Person at 67% of Average Wage, No Child, and a Single Person at 67% of Average Wage with Two Children, 2013, in %.

Country	**Single no child**	**Single two children**	**Difference between column 2 and 3**
1	**2**	**3**	**4**
Ireland	21.1	-24.9*	-24.9*
New Zealand	13.3	-17.1*	-17.1*
Canada	26.3	-6.3*	-6.3*
Australia	21.8	-2.9*	-2.9*
Slovenia	13.0	38.5	25.5
Luxembourg	4.4	29.9	25.5
Denmark	11.2	36.6	25.4
Czech Republic	39.3	14.3	25.0
USA	**29.3**	**11.1**	**18.2**
Poland	**34.7**	**29.6**	**5.1**
Turkey	36.5	35.5	1.0
Korea	18.3	17.4	0.9
Chile	7.0	6.1	0.9
Mexico	13.9	13.9	0
OECD	**32.2**	**17.2**	**15.0**

* Net incomes of households of single parents with two children and low wages exceeded their gross wages. This was due to specific allowances addressed to this group of households.

Source: OECD (2014)

Ireland provides the largest reduction of taxes for a single worker with two children. Similar allowances addressed to these households are also used in New Zealand, Canada and Australia. In some EU countries, the differences between the taxation of singles without children and with two children reach 25%. In the US, this difference is 18.2% and it is slightly higher (by 3.2%) than the average for the OECD. Poland ranks 30th (among 34 OECD countries) with a difference of only 5.1%.

Table 3.5: Tax Wedge for a Single Person at Average Wage, No Child, and One-Earner Married Couple at Average Wage, Two Children (in %)

Country	Single no child	Married couple two children	Difference between column 2 and 3
1	2	3	4
Czech Republic	42.4	20.5	21.9
Slovenia	42.3	23.1	19.2
Ireland	26.6	6.8	19.1
Hungary	49.0	34.1	15.9
Germany	49.3	33.7	15.6
USA	**31.3**	**20.3**	**11.0**
Poland	**35.6**	**29.8**	**5.8**
Israel	20.7	17.4	3.3
Japan	21.4	19.0	2.4
Turkey	38.6	37.4	1.2
Mexico	19.2	19.2	0
Chile	7.0	7.0	0
OECD	**35.8**	**26.3**	**9.5**

Source: OECD (2014)

Data presented in Table 3.5 show that in the tax systems of the OECD countries, preferences related to raising children apply also to employees who achieve income at the level of the average wage. In the EU, the burden for families with two children is about a 12% lower. In the US, the differences are somewhat higher than the average for the OECD. In Poland, a married couple with two children has a tax burden of merely 5.8% lower than singles with the same income.

Table 3.6: Tax Wedge for a Single Person at 167% Of Average Wage, No Child and Two-Earner Married Couple, One at Average Wage and Other at 67%, Two Children, 2013 (in %)

Country	Single no child	Married couple two children	Difference between column 2 and 3
1	**2**	**3**	**4**
Luxembourg	44.3	24.3	19.9
Ireland	38.5	19.2	19.3
Belgium	60.9	48.7	12.2
Slovenia	46.1	34.3	11.8
Sweden	50.5	38.9	11.6
USA	**36.2**	**26.7**	**9.5**
Estonia	40.8	36.3	4.5
Korea	22.9	19.0	3.9
Poland	**36.2**	**32.5**	**3.7**
Turkey	42.1	38.8	3.3
Chile	7.8	6.6	1.2
OECD	**40.3**	**31.2**	**9.1**

Source: OECD (2014)

Also, data on wealthier households (167% and 133% of average wage) show that in the countries of the European Union, the redistributive function plays a greater role than on average in the OECD (Tables 3.6 and 3.7). This does not apply, however, to Poland, because the tax wedge for families with children and without children is similar, and is the lowest among OECD countries.

Table 3.7: Tax Wedge for Two-Earner Married Couple, One at Average Wage and the Other at 33% of Average Wage, No Child and Two Children, 2013 (in %)

Country	No child	Two children	Difference Between column 2 and 3
1	**2**	**3**	**4**
Hungary	47.7	36.2	11.5
Czech Republic	40.2	29.7	10.5
Slovenia	40.0	30.5	9.5
Luxembourg	28.3	18.8	9.5
Austria	45.2	38.1	7.1
USA	**29.8**	**24.8**	**5.0**
Poland	**34.7**	**31.3**	**3.4**
Greece	42.0	40.6	1.4
Korea	20.3	18.9	1.4
Spain	37.5	36.4	1.1
Turkey	38.4	38.1	0.5
Mexico	16.9	16.9	0
OECD	**32.9**	**28.3**	**4.6**

Source: OECD (2014)

Taxation of labor in "*old*" UE countries, such as Ireland, Belgium, Luxembourg, Germany and new UE member such as Slovenia, Czech Republic, Hungary demonstrate the most family oriented systems. On the other hand, such systems are seen to a very limited extent in Korea, Turkey, Chile, Mexico and also in Poland. In all these tables, Poland is situated at the bottom of the ranks. The data also show that the tax system applied in the United States is moderate. Preferences related to the financial and family situation of the taxpayer are similar and often exceed the average tax wedge in the OECD by a few percentage points.

The structure of the tax wedge

The tax wedge consists of three components:

- Personal income tax (PIT).
- Social security contribution paid by employee.
- Social security contribution paid by employer.

The internal structure of tax wedge in OECD countries is very diversified (see Appendix 3.1). The OECD report (Table 3.8) shows that the structure of the tax wedge of employees receiving an average wage is very diversified. Among the 34 OECD countries, only two are unusual. In New Zealand, income tax is only on individuals (16.9%) while neither employees nor employers are burdened with social security contributions. In Chile, employees whose income does not exceed the amount of the average wage are charged only with social security contributions (7%), and employers are not charged. In Chile, employees pay income tax when their annual income exceeds $10,000. Currently, the average monthly wage stands at approx. $700, or $8,400 per year. The data obtained at the Embassy of Chile show that, out of the 8.5 million employed, only about one million of employees pay income tax.

In the other 32 countries belonging to OECD, the tax wedge is composed of PIT and social security contributions. Without taking into account New Zealand and Chile, it turns out that at the opposite poles of the tax wedge for a single person who is childless and receiving an average salary are Denmark and Poland. In Denmark, SSC account for only 6.3% of the tax wedge, while in Poland, PIT accounts only for 16.6% of tax burden on labor. The rest, 83.4% of the tax wedge, are contributions including old age pension, disability pension, health, accident and others. This indicates that high contributions are the "*Achilles heel*" of the Polish tax system.

The internal structure of the tax wedge in the United States is close to the average although the share of PIT is slightly larger than on the average in the OECD. The burden of contributions on employees is lower.

Table 3.8: Structure of Tax Wedge of Average Income Earner, Single, No Child, 2013 (in %)

Country	Tax wedge	Tax category			Structure in %		
		PIT	SSC employee	SSC employer	PIT	SSC employee	SSC employer
New Zealand	16.9	16.9	0.0	0.0	100.0	0.0	0.0
Denmark	38.2	35.8	2.7	0.0	93.7	6.3	0.0
Australia	27.4	21.8	0.0	5.6	79.6	0.0	20.4
Iceland	33.4	25.9	0.4	7.1	77.5	1.2	21.3
Norway	37.3	18.9	6.9	11.5	50.7	18.5	30.8
United States	31.3	15.4	7.0	8.9	49.2	22.4	28.4
Czech Republic	42.4	8.8	8.2	25.4	20.8	19.3	55.9
Slovakia	41.1	7.1	10.2	23.8	17.3	24.8	57.9
Greece	41.6	7.1	12.9	21.5	17.1	31.0	51.9
Poland	35.6	5.9	15.3	14.4	16.6	43.0	40.4
Chile	7.0	0.0	7.0	0.0	0.0	100.0	0.0
OECD Average	35.8	13.3	8.3	14.2	37.4	23.3	40.3

Source: OECD (2013)

Conclusions

1) The level of the tax wedge for a single person, childless, receiving an average wage in Poland is almost identical to the value of the average for OECD countries (35.6% in Poland and 35.8% OECD average). In the US, the tax wedge calculated in this way is slightly lower - 31.3%.

2) Large differences exist however in the comparative analysis of the tax wedge for households with different incomes (67%, 100%, and 167% of the average wage) and different family situations (singles without children and a family with two children). The redistributive aspects of

the tax wedge are used to the greatest extent in the countries of Western Europe oriented on the implementation of the welfare state policy. The United States pursues a more liberal policy in terms of redistribution but ranks slightly higher than the OECD average. In Poland, however, taxation of labor neglects the financial situation of low-income workers and those with dependent children. Such an assessment of the Polish tax wedge also results from the studies covering the period 2000-2012 (Kryńska, 2014). These analyses also confirm that family policy in Poland differs significantly from that carried out in other EU countries (Rękas, 2012).

3) The internal structure of the tax wedge in the United States can be regarded as similar to that of other OECD countries. However, the structure of the tax wedge in Poland is unusual because of the very large share of social security contributions. The contributions represent 83.4% of the tax wedge, which places Poland on the penultimate place among OECD countries.

4) The conclusions concerning Poland provoke three questions:
   - why is it happening?
   - what are the effects of this situation?
   - what should be done? (recommendation)

When we look at the taxation of labor in 2013, we looked back to the beginning of transition of Polish economy and introduction of tax reform in Poland. In a centrally planned economy, employees did not pay any taxes. State owned enterprises paid 20% tax which was put into total wage fund and social security contributions. According to established income intervals, 95% of taxpayers were situated in the first rate (20%). This enabled the introduction of tax reform smoothly and without social resistance but on the other hand, it made it impossible to use progressive taxes as a tool of redistribution of income. The same applies to social security contribution. Their rate is not connected with the financial and social status of employee.

5) Adverse effects of low diversity of tax wedge in Poland are as follows:

- increased unemployment in the group of low-skilled and low-earn workers since it is difficult to enter the labor market and remain employed.
- development of the informal sector to avoid labor taxation.
- impoverishment of families with dependent children.

The level of Poland's tax wedge can be considered moderate compared to the other EU countries. There is no possibility to decrease labor taxation in Poland because of economic and demographic reasons. However, the diversity of tax wedge in different cross-sections should be higher. It is necessary to decrease tax burden on low-skilled and low-earned workers to help them to enter the labor market. Such solutions are used in many western EU members.

Changes in PIT and SSC should be more family oriented (for example, higher level of tax free income, more tax rates with higher progressivity, more reliefs and allowances referring to family situation).

Acknowledgements

This paper was written as a part of the research project DEC-013/11/B/HS4/00684, financed by National Science Centre, Poland.

References

Eurostat. (2014). *Taxation Trends in European Union.* European Commission. Retrieved from http://ec.europa.eu/taxation_customs/sites/taxation/files/resources/documents/taxation/gen_info/economic_analysis/tax_structures/2014/report.pdf.

GUS. (2015). *Rocznik Statystyczny Rzeczypospolitej Polskiej 2015 [Statistical Yearbook of the Republic of Poland 2015].* Główny Urząd Statystyczny [Central Statistical Office].

Informacja dotycząca rozliczania podatku dochodowego od osób fizycznych za lata 2009-201 [Information on the settlement of income tax from individuals for the period 2009-2014]. (2009-2014). Ministerstwo Finansów, Departament Podatków Dochodowych. Retrieved from http://www.finanse.mf.gov.pl/documents/766655/2210514/Wykaz+organizacji+po%C5%BCytku+publicznego,+kt%C3%B3re+w+2013+r.+otrzyma%C5%82y+1+proc.

Krajewska, A. (2013). The Effect of the Financial Crisis on the Taxation of Consumption, Labor and Capital in the European Union. *Comparative Economic Research. Central and Eastern Europe, 16*(3), 29-47.

Kryńska, E. (2014). Labor Taxation in Poland Compared to The Other OECD Countries. *Comparative Economic Research. Central and Eastern Europe, 17*(3), 47–62.

OECD. (2013). *OECD Economic Outlook 2013* (Issue 2). Paris, France: OECD Publishing. DOI: http://dx.doi.org/10.1787/eco_outlook-v2013-2-en.

OECD. (2014). *Taxing Wages 2014.* Paris, France: OECD Publishing. DOI: http://dx.doi.org/10.1787/tax_wages-2014-en.

Piketty, T. (2015). *Ekonomia nierówności [The Economics of inequalities].* Warsaw, Poland: Wydawnictwo Krytyki Politycznej.

Pomerleau, K. (2013). Summary of Latest Federal Income Tax Date. *Tax Foundation Fiscal Fact, 408.* Retrieved from https://files.taxfoundation.org/legacy/docs/ff408.pdf.

Pomerleau, K. (2014). A Comparison of the Tax Burden on Labor in the OECD. *Fiscal Fact, 434.* Retrieved from https://files.taxfoundation.org/legacy/docs/FF434.pdf.

Praca w Unii Europejskiej – podatki i składki. Polska na tle Europy [Working in the European Union - taxes and contributions. Poland vs. Europe]. (2015). Raport PwC. PwC Report. Retrieved from http://www.pwc.pl/pl/media/2015/2015-03-24-praca-w-ue.html.

Rękas, M. (2012). Ulgi prorodzinne w wybranych krajach UE [Pro-family relief in selected EU countries]. *Prace Naukowe Uniwersytetu Ekonomicznego we Wrocławiu, 245,* 418-431.

Appendix 3.1. Tax wedge of average income earner by OECD Country, 2013

Country	Rank	Total Tax Wedge (%)	Income Tax (%)	Social Security Contributions	
				Employee (%)	Employer (%)
Belgium	1	55.8	22.0	10.8	23.0
Germany	2	49.3	16.0	17.1	16.2
Austria	3	49.0	12.6	14.0	22.6
Hungary	3	49.0	12.5	14.4	22.2
France	5	48.9	10.4	9.8	28.7
Italy	6	47.8	16.3	7.2	24.3
Finland	7	43.1	18.4	6.2	18.6
Sweden	8	42.9	13.7	5.3	23.9
Czech Republic	9	42.4	8.8	8.2	25.4
Slovenia	10	42.3	9.4	19.0	13.9
Greece	11	41.6	7.1	12.9	21.5
Portugal	12	41.1	13.1	8.9	19.2
Slovak Republic	12	41.1	7.1	10.2	23.8
Spain	14	40.7	12.8	4.9	23.0
Estonia	15	39.9	13.0	1.5	25.4
Turkey	16	38.6	11.6	12.9	14.2
Denmark	17	38.2	35.8	2.7	0.0
Norway	18	37.3	18.9	6.9	11.5
Luxembourg	19	37.0	15.1	11.0	11.0
Netherlands	20	36.9	14.3	14.2	8.4
Poland	21	35.6	5.9	15.3	14.4
Iceland	22	33.4	25.9	0.4	7.1
Japan	23	31.6	6.7	12.2	12.8
United Kingdom	24	31.5	13.3	8.5	9.8
United States	25	31.3	15.4	7.0	8.9
Canada	26	31.1	13.7	6.6	10.8
Australia	27	27.4	21.8	0.0	5.6
Ireland	28	26.6	13.3	3.6	9.7
Switzerland	29	22.0	10.2	5.9	5.9
Korea	30	21.4	4.6	7.5	9.3
Israel	31	20.7	8.4	7.5	4.8
Mexico	32	19.2	7.5	1.2	10.5
New Zealand	33	16.9	16.9	0.0	0.0
Chile	34	7.0	0.0	7.0	0.0
OECD Average	N/A	35.8	13.3	8.3	14.3

Source: OECD (2014)

Chapter 4

Women and Men in the Labor Market in Poland and Other EU Countries

Walentyna Kwiatkowska[3]

Abstract

The paper is focused on the position of women and men in the labor markets of Poland and other EU countries. Three labor market indicators are used for measurement: activity rate, employment rate and unemployment rate. The analysis includes the Polish national economy and the EU28 in the years 2005–2014. The goal of the paper is to show changes in the position of women in the labor market in comparison to the position of men in the period mentioned. It attempts to verify two hypotheses. First, the position of women in the labor market is significantly worse than the position of men. Second, the position of women in relation to the position of men is better with the passage of time in the analysis period. The empirical analysis of the paper is based on the official statistical data coming from the Labor Force Survey in Poland and from Eurostat. The data are prepared in such a way that the position of women can be compared with the position of men both for aggregated magnitudes as well as for narrower groups of labor force. These groups are defined by using such criteria as age and educational level. The conducted analysis leads to following conclusions. First, the female employment rate is significantly lower than that of men. In 2014, the female employment rate in Poland amounts to 44.3% and the male rate was higher and amounts to 59.8%. Second, the female rate of economic activity is lower than this rate of men. However, there have occurred insignificant increases of female activity rates in the investigated period from 47.7% to 48.5%. Nevertheless, the male activity rate is much higher: 62.8% in 2005 and 64.7% in 2014. The stock of inactive persons is dominated by women. Third, the female unemployment rate is higher than the unemployment rate of men on the Polish labor market. In 2014, the female unemployment rate accounted to 8.7% and the male rate to 7.6%. Also, the research indicates that women are

---

[3] wkwiatk@uni.lodz.pl

one of the groups at high risk of unemployment. These rates for females are less favorable than the rates for men not only in Poland but also in the clear majority of the EU countries.

Introduction

The issue of equal treatment of women and men in the labor market is one of the fundamental principles of the legal system of the European Union, as well as Poland. This issue has been legally authorized in the Equal Treatment Directive (No. 76/207) enacted on 9 February 1976 (Golinowska, 1999). The Directive stresses the equal treatment of women and men in regards to access to employment, vocational training and promotion, as well as in regards working conditions and social security. The principle of equal treatment clearly implies that there should be no direct or indirect discrimination on the grounds of sex, marital or family status. To eliminate wage discrimination, the European Community adopted the Equal Pay Directive (75/117) in 1975, which states that for the same work or work of equal value, all forms of discrimination based on sex must be eliminated.

It is worth noting that equality between women and men is guaranteed in all the basic human rights documents, including the UN Universal Declaration of Human Rights, the European Convention on Human Rights, the European Social Charter and also treaties and employment strategies adopted by the European Union (Tendera-Waszczuk, 2010). The revised European Employment Strategy adopted at the EU summit in Brussels in 2003 is particularly important in this respect. It is currently based on three pillars: full employment, improving quality and productivity at work and strengthening social cohesion and social inclusion (Knapińska, 2012). It is the latter third objective that underlines the crucial importance of employment for achieving social inclusion and therefore, involves supporting access to employment and combating discrimination in the labor market. The Polish Constitution and the Labor Code contain basic rules which play a major role in combating discrimination in access to employment in Poland. These are consistent with the priorities of Member States' policies on employment.

Against the background of these legal guarantees for implementation of the principle of equal treatment of women and men in the labor market, the question arises whether, in practice, this principle is fully respected. Therefore, the primary objectives of this study are to assess and describe the changes in the position of women in the labor market in relation to the position of men in Poland and other EU countries in the period between 2005 and 2014. This assessment is based on a comparison of the changes in economic activity rate, employment rate, and unemployment rate for men and women. This objective is used to examine a hypothesis suggesting an inferior position of women relative to men in the labor market in Poland and most EU countries. Empirical analyses are based on official statistics from the Labor Force Survey in Poland and Eurostat.

Economic activity of men and women in Poland and the EU in the years 2005–2014

Economically active persons include those who are looking for work and are capable and ready to work under typical conditions existing in the economy. These persons represent the supply side of the labor market and characterize the size of the labor force. To compare and assess the size of changes in the economic activity of women and men in Poland and other EU countries, we have used the rates of economic activity. Activity rate is a percentage characterizing the economically active population in the whole population of a given category (GUS, 2015a, b). Changes in overall activity rates of women and men in Poland in the years 2005–2014 are presented in Table 4.1.

Table 4.1: Economic Activity Rate of the Population Aged 15 and More, Overall and by Sex, in Poland in the years 2005–2014, in the 4th Quarter (%)

Years	Overall	Females	Males
2005	55.2	48.1	62.9
2006	54.1	46.7	62.3
2007	54.1	46.7	62.2
2008	54.7	47.1	63.1
2009	55.1	47.5	63.5
2010	55.4	47.5	63.9
2011	55.7	48.0	64.2
2012	56.0	48.3	64.4
2013	56.1	48.5	64.4
2014	56.3	48.5	64.7

Source: GUS (2014)

In the years 2005–2014, the activity rate of the population aged 15 and more in Poland increased slightly by 1.1%, reaching 56.3% in 2014. Activity rates for women were lower than the overall rates and significantly lower than the activity rates for men. In the years under study, activity rates for women did not reach 50%. Their maximum height of 48.5% marked the years 2013–2014. Activity rates for men exceeded 62% in the period considered, reaching the highest level of 64.7% in 2014. The difference between economic activity rates for women and men is very high, increasing from 14.8% in 2005 to 16.2% in 2014.

The economic activity of persons depends on many factors: demographic, social, and economic, including preferences in education, family model, job opportunities or age (Kryńska & Kwiatkowski, 2013). The degree of economic use of the potential labor resources in the case of women is relatively low in Poland (see Table 4.2). Women dominate the categories of inactive persons or the economically inactive. Their share in the years 2005–2014 was above 61%, while the share of men was only 38–39%.

Table 4.2: The share of females and males in economically inactive persons aged 15 and more in Poland, in 2005–2014, in the 4th quarter

Years	Females		Males	
	In thousands	In %	In thousands	In %
2005	8,515	60.6	5,536	39.4
2006	8,765	60.9	5,629	39.1
2007	8,789	61.0	5,628	39.0
2008	8,733	61.4	5,491	38.6
2009	8,695	61.5	5,454	38.5
2010	8,471	61.3	5,355	38.7
2011	8,407	61.2	5,322	38.8
2012	8,369	61.3	5,287	38.7
2013	8,326	61.1	5,295	38.9
2014	8,310	61.4	5,232	38.6

Source: GUS (2006, 2007, 2014). Author's own calculations

The economic passivity of women as illustrated by Figure 4.1, results from the following reasons: (1) the possibility of early retirement, (2) participation in further education and training to raise the level of education and professional qualifications, (3) family and home duties related to motherhood and bringing up children and caring for elderly family members (four times higher proportion of women in implementing these duties than men), (4) illnesses and disabilities, and (5) discouragement after ineffective job searches.

Figure 4.1: Structure of Economically Inactive Females and Males by Reasons for Inactivity in Poland in 2014 (%)

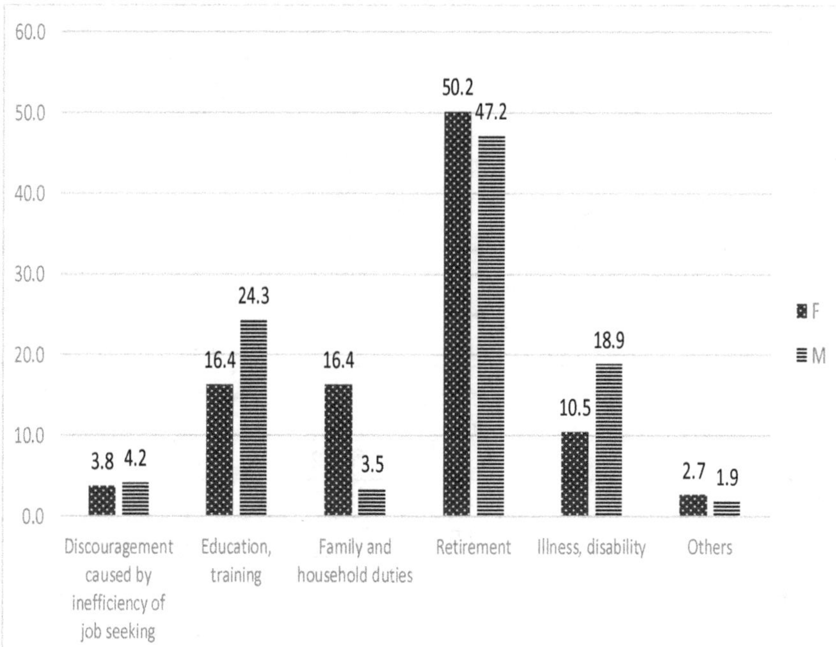

Source: GUS (2015). Author's own calculations

A more complete assessment of the degree of economic activity of women and men in Poland is achieved by comparing it with economic activity rates in EU member states. Data on the subject are shown in Table 4.3. In this table, an age group 15–64 years is introduced, representing the thresholds of the working age according to the Eurostat definition and used for international comparisons.

Table 4.3: Economic Activity Rate of the Population Aged 15 to 64 Years by Sex in the European Union 28, in the years 2005 and 2014(%)

Countries	Females		Males	
	2005[a)]	2014[b)]	2005[a)]	2014[b)]
EU28	62.2	66.8	77.3	78.3
Belgium	59.5	63.3	73.9	72.8
Bulgaria	57.3	65.2	67.0	72.3
Czech Republic	62.4	66.4	78.4	81.6
Denmark	75.9	75.6	83.6	81.3
Germany	66.9	73.0	80.6	82.7
Estonia	67.9	71.7	73.6	79.2
Ireland	60.8	62.5	80.6	77.0
Greece	54.5	59.1	79.2	75.5
Spain	58.9	69.2	80.9	79.7
France	64.8	67.4	75.2	75.6
Croatia	56.7	60.9	70.0	71.7
Italy	50.4	55.4	74.6	74.0
Cyprus	62.5	70.5	82.9	79.8
Latvia	65.1	70.6	74.4	78.2
Lithuania	65.2	71.6	72.4	75.9
Luxembourg	57.0	65.0	76.0	78.0
Hungary	55.1	61.2	67.9	73.9
Malta	36.4	50.8	78.5	80.1
Netherlands	70.0	74.3	83.7	84.3
Austria	65.6	70.6	79.3	80.0
Poland	**58.1**	**61.5**	**70.8**	**74.9**
Portugal	67.8	69.9	78.9	76.7
Romania	55.3	56.4	69.4	74.3
Slovenia	66.1	66.6	75.1	75.0
Slovakia	61.5	63.3	76.5	77.9
Finland	72.8	72.4	76.6	76.0
Sweden	76.3	78.2	80.9	82.9
United Kingdom	68.8	71.5	82.3	82.0

a) Annual averages b) 2014 4Q

Source: Eurostat Database (2016b)

The data in Table 4.3 show that the activity rates for women in Poland are lower than the average rates for EU28 and the difference between them increased from 4.1% in 2005 to 5.3% in 2014. Activity rates for women in 2014 in Greece, Italy, Malta, Romania, and Hungary are lower than in Poland. In 11 countries, women's activity rates are relatively higher, at the level of over 70%. Sweden has the highest rate of over 78%, followed by Denmark, Germany, the Netherlands, Finland, Great Britain, Austria, and countries admitted to the Union in 2004, such as Estonia, Cyprus, Latvia, and Lithuania.

In all 28 EU countries, activity rates for men are significantly higher than activity rates for women in both years examined. The highest activity rates for men are over 80% in 2014 in Sweden, Great Britain, Austria, the Netherlands, Malta, Germany, Denmark, and the Czech Republic. In other countries, these rates are higher than 70%. However, in 2005, lower rates could be seen, e.g., in Bulgaria, Hungary, and Romania. In Poland, the activity rates for men are lower in the years under study than average rates for EU28 in 2005 by 6.5%, and in 2014 the difference decreased to 3.4%.

Employment rates

Employment rates are used to describe the changes in the level of employment in Poland and other EU member states. Employment rate is a percentage of the employed persons of a given category in the total population of a given category. Overall employment rates for women and men aged 15 and older in the years 2005 to 2014 are presented in Table 4.4.

Table 4.4: Employment Rate of the Population Aged 15 and More by Sex in Poland in the Years 2005–2014 (%)

Years	Total	Females	Males
2005	45.9	39.2	53.2
2006	47.5	40.3	55.5
2007	49.5	42.3	57.4
2008	51.0	43.5	59.3
2009	50.4	43.3	58.3
2010	50.2	42.8	58.2
2011	50.3	42.8	58.5
2012	50.4	43.0	58.4
2013	50.6	43.4	58.5
2014	51.7	44.3	59.8

Source: GUS (2015)

The data in Table 4.4 show that in all three groups, an upward trend for these rates in the years 2005–2008 which stops in the years 2009–2010 as a result of the economic downturn, and then, the rates increase relatively slightly in subsequent years. Employment rates for women in all investigated years are lower than the overall employment rates and employment rates for men. Despite the increase in the employment rate for women in 2014 compared to 2005 by 5.1%, the difference between the level of this rate and the employment rate for men increases from 14% in 2005 to 15.5% in 2014. In relation to the overall employment rate, the rates for women are lower in 2005 by 6.7%, and in 2014 by 7.4%. The data indicate a poorer position for women in the labor market in relation to that of men since their rate of employment indicates that only 44 women per 100 were employed in 2014.

As already mentioned, the employment rates for men and women are characterized by relatively small values. Comparable rates from Eurostat are presented in Table 4.5. These concern people aged 15–64 years, hence the difference in their levels for Poland in relation to the rates in Table 4.4.

Table 4.5: Employment Rate of the Populations Aged 15 to 64 Years, by Sex in the European Union 28, Japan and United States, in the Years 2005 and 2014, Annual Averages (%)

Countries	Females		Males	
	2005	2014	2005	2014
UE28	56.1	59.6	70.7	70.1
Belgium	53.8	57.9	68.3	65.8
Bulgaria	51.7	58.2	60.0	63.9
Czech Republic	56.3	60.7	73.3	77.0
Denmark	71.9	69.8	79.8	75.8
Germany	59.6	69.5	71.3	78.1
Estonia	63.1	66.3	66.7	73.0
Ireland	58.3	56.7	76.9	66.9
Greece	46.1	41.1	74.2	58.0
Spain	51.8	51.2	75.1	60.7
France	58.4	60.9	69.2	67.7
Croatia	48.6	50.0	61.7	59.1
Italy	45.3	46.8	69.9	64.7
Cyprus	58.4	58.6	79.2	66.0
Latvia	59.3	64.3	67.6	68.4
Lithuania	59.6	64.9	66.4	66.5
Luxembourg	53.7	60.5	73.3	72.6

Hungary	51.0	55.9	63.1	67.8
Malta	33.4	49.3	73.5	74.9
Netherlands	66.4	68.1	79.9	78.1
Austria	62.0	66.9	75.4	75.2
Poland	**46.8**	**55.2**	**58.9**	**68.2**
Portugal	61.6	59.6	73.3	65.8
Romania	51.5	53.3	63.7	68.7
Slovenia	61.3	60.0	70.4	67.5
Slovakia	50.9	54.3	64.6	67.6
Finland	66.5	68.0	70.3	69.5
Sweden	70.4	73.1	74.4	76.5
United Kingdom	65.8	67.1	77.7	76.8
Japan	57.4[a)]	63.6	80.0[a)]	81.5
United States	65.4[a)]	63.0	77.2[a)]	73.5

[a)] 2004

Source: *Eurostat Database (2016a)*

In 2005, Poland, with an employment rate for women of 46.8%, ranked fourth from the bottom ahead of Malta, Italy, and Greece. The difference between the employment rate for women in Poland and the EU28 was 9.3%. In relation to Sweden and Denmark, where these rates exceed 70%, the difference was more than 24%. At the end of the period examined, the employment rate for women in Poland was ahead of only seven EU countries (Greece, Spain, Croatia, Italy, Malta, Romania, and Slovakia). The employment rate was lower by 4.4% than the average for the EU28, by more than 17% than Sweden, and by 14% than Denmark and Germany. Despite some improvement in Poland's position in the ranking, it should be recognized that the situation of women in the labor market is still unsatisfactory. It is worth noting that the employment rates for women in the EU28 were lower than those in countries such as the United States and Japan. It should also be added that, in accordance with European Council Decision (2003/578 / EC) of 22 July 2003, an employment rate for women of working age was expected to reach 60% in 2010 (Głąbicka, 2006). In 2014, this rate was reached and exceeded only by the developed countries of the EU15, as well as by those newly adopted in 2004: The Czech Republic, Estonia, Lithuania, Latvia, and Slovenia. In the new "*Europe 2020*" Strategy, the employment rate for the population aged 20–64 in the target year was to rise to 75%, a big challenge for the Polish economy (European Commission, 2010).

Data in Table 4.5 show the improvement in the situation of men in the labor market in Poland in the period examined. Their rate of employment increases from the lowest level among the other Member States (58.9% in 2005, the last place in the ranking) and in 2014, approaches the average rate for EU28. The difference decreases from 11.8% to 1.9%. Lower employment rates for men are found in Belgium, Bulgaria, Estonia, Ireland, Greece, Spain, France, Cyprus, Lithuania, Hungary, Portugal, Slovenia, and Slovakia. The highest employment rates for men, above 75%, are in Sweden, Great Britain, Austria, the Netherlands, Germany, Denmark, and the Czech Republic. Higher rates, over 80%, are characteristic of Japan and over 73%, for the United States. However, the employment rates for women and men in the United States decline in the period examined, presumably due to the financial and economic crisis.

An important criterion for the assessment of opportunities for women and men in the labor market is the level of their education. The data are shown in Table 4.6.

Table 4.6: Employment Rate of Females and Males Aged 15 and More by Level of Education in Poland in the 4th Quarter 2005 and 2014 (%)

Educational level	Females		Males	
	2005	2014	2005	2014
Tertiary	73.6	74.2	75.6	80.1
Post-secondary and Vocational secondary	52.2	50.6	64.8	70.0
General secondary	33.3	36.0	43.1	56.3
Basic vocational	42.7	44.0	61.4	62.4
Lower secondary, primary and incomplete primary	12.0	9.3	23.1	22.6

Source: GUS (2006, 2015)

Analyzing the data in Table 4.6, it should be noted that employment rates for women and men are the highest for those with higher education in both years. The female employment rate reaches more than 74% in 2014, an increase of 0.6% compared to 2005. In contrast, a much larger increase is seen in the employment rate for men with higher education which reached 80% in 2014, an increase of 4.5%. Despite having higher education, a much smaller proportion of women are employed compared to men. In 2014, the difference between the employment rates for women and men increases from 2% in 2005 by 5.9%. However, it should be noted that the high level of education ensures women a better position in the labor market. Knowledge and high qualifications are in demand from both men and women to ensure the innovation and competitiveness of the Polish economy.

In the period examined, the employment rate for women with post-secondary and vocational secondary education decreases in favor of men (the difference in 2014 was 19.4%). The employment rates for women with secondary and vocational education are significantly lower in comparison to employment rates of men. In the case of the lowest education levels, employment rates for women and men decrease, reflecting the qualitative transformations in the labor market and the decline in labor demand for low-skilled and very low-skilled workers.

During the period examined, one can observe diversity in the employment of women and men by different age groups.

Table 4.7: Employment Rate of Females and Males Aged 15 and More by Age in Poland in the 4th Quarter 2005 and 2014 (%)

Age	Females		Males	
	2005	2014	2005	2014
15–24	20.2	21.1	25.7	30.4
25–34	63.8	71.3	80.0	85.1
35–44	71.0	75.9	82.3	88.2
45–54	58.9	74.0	70.3	80.1
55 and more	10.5	16.6	22.6	32.7
in working age	53.1	64.0	63.5	72.3

Source: GUS (2006, 2015)

The data in Table 4.7 show that in 2014 compared to 2005, the percentage of employed women in the age groups 25–34, 35–44 and 45–54, increases to over 70%. The highest employment rate among women takes place in the mobile age group (35–44 years) reaching about 76% in 2014, while the highest increase in the rate (by 15.1%) is noted for women aged 45–54 years. Presumably, such positive effects are a result of increased activation programs in the labor market aimed at the group of women. However, the employment rates for men in the same age groups are significantly higher in both years examined. The percentage of employed men aged 35–44 years exceeds 88% in 2014. Among the younger aged 25–34 year-old males, it is 85%. The difference in relation to the rate of women is about 14% which probably has been affected by the need to balance their family roles with professional roles.

Numerous studies indicate that women are losing the competition with men because of social privileges (e.g., the developed legal protection of motherhood and job) and their smaller availability (according to the employers) and frequent absences due to the care of sick children and other family members (Matysiak, 2009; Kalinowska-Sufinowicz, 2013).

Women aged 15–24 years have relatively low and relatively stable employment rates (20–21%), while in the same age group of men, these rates are higher with a range of 25–30%. Both these groups include graduates of different types of schools for whom taking up their first job is often particularly important for their professional development, to gain practical skills, and to become independent. The low employment rates for these groups are therefore an important social problem in the Polish economy.

The lowest percentage of employed women is characterized by age group 55 years and over, despite some increase to 16.6% in 2014. The percentage of employed men in this age group is twice as high, which may result from the fact that women, as a result of lower retirement age, could retire earlier. Due to an expected decline in labor supply and concerns about the efficiency of the pension system, the Polish Parliament has enacted the Act of 11 May 2012, which commenced, starting from 1 January 2013, the process of raising the retirement age up to 67 years, with no difference between women and men (2012).[4]

Table 4.8 compares the situation of women and men in the labor market. Their share in employment by so-called major occupational groups is taken into account along with the demonstration of the relationship between their wages (Kwiatkowska, 2015).

Table 4.8: Employed Persons by Sex and Selected Occupational Groups in Poland in 2014 (%)

	Females	**Males**	**The female-to male earnings ratio***
Total	100.0	100.0	0.83
Managers	5.3	6.8	0.73
Professionals	26.2	12.7	0.75
Technicians and associate professionals	13.8	10.5	0.77
Clerical support workers	8.8	4.7	0.98
Service and sales workers	19.8	9.1	0.87
Skilled agricultural, forestry and fishery workers	9.7	10.9	0.95
Craft and related trades workers	4.4	23.5	0.69
Plant and machine operators and assemblers	2.8	15.2	0.82
Elementary occupations	9.0	5.1	0.84

*Without enterprises employing less than 9 people

Source: ***GUS (2014, 2015)***

[4] The changes were met with various social and political assessments; see Pacud (2016).

Equal treatment of men and women in employment and wages for work of the same type, quantity and quality are important principles contained in the Polish Labor Code and the ILO Convention No. 100 (Polish labor code..., 1998). The data in Table 4.8 show that the wages of females are lower than the wages of males in each occupational group. The average monthly wages and salaries of women and men are almost the same in the group of clerical support workers and in service and sales workers where women dominated among employed people. But in the other occupational groups, for example, professionals, the wages of women are lower (only 75% of men's wages); despite the fact that this group is predominated by women.

Unemployment rates for women and men

Gender is the main distinguishing demographic feature of the unemployed. The analysis of unemployment rates indicates that the risk of unemployment among women is higher than among men. This is evidenced by higher rates of female unemployment in relation to male unemployment rates.

Table 4.9: Unemployment Rates by Gender in Poland in the Years 2005–2014 (%)

Years	Women	Men	Total
2005	18.3	15.4	16.7
2006	13.7	11.0	12.2
2007	9.4	7.8	8.5
2008	7.6	6.0	6.7
2009	8.8	8.2	8.5
2010	9.9	8.9	9.3
2011	10.8	8.8	9.7
2012	11.1	9.3	10.1
2013	10.5	9.1	9.8
2014	8.7	7.6	8.1

Source: GUS (2014)

Downward trends in unemployment rates are strongly dependent on the economic situation and labor market situation in Poland. Improvement in the economic situation in 2005–2008 has contributed to a significant decline in the unemployment rate for men and women. The downturn in 2009–2012 results in an increase in the unemployment rate, particularly of women, to over 11%. It is not until 2014 that the difference between unemployment rates for men and women decreases to 1.5. This should be viewed positively as it indicates less risk of unemployment for women.

In the vast majority of member states, not only in Poland, the unemployment rate for females is higher than the unemployment rate for males.

Table 4.10: Unemployment Rates of Females and Males in the European Union, Japan, and United States in the Years 2005 and 2014, Annual Average (%)

Countries	Females		Males		<25 years
	2005	2014	2005	2014	2014
UE28	9.7	10.3	8.4	10.1	22.2
Belgium	9.5	7.9	7.6	9.0	23.2
Bulgaria	10.0	10.4	10.3	12.3	23.8
Czech Republic	9.8	7.4	6.5	5.1	15.9
Denmark	5.3	6.8	4.4	6.4	12.6
Germany	10.9	4.6	11.4	5.3	7.7
Estonia	6.9	6.8	9.2	7.9	15.0
Ireland	4.1	9.4	4.6	12.9	23.9
Greece	15.4	30.2	6.2	23.7	52.4
Spain	12.0	25.4	7.1	23.6	53.2
France	9.7	10.1	8.2	10.5	24.1
Croatia	14.4	18.3	11.8	16.5	45.5
Italy	10.1	13.8	6.2	11.9	42.7
Cyprus	6.5	15.1	4.4	17.1	35.9
Latvia	10.0	9.8	10.1	11.8	19.6
Lithuania	8.5	9.2	8.1	12.2	19.3
Luxembourg	6.1	6.0	3.6	5.9	21.2
Hungary	7.4	7.9	7.0	7.6	20.4
Malta	8.4	5.4	6.3	6.2	11.8
Netherlands	5.8	7.8	4.9	7.2	12.7
Austria	5.5	5.4	4.9	5.9	10.3
Poland	**19.4**	**9.6**	**16.7**	**8.5**	**23.9**
Portugal	8.8	14.5	8.7	13.8	34.7
Romania	6.4	6.1	7.7	7.3	24.0
Slovenia	7.1	10.6	6.1	9.0	20.2
Slovakia	17.4	13.6	15.6	12.8	29.7
Finland	8.6	8.0	8.2	9.3	20.5
Sweden	7.6	7.7	7.7	8.2	22.9
United Kingdom	4.3	5.8	5.2	6.4	16.9
Japan	4.5*	3.4	3.9*	3.8	6.3
United States	3.7*	6.1	4.7*	6.3	13.4

* 2007

Source: ***Eurostat Database (2016a)***

In 2005, the unemployment rate for women in Poland is one of the highest in the EU28. However, in 2014, the unemployment rate for women in Poland (9.6%) is lower than the average in the EU28 (10.3%). In 2014, the highest unemployment rates of females, amounting to over 25–30%, are characteristic of Greece and Spain, countries particularly affected by the financial and economic crisis.

The lowest unemployment rates for women (6%) are observed in highly developed countries, with a developed services sector, such as Germany, Luxembourg, Austria, and the United Kingdom. Very low unemployment rates for women and men in relation to the average rate for the EU28 are characteristic of Japan and the United States.

In some countries, the unemployment rates for men are slightly higher than the unemployment rates for women, e.g., in Bulgaria, Estonia, Ireland, Latvia, Lithuania, Romania, Finland, Sweden, and the UK. Increase in the unemployment rate for men is associated generally with the loss of their jobs in the fields of the economy sensitive to economic fluctuations, especially in the private sector, construction, and industrial production. These employ a significant proportion of men. On the other hand, as part of the process of improving the situation of unemployed women, a significant role should be attributed to implementation of professional activation programs, the development of flexible forms of employment, and ever more effective implementation of gender equality in the labor market as a result of legal and institutional anti-discrimination solutions.

Table 4.10 also shows the unemployment rate for younger people aged 25 years in 2014 in the EU28. In 2014, in countries such as Greece and Spain, the percentage of unemployed persons exceeds 50%. The unemployment rate for young people in Croatia and Italy is equally high, above 40%. In Poland, the unemployment rate for people up to 25 years (about 24%) is higher than the average for the EU28. Germany can boast of the lowest unemployment rate (7.7%). This is 1.4% higher than the rate in Japan. It can be argued that the situation of young people on the labor market is very difficult in a fairly large group of EU28 countries. Factors determining their chances on the labor market include the level and type of education, the effectiveness of job search, and the ability to adapt to changes in the labor market.

Educational qualifications are still the best insurance against unemployment. The risk of unemployment is the lowest in the groups of females and males with tertiary education. The highest rates of unemployment and the associated risk of unemployment occur among females and males with lower secondary, primary and incomplete primary education.

Figure 4.2: Unemployment Rates of Females and Males by Level of Education in Poland in 2014 (%)

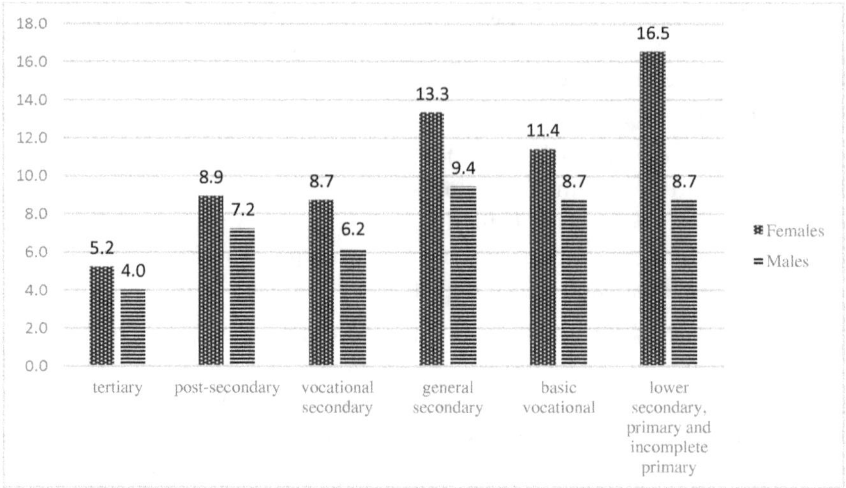

Source: GUS (2014)

The figure shows clearly that, despite the same level of education, women account for a higher percentage of the unemployed. The lower the educational level, the greater the difference between unemployment rates for women and men (from 1.2% for a higher education to about 8% for the lowest).

Conclusions

The following conclusions may be drawn from these analyses.

1) In the years 2005–2014, economic activity of women has been significantly lower than that of men. The difference between the activity rates for women and men in 2014 is 16.2%. This demonstrates an inferior position for women in the labor market.
2) The group of inactive persons is dominated by women (61.4% in 2014). The main reasons for their employment inactivity are: retirement, education training, family and household duties.
3) The female employment rate is significantly lower than this rate of men. In 2014, the female employment rate amounted to 44.3% and the male rate was higher and amounted to 59.8%. This is a manifestation of discrimination processes in the labor market.

4) In Poland, the female rate of economic activity and the female employment rate are lower than these rates in the highly developed EU member states.
5) The female unemployment rate is higher than unemployment rate of men in the Polish labor market. In 2014, the female unemployment rate accounted for 8.7% and the male rate for 8.1%, i.e., the degree of unemployment risk among women declined although a significant number of them are not economically active.
6) Average monthly gross wages and salaries of women are lower than the wages and salaries of men. This difference exists although the levels of education and the professions of women and men are the same.
7) In order to improve the situation of females in the labor market, the governments of the member states of the European Union must implement the requirements of the pro-employment economic policy and thus improve the quality of human capital and effectively implement gender equality in the labor market within the framework of the anti-discrimination legal and institutional solutions.

References

European Commission. (2010). *Communication from the Commission Europe 2020. A strategy of smart, sustainable and inclusive growth.* (COM (2010) 2020). Retrieved from http://ec.europa.eu/eu2020/pdf/COMPLET%20EN%20BARROSO%20%20%20007%20-%20Europe%202020%20-%20EN%20version.pdf.

Eurostat Database. (2016a). *Employment rates for selected population groups.* Retrieved from http://ec.europa.eu/eurostat/statistics-explained/index.php/Employment_statistics.

Eurostat Database. (2016b). *Populations, activity and inactivity, activity rates by sex.* Retrieved from http://ec.europa.eu/eurostat/statistics-explained/index.php/Employment_statistics.

Głąbicka, K. (2006). *Socjalny wymiar Europy. Od niewolnictwa do obywatelskości [Monograph] [Social dimension of Europe. from slavery to citizenship].* Wydawnictwo Politechniki Radomskiej [Publisher Technical University of Radom].

Golinowska, S. (1999). *Polityka społeczna Unii Europejskiej i jej konsekwencje dla Polski [Social policy European Union and its consequences for Poland].* Warsaw: IPiSS.

GUS. (2006). *Rocznik Statystyczny Rzeczypospolitej Polskiej 2006 [Statistical yearbook of the Republic of Poland 2006].* Główny Urząd Statystyczny [Central Statistical Office].

GUS. (2007). *Rocznik Statystyczny Rzeczypospolitej Polskiej 2007 [Statistical yearbook of the Republic of Poland 2007].* Główny Urząd Statystyczny [Central Statistical Office].

GUS. (2014). *Aktywność ekonomiczna ludności Polski [Labor force survey in Poland].* Główny Urząd Statystyczny [Central Statistical Office].

GUS. (2015a). *Aktywność ekonomiczna ludności Polski [Labor force survey in Poland].* Główny Urząd Statystyczny [Central Statistical Office].

GUS. (2015b). *Aktywność ekonomiczna ludności Polski. [Labor force survey in Poland the 4th quarter 2014].* Główny Urząd Statystyczny [Central Statistical Office].

Kalinowska-Sufinowicz, B. (2013). *Polityka społeczno-gospodarcza państwa wobec pracy kobiet [Socio-economic policy of the state towards women's work].* Poznan: Wydawnictwo Uniwersytetu Ekonomicznego w Poznaniu.

Knapińska, M. (2012). *Wspólny europejski rynek pracy. Geneza – Rozwój – Funkcjonowanie [Common European labor market. genesis – development – functioning].* Poznan: Wydawnictwo Uniwersytetu Ekonomicznego w Poznaniu.

Kryńska, E. & Kwiatkowski E. (2013). *Podstawy wiedzy o rynku pracy [Basic knowledge about the labor market].* Lodz: Wydawnictwo Uniwersytetu Łódzkiego.

Kwiatkowska, W. (2015). The differentiation of wages in Polish economy in the years 2005–2012. *Olsztyn Economic Journal, 10,* 37-61.

Matysiak, A. (2009). Zatrudnienie kobiet w Polsce a posiadanie dzieci: bariera czy warunek? [Employment of women in Poland and having children:

barrier or condition?] In Kotowska, I. E. (Ed.). *Strukturalne i kulturowe uwarunkowania aktywności zawodowej kobiet w Polsce [Structural and Cultural Conditions of Women's Professional Activity in Poland]*. Warsaw: Wydawnictwo Naukowe SCHOLAR.

Pacud, R. (2016). Dylematy stanowienia wieku emerytalnego [Dilemmas About Setting Up Retirement Age]. *Polityka Społeczna*, 2.

Polish labor code No. 21, Item 94. (1998). *Journal of Laws*. Retrieved from http://isap.sejm.gov.pl/DetailsServlet?id=WDU19980210094.

Tendera-Waszczuk, H. (Ed.). (2010). *Polityka społeczna Unii Europejskiej po wschodnim rozszerzeniu [European Union social policy after the eastern enlargement]*. Cracow: Polskie Towarzystwo Ekonomiczne.

The Act of 11 May 2012 amending the law on retirement and disability pensions from the Social Insurance Fund and other acts, (*Dz. U.* of *2012*, No. 107, *item 637*).

(2012). Poland Journal of Laws 2012.

Chapter 5

The Efficiency of Employee Representation in Corporate Governance in the Selected EU Countries

Stanisław Rudolf [5]

Abstract

The participation of workers' representatives in the bodies of corporate governance continues to raise controversy. The purpose of the study is to determine the effect of employee representation in the corporate governance bodies on the economic and social performance of companies in Germany and Sweden. These countries share well-established principles of democracy, but differ in terms of their corporate governance systems (two-tier, one-tier), levels of concentration of capital and the position of institutional investors, mainly banks, as well as the scope of employee representation. In both countries, unique models of employee representation have been created, generating beneficial results for both companies and employees. The experiences of these countries can be widely used in Polish conditions.

Introduction

Irrespective of the form of its system, dualistic or monistic, employee representation in the bodies of corporate governance has always raised a great deal of controversy. The dispute over that issue refers to its political, ideological and economic aspects. Further considerations presented in the following study are mainly focused on the latter group of aspects, because in a long-term perspective, they decide about the existence of employee representation. Theoretical and empirical considerations which have been recently carried out do not provide any explicit answer to the question about the influence of employee representation on company operations.

---

[5] rudolfs@uni.lodz.pl

The supporters of such representation indicate benefits that it can bring to the company as well as to its employees. They indicate that long-standing employees come as a particular type of human capital that incurs residual risk, which is quite similar to the risk incurred by the owners, and in that way, they deserve their proper representation at the level of the corporate board of their company (Fauver & Fuerst, 2006). Such representation may also result in numerous benefits for the employees, as they can actively monitor activities of the board, protect their own interests, and become a channel for information exchange between the employees and the management (Roberts & Van den Steen, 2000). However, the opponents of employee representation claim that it may contribute to the worsening of the economic performance of the company because of their pressure for pay increases and defense of their jobs. They also mention the longer time required to make decisions and the fact that such decisions are of poor quality. In their opinion, employee representation in corporate governance leads to an increase in agency costs, considering the escalation of the conflicts of interest between employees and shareholders (Faleye et al., 2006).

The purpose of this paper is to determine the influence exerted by employee representation in the bodies of corporate governance on economic and social performance of companies. The influence of such representation has been analyzed with the consideration of the dualistic and monistic systems. First, the German experience is presented, in which employees enjoy broad representation in corporate boards. Then the Swedish experience is discussed where employee representation is also present in supervisory boards. It should be noticed that in the dualistic system, which is very popular in the EU countries, employee representation in supervisory boards has had a long-standing tradition, whereas in the monistic system, it is still scarce. Therefore, the Swedish experience in that field becomes even more valuable for the discussion.

Efficiency of employee representation in German supervisory boards

The German system of corporate governance is commonly considered to be a classical model of such supervision in the dualistic system. It consists of a supervisory board and company management. Such a model fosters the participation of employee representation in corporate boards in terms of their control and supervisory rights whereas company operations are run by the company management. Contrary to other countries where that model is applied, in Germany, employee representation in corporate boards has the broadest scope and it is of a statutory nature. The scope of such representation in a supervisory board grows with the size of the company (Clarke, 2006).

The types of employee representation in the supervisory boards of companies

Employee representation has had a long-standing tradition in the German supervision system. It was implemented in 1920 when a relevant legal act ensured one or two seats in supervisory boards for employees. Such representation functioned until 1934 when it was suspended by the Nazis. It came back after the Second World War, in 1947 (Charkham, 1994). The current system of supervision is quite complicated. It is regulated by three separate legal acts, with a differentiated share of employee representation in supervisory boards. Their short presentation is provided below (HBS & ETUI, 2004).

The most numerous and historically, the oldest employee representations in supervisory boards were introduced by the legal act of 1951. The act refers to the companies in the mining industry as well as the iron and steel smelting industry, which employ at least 1000 workers. The size of the board depends on the size of the company, and such boards are relatively large, often consisting of 11, 15 or 21 members. In accordance with the act, investors, as well as employees, are represented in the board, following the parity principle. Constituted in such a way, the board appoints a so-called neutral member who should represent the public interest. The neutral member holds a casting vote if other partners cannot reach an agreement. The seats for the employees also include the seats for the trade union representatives. For example, in a board of 11 members, the employees are entitled to have five seats. However, only two seats out of those five are for the employees; two seats are taken by the local trade union representatives (unions in Germany are outside the enterprise) and the fifth seat is held by a member of the board appointed by the central authorities of the particular union. There are 50 companies subject to that legal act.

In 1952, there was another legal act established to determine the second type of employee representation in supervisory boards. It was amended in 1972. In accordance with that act, the companies which employ at least 500 workers (excluding enterprises from the sectors of mining and iron smelting industry, as mentioned above) must allow their employee representatives to take 1/3 of the seats in their supervisory boards. While appointing members, the employee representatives directly elected by the workers are given priority to take those seats. Thus, if the workers are entitled for one or two seats, these seats are taken by the employees of the company. If there are more seats for the company staff, they can be taken by the representatives of the trade unions. In accordance with the act, a supervisory board may consist of between three and 21 members. There are approximately 2000 companies which are subject to that act.

The third and the latest type of employee representation were introduced by the legal act of 1976. It came as a final result of intensive activities of trade unions which fought for the extension of employee representation in supervisory boards. The act refers to large enterprises which employ over 2000 employees. It should be noticed that approximately 1/3 of the whole German labor force is subject to that legal act. It has introduced the parity system to the share of seats in supervisory boards for the representatives of investors and employees. Contrary to the solution that governs the mining and smelting industries, a supervisory board appoints a chairperson and a deputy chairperson subject to a two-thirds majority of votes, but one of them must be the representative of the investors and the second one – the representative of the employees. If such representation turns out to be impossible, then the representatives of the investors appoint the chairperson of the board and the representatives of the employees elect the deputy chairperson. It should be also mentioned that if the number of votes is inconclusive, the vote of the chairperson counts double. In practice, a chairperson of the board is almost always a representative of the investors. It means that the representatives of the investors prevail in the supervisory board by one vote. The board may consist of 12, 16 or 20 members. There are over 750 companies subject to that one act.

It should be emphasized that according to the current legal regulations, the representatives of investors and the representatives of employees (including trade unions) should represent the interests of their company. This is obvious for the representatives of investors; however, one might have some doubts whether it is obvious for the representatives of employees, while looking at their behavior. The interests of employees are not always in line with the interests of their company as a whole. The research carried out on that issue indicates that the representatives of employees in supervisory boards usually do represent the interest of their company. The fact that the voting carried out by supervisory boards rarely follows the pattern "*investors – employees*" also proves that statement. The exemptions from that rule are relatively rare, and they occur when a company neglects the interests of its employees, or it violates previous agreements with the employees. It is worth noting that employees' representatives on the board have the same rights as other members of the board.

The author of the article believes that the high share of employee representation in corporate governance in some way neutralizes the high level of capital concentration in Germany, which is much higher than in other Western countries. At the beginning of the 21st century, almost each large company had its shareholders who held controlling interests, and it was usually the capital of the family or the capital of institutional investors, such as banks, insurance companies, or some other enterprises (Roe, 2003). An important feature of German economy is its high institutionalization of property. It is estimated that in Germany over 50% of share capital is owned by institutional investors, whereas individual investors own only about 20% of share capital. In 18 out of 20 German corporations with the capital over USD 500 million, there have been shareholders who own 20% or more of the share capital. In the USA, there have been only two such companies (Roe, 2003).

Among institutional investors, banks play a particular role as they collect the most share capital. Their leading position in the German supervision system additionally results from the fact that they also hold individual shares in escrow, and based on that, they can vote as deputies during the general meetings of shareholders. All that contributes to the fact that banks significantly and often decisively affect operation of companies. Therefore, German companies rarely use the stock exchange to raise funds for their operation or further development. Their close relations with banks result in the fact that banks have become their main source of credits. It explains the fact that the German stock exchange is relatively small, and it comprises only 600 companies.[6]

Generally, it is possible to state that the concentration of capital and co-decision processes in Germany have been developed in a kind of symbiosis. Let us try to look for the reasons for such a symbiosis and the factors which determine such a result. Historically, the concentration of capital has occurred earlier. Co-decision is a political and social reaction to such concentration. The political character of such representation is particularly easy to observe in the context of the legal act of 1951, which implemented a wide scope of such representation in companies from the mining and smelting industries. Since companies granted their support for the Nazis after the war, it has been decided to submit them under the social control, taking the form of a broad employee representation in the supervisory boards.

To sum up this part of our considerations, it is possible to state that the German system of corporate governance, with its principles of employee participation and co-decision at the level of enterprises, follows a general concept of the current political system which functions in that country, soundly based on the principles of democracy. Similar principles are employed there at other levels of the state structure, i.e., at the regional and central levels. Commentators on the German system refer to it as to "*social governance*", not without a good reason (Clarke, 2006).

---

[6] In February 2016, Deutsche Vorse listed only 611 companies, 548 of which were national companies. The listed companies were the largest ones; hence the stock exchange was one of the top ten stock exchanges in terms of the value in the world (data provided by FESE).

The influence of employee representation on the agency costs

Let us now consider whether employee representation in corporate governance serves only the purposes which refer to the implementation of democratization processes at the level of a company. In their survey carried out in 2004, L. Fauver and M.E. Fuerst formulated a hypothesis, stating that such representation leads to the reduction in agency costs, and that it is manifested in the counteraction against excessive remuneration for the management (2006). The survey is based on the sample of 59 public companies with employee representation in their supervisory boards and on the sample of 59 companies without such representation. The average remuneration per one member of the management is calculated for all these 118 companies. In the research, a classical model of regression is applied to indicate that the remuneration for the management members in the companies with employee representation in their supervisory boards is lower than in other companies. Differences are not large and do not affect rather the efficiency of management. The authors of the survey state that the obtained results do not come from a position against high payments for the management members. The employee representatives focus their activities mainly on the maintenance of some proportions between the remuneration for the management members and the remuneration for the employees. Hence, it results in some limitation in the remuneration for the management members.

The authors also focus their research on the influence of employee representation in supervisory boards on the reduction of the agency costs in their broader aspect. The subject of the research focus on excessive expenses which generate costs, for example: excessive office room, rich office equipment, and unnecessary real estate or investment projects which will not generate any profits. Using the regression model, the authors indicate that the expenses in the companies with employee representation in their supervisory boards are lower than in the companies without such representation. The employee representatives monitor all the expenses of that kind, efficiently limiting any costs involved (Fauver & Fuerst, 2006).

The influence of the scope of employee representation on the goodwill of the company

The research has been also focused on the influence exerted by employee representation in the supervisory board on the operations of the company. The research indicates that small or reasonable participation of employee representation in corporate governance may contribute to the growth in the goodwill of the company; however, its excessive participation may lead to the opposite results. G. Gorton and F. Schmid present such a conclusion, and they indicate that an increase in employee participation in the supervisory board horizontally from a share of one-third to one half becomes detrimental for the goodwill of the company (2004). In their opinion, the relations between the goodwill of the company and the scope of employee representation in the supervisory board take the form of an upside-down letter U.

At first, the growing participation of employee representatives in the supervisory board (the left part of the upside-down U) contributes to the growth in the goodwill of the company. It comes as a result of information supplied by the employees, which contributes to the increase in the quality pertaining to decisions made by the board. The employee representatives in the board provide unique knowledge about the discussed problems, and that fact generally decides about the positive role of co-decision processes. The fact can be proved by the opinions provided by the Presidents of such corporations as Daimler-Chrysler or German Railway Transportation System. Jurgen Schrempp, the President of that first corporation states that the cooperation with the trade unions and the employee representatives was crucial for the reduction of costs and maintenance of posts during the negotiations with Mercedes-Benz. Hartmut Mehdorn, the President of the latter company states that the reduction of costs in German railways would not be possible without the involvement of the employee representatives in the supervisory board (Gorton & Schmid, 2004).

According to Fauver and Fuerst, employee representation also contributes to the reduction of antagonisms in the company, and it makes the staff more willing to solve current problems (2006). It also naturally results in synergy in providing value for the shareholders. Employee co-decision brings new energy to the company. Its employees feel that they are an important part of the company and they become responsible for the success of the company. It should be also noticed that the reliable information on the company strategy or expected profits for the employees and trade unions decrease the number of shutdowns and strikes. At the same time, the research indicates that the representatives of trade unions in the supervisory board do not contribute to the increase in the goodwill of the company. It results from the fact that the trade unions, contrary to the representatives of the employees in the board, do not work for the company.

The above mentioned authors state that a further increase in the participation of the employee representatives in the supervisory board (the right side of the upside down U letter) may result in the fact that they will become a source of agency costs. Considering their position, the representatives may seek such benefits for the employees as high salaries or the selection of the technologies which will allow them to protect jobs. As a result, the implementation of the investors' objectives may become less important. M. J. Roe believes that the growing scope of co-decision may additionally result in the weakening of the position held by the supervisory board that could decrease the significance of the employee representation (1998). The author states that the abovementioned high concentration of capital plays an important role in corporate governance. It comes as a counterbalance for the high level of co-decision in a company.

The scope of bank representation in German supervisory boards may be interpreted in a similar way. Moderate participation of bank representatives in corporate boards results in the fact that corporations independently decide about their development and they face the attendant risk. Excessive participation of bank representatives, however, makes supervisory boards act in line with the interest of creditors. They avoid excessive risk while making their investment decisions. It means that they do not take full advantage of their opportunities.

German experience in the participation of employee representation in supervisory boards, as presented above, generally indicates its positive results. The research carried out in that field more often presents the advantages resulting from employee representation for companies and their employees. The research on the correlation between the scope of employee representation and its results for the operation of companies may be particularly interesting. Thus, it is possible to conclude that such representation should be maintained at a reasonable level, which is namely one third of the employee representatives in a supervisory board. It is worth noticing, however, that employee representation based on the parity principle in Germany results from a very high concentration of capital which is not observed in any other countries.

The results of employee representation in the Swedish system of corporate governance

Sweden enjoys a long-standing tradition of social democracy. It belongs to the group of the countries which have the highest level of employee membership in trade unions (Visser, 2006).[7] The participation of employee representation in corporate governance is not as old as it might seem at first. It has been implemented by an act in 1973, becoming more common in 1976. The act has been strongly criticized by the left- as well as the right-wing parties. Both

[7] The level of the organization of employees in trade unions had been evenly maintained at 80% for decades, and after 2000 it started to decrease slightly.

right-wing politicians and employers' organizations agree at most to voluntary invitation of employee representatives to meetings of the executive board. Meanwhile, the left-wing parties consider such representation as collaboration with the capitalistic system. In accordance with the act, in the companies employing at least 25 workers, the employees are entitled to appoint two representatives to the executive board. If the company employs over 1000 workers, then the number of employee representatives is three. The act stipulates that the number of employee representatives may not be higher than the number of other members of the board. It means that employee representation never constitutes the majority of the board. It should be mentioned that a Swedish executive board most often consists of between five and up to nine members (Berglund, Holmen & Rana, 2013).

The decisions which refer to the exercising of the right for delegating their representatives to the executive board are made by the local trade unions. They are regulated by a respective legal provision in the corporate collective agreement. However, the opinions on employee representation in executive boards are very different in Sweden. Some companies support this policy, indicating a number of positive results, whereas other enterprises criticize it, pointing out a lot of negative consequences of such representation. As a result, only half of Swedish companies entitled to delegate employee representatives to their executive boards exercise that right in practice. The reason for such a situation may result from a strong position held by trade unions, that additional representation may seem unnecessary.

Employee representatives have the same rights and obligations as other members of the board and they take the same responsibilities. Their votes count equally as the votes of the corporate board members appointed by the shareholders. The differences between them can be found mainly in their remuneration. Two thirds of employee representatives in corporate boards are not paid anything for their participation. Only 8% obtain remuneration at the level of payment obtained be other members of the board. The others obtain only some service allowances for their work in the corporate board (HBS & ETUI 2004).

In 1998, 25 years after the establishment of the abovementioned act, a wide-scale survey was carried out to evaluate employee representation in corporate boards and the efficiency of the act itself (Levinson, 2001). The survey was based on a sample of 36 Presidents of corporate board, 422 CEOs, 405 employee representatives of the LO trade union (blue-collar workers) and 433 representatives of the PTK trade union (white-collar workers). The results of the survey turned out to be very favorable for those representatives. A general evaluation of employee representatives in corporate boards presented by the leading managers of the surveyed companies is displayed in Table 5.1.

Table 5.1: The Activity of Employee Representatives in the Opinion of Presidents and CEOs (%)

	Evaluation provided by Presidents	Evaluation provided by CEOs
Very positive	23	19
Positive	46	42
Neither positive nor negative	26	30
Negative	5	8
Very negative	-	1
Total	100	100

Source: Levinson (2001)

Almost 70% of Presidents and over 60% of CEOs evaluate employee representatives in their corporate boards very positively and positively. They emphasize the fact that employee representation allows them to develop a favorable atmosphere for cooperation (respectively 61% and 64%). Due to their representation, employees can better understand decisions made by the management board (65% and 59%) and they accept the implementation of difficult decisions more easily (55%, 47%). Their presence makes the decision-making processes harder only to a little extent (13%, 12%). However, the respondents also observe that the presence of employee representatives in their corporate boards increases the risk of the disclosure of confidential information. It should be noticed that only 5% of Presidents and 9% of CEOs negatively assess the presence of employee representatives in their corporate boards.

The presidents and CEOs indicate that the intensity of activities performed by the employee representatives is generally very low and low (46%, 58%). Their high or very high intensity is rarely indicated (14%, 9%). The activity of employee representatives is manifested differently when it comes to some selected issues. It is much higher in regard to issues concerning production, work environment or reorganization of the company. Hence, it is possible to conclude that employee representatives are more active in respect of the issues which deal with employees' problems or the issues with which they are familiar or with which they have some experience.

The discussed research indicates that the participation of employee representation in corporate boards is generally advantageous for companies. The surveyed managers perceive it as a valuable asset in their companies. Eighty percent of them believe that this results from very good cooperation between the employee representatives and other members of the corporate boards. It should be also noticed that the number of positive opinions provided by the CEOs increases with the size of the company. It reaches the highest level in the companies which employ over 500 workers. The positive evaluation of employee representation in corporate boards provided by the managers is proved by their answers to the question about any possible decrease in the number of such representatives. The suggestion of limited employee representation in corporate boards has been raised during discussions concerning some possible amendments to the legal act. Up to 80% of the surveyed managers declare that there is no need for such a decrease and only 7% of them state that such a limitation is necessary (Levinson, 2001).

Let us now take a closer look at the evaluation of their participation in corporate boards provided by the employee representatives themselves. Generally, their opinions are positive, but at the same time, they are also critical. Critical opinions are more often formulated by the representatives of the blue-collar trade unions (LO) than the white-collar trade unions (PTK). The employee representatives complain about the fact that some decisions are made outside the corporate board (LO – 21%, PTK – 19%), that they rarely participate in the initial stages of meetings during which the particular issues are discussed, and they only participate in the final stage of the decision-making process. They rarely participate in setting the agenda of the board meetings. They also indicate that they are given insufficient time to prepare for a discussion before the board meetings (44%, 39%, respectively) and complain about the time constraints during those meetings (18%, 15%, respectively).

For many representatives, the problems analyzed during the board meetings are too complicated and difficult to understand (16%, 8%, respectively). The linguistic problems are less often mentioned, if there have been other than Swedish languages used, as well as inaccessibility of required information. The employee representatives assess their impact on decisions made by the corporate boards as limited, although in some cases, it has been assessed as significant. The respondents indicate close relations with their trade unions, and that it has mainly occurred before the board meetings. This is not surprising because some of them are trade union activists. One third of the surveyed companies have organized inter - trade unions consultations. The respondents value highly the benefits which result from employee representation in the corporate boards for the trade union operations. They consider their presence as very useful at the level of 65% (LO) and 58% (PTK). It is also worth mentioning that the employee representatives positively assess their relations with the CEOs of their companies (Levinson, 2001).

Employee representation in Swedish corporate boards has been the subject of some more recent surveys. The survey run by T. Berglund, M. Holmen and R. Rana (2013) deserves our particular attention. The authors try to answer the previously posed question referring to the reasons for relatively low participation (50%) of employee representation in the management boards of the companies which are entitled to have such representation. They try to determine the consequences which result from such representation and which must be faced by the companies. The survey has been carried out on the sample of 226 companies listed on the stock exchange (excluding the companies from the financial sector). Almost half of those companies (106) have employee representation in their corporate boards. The survey was carried out in the years 2001-2007 and it was based on the annual reports provided by those companies and information collected by the relevant institutions.

First of all, a frequently used argument stating that companies increase the number of their board members to weaken the impact of employee representation has been disproved. The research indicates that large companies accept employee representatives much easier than small and medium-sized enterprises. The survey also indicates that employee representatives are included in corporate boards significantly less often, if there are some foreigner members. Employee representatives have declared that they are not ready to make decisions in a situation in which their company is involved in competition in the international markets. The fact that the foreign member of the corporate board might feel unprepared for the presence of employee representatives has been also taken into consideration.

The research indicates a negative correlation between employee representation in a corporate board and the risk incurred with the operations of a company. The study also shows that workers are less likely to be represented on the boards of companies whose activities are exposed to a serious risk. Apparently, the trade unions which make operational decisions are afraid to take responsibility for their representatives' participation in risky decisions. Another factor which affects decisions about delegating employee representatives to the corporate board is the required labor involvement. Considering that aspect, the companies characterized by high labor involvement are preferred. Hence, it is possible to make a general statement that the positive influence on delegating employee representation to corporate boards is affected by such factors as the low risk of operations performed by a company, high labor involvement, and the national character of a company.

Let us check the results of employee representation in the corporate boards of the companies in comparison to the companies which did not have such representations. The most observable result is the lower fluctuation of employees in the companies with employee representation in their corporate boards. It has been confirmed by the results of the previously discussed survey which indicates that the activity of employee representatives has been generally maintained at a low level, except for cases involving employee issues. As a result, their influence on employment stability can be observed. The survey also indicates that changes at the level of the CEOs are less often in the companies which have the employee representatives in their corporate boards. It may result from their support for the current corporate board as well as from their concern about the long-term stability of the company.

To sum up this part of our considerations, it is possible to state that employee representation in the Swedish system of corporate governance should be generally assessed in a positive way. Almost 40 years of experience with employee representatives in corporate boards indicate that, considering its social and economic aspects, their presence is mostly advantageous for the companies. It should be also emphasized that the Swedish system of corporate governance is flexible, and employees and trade unions make their own decisions about delegating their representatives to corporate boards.

Conclusions

The considerations presented above indicate that in the countries with well-established democratic principles, among which Germany and Sweden can be listed, employee representation in corporate governance usually brings advantageous social and economic results. It should be emphasized that those countries are very much different from each other in almost every respect, except for the abovementioned democratic principles. They also differ in terms of corporate governance (dualistic or monistic), the level of capital concentration, the position taken by institutional investors, mainly banks and the scope of employee representation. Both these countries have developed their own unique models of employee representation, adjusted to the current economic, social and political conditions. In the German model, the abovementioned high level of capital concentration has been considered, whereas in the Swedish model, the high ranking of trade unions has been taken into consideration.

So far, our experience in this respect has been very modest. The code of commercial companies does not require employee representation in corporate boards. However, it does not forbid it. Employee representatives are included in numerous corporate boards under the authority of the privatization acts. They are often treated there as necessary evil. There have been several attempts aiming at the limitation or cancellation of such representation in corporate boards by providing amendments to the Act on privatization and commercialization of state companies of 1996, by the virtue of which employee representatives retain their seats in a corporate board also after the end of the privatization process.

The experience presented above allows us to conclude that Poland should also develop its own model of corporate governance, adjusted to the current conditions. The discussed experience also indicates that employee representation should be maintained at a reasonable level. It should not be too high, as the excessive participation of employees in the management board may bring negative results for the operation of the company, as it sometimes happens in Germany. In most EU countries where the dualistic system is applied, such representation is one third of all the board members. Such a level may be recommended for Poland. Poland should immediately start working on the development of its own model of employee representation and the implementation of relevant legal regulations to the code of commercial companies. Such a solution will be more advantageous than waiting for the EU ordinance which may impose a model that may be not the most suitable one for Poland.

References

Berglund, T., Holmen, M., & Rana, R. (2013). Causes and consequences of employee representation on corporate boards. Paper presented at the conference, *Twenty years after Cadbury, ten years after Sarbanes-Oxley: challenges of corporate governance.* University of Bath.

Charkham, J. P. (1994). *Keeping good company. a study of corporate governance in five countries.* Oxford: Oxford University Press.

Clarke, A. D. (2006). German corporate governance provision for employees: Lessons for Australia. *Southern Cross University Law Review, 10.* Retrieved from http://www3.austlii.edu.au/au/journals/SCULawRw/2006/1.pdf.

Faleye, O., Mehrotra, V., & Morck, R. (2006). When labor has a voice in corporate governance. *Journal of Financial and Quantitative Analysis, 41*(3), 489-510.

Fauver, L., & Fuerst, M. E. (2006). Does good corporate governance include employee representation? Evidence from German corporate boards. *Journal of Financial Economics, 82,* 673-710. Retrieved from http://corpgovcenter.utk.edu/Research/FauverandFuerstJFEGermanLaborPaper.pdf.

Gorton, G., & Schmid, F. (2004). Capital, labor, and the firms: A study of German codetermination. *Journal of European Economic Association, 2*(5), 863-905.

HBS & ETUI. (Eds.). (2004). *Workers` participation at board level in the EU – 15 countries. Reports on the national systems and practices.* (2004). Brussels: Hans Bockler Foundation / European Trade Union Institute.

Levinson, K. (2001). Employee representatives on company boards in Sweden. *Industrial Relation Journal, 32*(3), 264-274.

Roberts, J. & Van den Steen, E. (2000). Human capital and corporate governance. In J. Schwalbach (Ed.). *Corporate governance: A volume in honor of Horst Albach* (pp. 128-144). Berlin: Springer Velag.

Roe, M. J. (1998). German co-determination and German securities markets. In K. J. Hopt, et.al. (Eds.). *Comparative corporate governance, state of the art and emerging research.* Oxford: Oxford University Press, Oxford.

Roe, M. J. (2003). Political determinants of corporate governance: Political context, corporate impact. (Discussion Paper No. 451). Harvard Law School, Cambridge, MA. Retrieved from http://www.law.harvard.edu/programs/olin_center/papers/pdf/451.pdf.

Visser, J. (2006). Union membership statistics in 24 countries. *Monthly Labor Review, 1*(44), 38-49.

Chapter 6

The Role and Position of Works Councils in the Polish System of Labor Relations

Stanisław Rudolf[8] and Katarzyna Skorupińska[9]

Abstract

The change of political and economic system, which took place first in Poland in 1989 and later in many other countries of Central and Eastern Europe, had not generally led to democratization of labor relations. This happened because both the trade unions and employers were not interested in transferring decision-making powers to employees. Attempts to create works councils or introduce workers' representatives to supervisory boards of companies, were treated by trade unions as competing with each other, so they were opposed to them. As a result, the introduction of works councils in Poland was forced by the relevant EU Directive. The empirical research presented in this chapter examined the functioning of works councils created in such a way. These councils, due to the said restrictions, did not bring significant changes in labor relations.

Introduction

Under the communist system, which functioned in Poland and some other so-called socialist countries, it was difficult to talk about real employee participation. Existing unions, uniting the vast majority of employees, were under the control of communist parties. Communist propaganda made employees believe that they were the ruling class, that their interests were most important. Leaders of the nation appealed to employees in difficult times, in order to obtain their support, etc. In practice, however, employees were effectively manipulated by the ruling elite and treated in an instrumental way. It should also be emphasized that trade unions effectively performed social functions, providing employees with cheap meals, nurseries, kindergartens, sanatoriums, and holidays abroad.

[8] rudolfs@uni.lodz.pl

[9] kasiasko@uni.lodz.pl

It is worth noting that the restriction of freedoms in the communist system also concerned employers. Without closer study of these limitations, it is difficult to explain the attitude of employers during transition, especially their attitude to employee participation. In general, the condition of employers in that period should be assessed as very difficult if only because there were no employers' organizations taking care of their interests. In contrast, the condition of employees, united in mass trade unions, was much more favorable. In this system, employers were subject to manipulation: they were appointed to managerial positions by the Party committees and, in a similar way, removed. This was often the case with lower level managerial positions.

Employers were also largely incapacitated in carrying out their daily duties. In particular, this applied to decisions on matters of production. These were restricted on the one hand by the plan imposed on them, and on the other, by numerous indicators which had to be taken into account, that a number of which at their peak exceeded 20 in Poland. As a result, employers did not decide on the size of the production, suppliers, about customers and prices, etc. The frustration of employers was additionally also growing, because they were continuously juxtaposed with the employees as the most important social group in the workplace. This made it difficult even to maintain the discipline of work. Industrial relations were further deteriorated by the introduction, in some countries, of the system of pseudo-self-government, in the form of workers' councils or similar institutions (The Act on Employee Self-Government, 1981). These councils were granted extensive powers, including the right to appoint and dismiss the director. While exercising these powers, they did not bear any responsibility.

The change of the political and economic system which took place in Poland in 1989 did not eliminate the pre-existing antagonisms and conflicts in labor relations. New problems emerged, arising from the tensions posed by transformation (Kohl & Platzer, 2004). It should first be noted that the new system had brought a fundamental change in the position of the social partners. The myth of a leading role of the working class had been dispelled, which was due to a significantly high level of unemployment, especially in the initial period of transformation (Gardawski, 1999). At the same time, employers (at least those private) began to exercise their powers in the company, keeping them entirely for themselves. They reacted nervously to any initiative aimed at extending employee participation, seeing in it the return to the previous system. Employers, organized in employers' organizations, effectively torpedoed attempts to extend such participation.

In the parliamentary system, the scope of employee participation, at least that of an indirect nature, is the resultant of the power of trade unions, which at least theoretically should encourage its development. Also important is the power of employers' organizations, which are usually opposed to employee participation, as well as of the determination of the ruling political parties, whose support depends on the represented political option. In practice, the social partners may represent different views from the above-mentioned, which brings unpredictable results. This model also applies to Poland.

The adaptation process of works councils

We will now examine the nature of labor relations existing in Poland, using the example of the adaptation of the so-called works councils to the Polish legal system. While joining the EU, Poland committed to introduce EU directives into the Polish legal system. One of them was a directive of the European Parliament from 2002 establishing general conditions for informing and consulting employees (The European Parliament..., 2002). The Polish Parliament adapted the Directive in 2006, adopting the relevant Act (Act on informing employees..., 2006). On one hand, the adoption of the Act can be considered a success since it ended a nearly 20-year-long discussion on works councils and earlier abortive attempts to implement them. On the other hand, the adoption of the Act can be regarded as a failure. Its adoption was preceded by a long debate, accompanied by considerable controversy. The draft law was particularly called into question by the trade unions, which since from the beginning regarded the councils as their competition. Realizing the impossibility of blocking the Act, the unions tried to affect its shape, in such a way that would not jeopardize their monopoly position in the workplace. The employers' organizations also lobbied to reduce the powers of councils.

Admittedly, the Parliament adopting the Act took into account the demands of both employers and trade unions. As a result, we have received works councils with very limited powers, very modest in number, and most importantly, subordinated to trade unions, at least in those workplaces where they existed. Therefore, the Act differed significantly from the Western legislation (Rudolf, 2006). The Act provided that, wherever there were representative trade union organizations, precisely they, and not all workers – as was provided in the Directive, were to elect the members of works councils. The dominant position of trade unions extended also over those enterprises which at the time of the elections to the council had no unions, and members of the council were elected by all employees. However, if trade union organizations were later established in such enterprises, then the previously elected councils were dissolved and trade unions elected new members (Act on informing employees..., 2006).

This solution, as mentioned, was incompatible with the Directive, which states unequivocally that the council should represent all employees at the workplace (Wratny, 2006). According to the Confederation of Polish Employers, such regulation also violated also the provisions of the Constitution because it unlawfully differentiated employee rights depending on their union membership (Skorupińska, 2015a). After a long discussion on this subject, the Constitutional Court ordered to amend the amendment of certain provisions of the Act, to guarantee for its compliance with the Directive. The Polish Parliament amended the Act in May 2009 (The Act of 22 May 2009..., 2009). The new provisions make the council representative of all employees. Election of council members is organized by the employer, who covers the costs associated with it, as well as the costs of the council's work. The council can be established at the request of at least 10% of employees.

The said weakness of the Polish works councils manifests itself both in their limited range in Polish enterprises, as well as in their small number. The Act requires employers to establish councils in enterprises employing at least 50 employees. For a country like Poland, where small companies prevail, this is a serious limitation. In several other Central and Eastern European countries, the employment threshold is lower and amounts to 30 employees (Estonia), 25 employees (the Czech Republic) and 20 workers (Romania, Slovenia, and Lithuania). For comparison, in some 'old' EU countries (i.e., Germany, Austria) such obligation even applies to companies employing at least five employees. The small size of Polish councils is also noteworthy - by far the lowest in the EU. There are only three members in councils in the largest group of enterprises employing 50 to 250 employees. The number of members rises to five in enterprises employing 251 to 500 employees and to seven in enterprises employing more than 500 workers. For comparison, works councils in Austria consist of five members in enterprises employing 101 to 200 employees. Above 200 workers in company, the number of councilors increases by one for every 100 employees until 1,000, after which it increases by one for every 400 employees. The Spanish works councils are even more numerous, i.e., in enterprises employing 101 to 250 workers, councils consist of nine members whereas in enterprises employing 751 to 1000 workers, composition of councils increases to 21 members. Afterwards, the number of members goes up by two for every additional 1,000 workers up to a maximum of 75 (Fulton, 2013).

The law requires employers to provide councils with information on the situation status of the company. The councils should especially be informed on issues related to the employment of employees, or, more generally, on personnel matters. Employers should therefore inform the council on the status, structure and expected changes in the size of the workforce employment and work organization. They should also provide information on the financial status of the company and about the prospects for its development, etc. The council has the right to present its views on matters relating to the functioning of the company and its economic situation (Rudolf, 2007).

The complicated process of developing the law on works councils substantially affected the scope of the functioning of these councils, and more specifically the changes in this scope. These changes are presented in Figure 6.1.

Figure 6.1: The Number of Works Councils in Poland in the Years 2006-2014

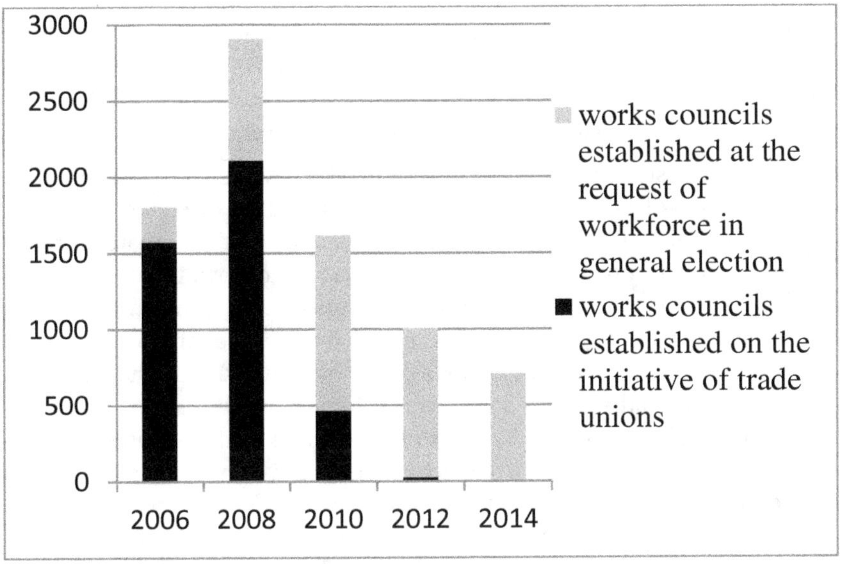

Source: K. Skorupińska (2015b).

Research of the Ministry of Labor and Social Policy shows that in 2007, a year after the adoption of the Act, nearly two thousand such councils were created. The vast majority of them, i.e., 80%, were established by representative trade union organizations and only 20% by all workers. More than half of the councils were set up in enterprises employing from 50 to 250 employees (Balsam, 2008). In 2008, the number of councils rose to nearly three thousand which was a result of the entry into force of the Act in its full extent (the 100-employee threshold was lowered to 50 employees). At the same time, the share of councils elected by all employees increased to nearly 30%. The amendment to the Act, which requires electing councils by all workers, brought a radical and progressive decline in their number. Trade unions, which were the main driving force behind the creation of works councils, lost their monopoly on determining the composition of the councils in unionized companies. After the amendment of the Act, unions did not have special privileges with respect to the election of councillors, although just as other employees they can recommend their candidates. In 2012, the number of works councils decreased to about 1,000 and in 2014 to about 700. Whereas the initial decline was related to the fact the trade unions could not elect council members, in recent years, the decline affected councils elected by all employees. The reasons for this decline were thought to include inter alia, the limited, in practice, competences of works councils, and a lack of trust in the new institutions of employee participation on part of employees. In addition, there was the still reluctant attitude of employers, who often effectively torpedo the employees' initiatives to appoint works councils (a request to set up the council must obtain the support of at least 10% of employees).

The results of empirical research

Information presented below comes from the research carried out on a national sample of 242 works councils. This was the first so extensive research on works councils in Poland. The main objective of the research project, funded by the National Science Centre, was to determine the role and importance of works councils in Polish enterprises. An attempt was made to determine whether the works councils are active, whether employers comply with the obligation to inform councils, and how effective is the activity of councils, etc. The survey was conducted using a questionnaire addressed to the chairman of the council. The list of companies and institutions for the survey came from the database of works councils developed by the Ministry of Labor and Social Policy (as of 31/12/2014). Survey questionnaires were sent to all 3429 councils in the database (both those which are still operating and those which went out of existence. In the sample of 242 works councils, most councils operated in enterprises in the processing industry (19% of the analyzed councils), services sector (17%), and public utilities (14.6%). A significant portion of councils also operated in the entities belonging to the sector "*health and social care*" (almost 11%) and the "*transport and storage*" sector (9%). Considering the ownership status of economic entities involved in the survey, it was found that those from the public sector (59%) outnumber the entities from the private sector (41%).

The activity of works councils

The activity of works councils can be measured by the frequency of their meetings, requests for information, presentation of their opinions to employers, and the forms of cooperation between councils and employees. It should be noted, however, that the first meeting of the council should adopt its rules of procedure, which specify the principles for its functioning. In particular, they should contain the rules concerning the frequency of meetings, the division of competences between the members of the council, or the rules for addressing the employer. However, as many as 13% of the analyzed councils have not developed this basic document of their functioning.

It should be noted that council meetings are not held too often. Only 30% of the surveyed councils held meetings not less frequently than at least once a month and only in their case, one can talk about fairly regular activity. It is difficult to talk about regular activity if the council meetings are held only once a quarter (about 34% of the surveyed councils), only twice a year (about 3% of councils), or even only once a year. As many as 20% of the surveyed councils meet "*as needed*", which might suggest that such meetings are held infrequently.

In general, works council meet in their full composition (88%), which is certainly beneficial given a small size of Polish institutions of participation.[10] The meetings of the council are very often (45.5% of councils) attended by a director or chairman of the board. Importantly, the meetings are also attended by other representatives of the employer (e.g. the chief accountant, legal counsel or in-house lawyer, a representative of the supervisory board, and the director of HR), which allows the council to obtain a lot of relevant information, which in many cases, is difficult to obtain in writing.

Under the Act, the information should be communicated to the council by the employer, in order to take into account expected changes and at the written request of the works council. The survey has shown that in almost half of the surveyed councils, both the employer and the works council took the initiative to provide information to the council. In turn, in 43% of the surveyed councils, the employer did not provide any information to the council, and the information was obtained only at the request of the works council. However, the activity of councils in this respect seems to be modest, because almost 15% of the surveyed councils have not even once applied for

---

[10] The size of the council depends on the number of employees employed by the employer and amounts respectively 3 persons - if the employer employs 50 to 250 employees; 5 persons - if the employer employs between 252 and 500 employees and 7 persons in the case of employing more than 500 employees (The Act on informing employees...., Op. cit. Article 3 Paragraph 1).

information from employers in the past year. More than 32% of councils applied for information only once or twice a year. Such a passive behavior by councils was certainly a result of their infrequent meetings.

In general, councils are satisfied with the scope of the information provided to them by employers. Only 12% of councils found this scope to be inadequate. Most responses define this scope as satisfactory (43.8%), which should be understood as a certain minimum scope, which allows the council to operate. A large part of councils defined this scope, as extensive (38.8%) or very extensive (5.4%), which may indicate a large availability of such information, making it possible to operate actively. The help of experts or consultants may increase the scope of information provided to councils. However, the surveyed councils rarely took advantage of such help (only 19%). This may confirm the thesis presented above about the weak activity of councils. The need for an expert or consultant appears only then if the council operates actively and cannot claim its rights from the employer. It should be pointed out, however, that councils used the information obtained to submit their opinion to the employer - as many as 73.6% of councils did it often or always.

The works council is a representative of all employees and is to serve their interests in the company. The survey has shown that cooperation with employees is based primarily on reporting their problems and proposals to members of the council (77% of councils use this form). In addition, the council refers to employees' proposals for solutions (one third of the analyzed cases), and members of the council meet regularly with employees of the workplace (24% of the surveyed councils). The works council should pass information obtained from the employer to employees, unless it threatens the company's business secrets, for which the employer reserved confidentiality (The Act on informing employees..., 2006). The most common way to communicate information to employees in the surveyed councils involves displaying information on bulletin boards (53%), direct contact with employees (about 42%), sending information electronically (about 10%), or posting information on the company's website (9.5%). However, given the relatively weak position of councils in enterprises in Poland, in as many as a quarter of the cases examined, chairmen of councils realize that their councils are not an effective representative of employees in dealing with the employer. This is mainly due to the limited powers of these institutions of participation, with the result that even council chairmen believe that the activities of their council are a mere formality (almost 40% of the analyzed councils).

The efficiency of works councils

Information presented above indicates that works councils in Poland have rather low position in the companies. Now, we will look closely at the effectiveness of their work, examining the scope and frequency of their consultations, their relationships with the company's management, and how their members are prepared to work in the council. The analysis will begin with the scope of consultations.

The role and position of the works council is strongly affected by the type of cooperation with the management of the company, or more specifically, by whether the relationship between them is limited to providing information or takes the form of consultation. The above forms of these relations substantially determine the impact of works councils on decisions taken in the company. When these relations are limited to providing information, then the councils practically have no, or a very limited impact on decision making. This impact may be far greater if these relations take the form of consultation. The said Act requires employers to provide information to works councils and to conduct consultations with them (The Act on informing employees..., 2006).

A defined amount of information is necessary to conduct consultation. This means that the scope of information provided determines the possibility of conducting consultations. But we cannot place an equality sign between the scope of information and the scope of consultation because the employer may in fact only provide information, engaging at the same time in no consultation at all. Both the limited scope of information provided to councils, analyzed above, and the low frequency of meetings of councils call into question the effectiveness of the consultation carried out by councils. The survey shows that in only 59% of enterprises, the employers do not only provide information to councils but also carry out consultations. In 34% of the surveyed enterprises, employers provide only information to councils while there is virtually no cooperation in 7% of the surveyed enterprises.

More detailed information on consultations with works councils is presented in Table 6.1. It presents the frequency of consultation.

Table 6.1: The Frequency of Consultations with Works Councils

Frequency of consultations	% of works councils
The employer rarely consults with the council	39.2%
Consultations are often held	30.4%
Consultations never take place	17.5%
The consultations are always held	12.9%

Source: Results of questionnaire survey

The data in Table 6.1 let us verify the previously presented information on consultation. They show that actually consultations are conducted in only about 43% of the companies surveyed (12.9% always and 30.4% often), because one cannot classify as consultations those which are held rarely or occasionally. There are signs that even such a scope of consultation might be greatly exaggerated, especially if we compare it with the frequency of council meetings. It is difficult to imagine conducting consultations always or often if more than 60% of councils held their meetings once a quarter or less frequently. It is worth noting that the scope of consultations conducted by councils was slightly lower in companies with unions than in those without.

Finally, we will demonstrate how the councils evaluate their position in the company, and what problems and barriers they face. We begin by pointing out that these are not entirely new institutions. In fact, many of them have had a 10-year period of activity, which means that they are in their third 4-year term. The survey shows that the councils have not yet determined what their appropriate role is. As we mentioned above, according to the nearly 40% of respondents, the work of the council is only a formality. A similar number of respondents is aware that the activities of the council are not highly valued by employees; they cite, among others, the lack of confidence in these relatively new institutions of employee participation and the atmosphere of distrust between the employer and employees. Above all, employees believe that the main reason for such a situation is a lack of experience and the absence of basic knowledge of law and economics among of the council members.

Councils are interested in improving their position in the enterprise, but they need an appropriate support mechanism for this. Unlike the trade unions, they do not have hierarchical structures at higher levels. Councils rarely cooperate with each other which mean that they do not exchange experiences with them, or consult. Figure 6.2 shows the types of support expected by councils.

Figure 6.2: Types of Support Expected by Works Council

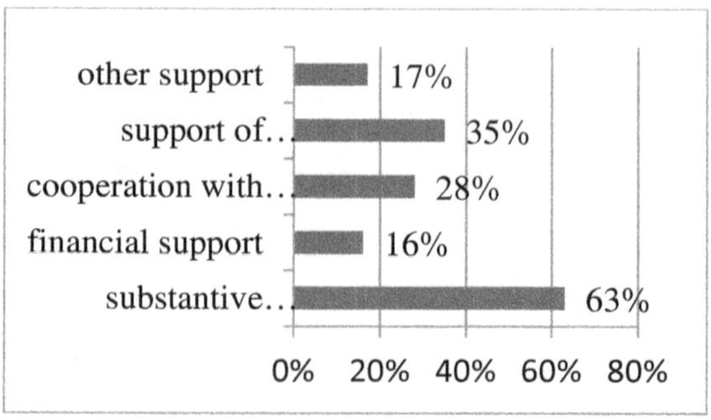

Source: Results of questionnaire survey

The expected forms of support for the works councils presented in Figure 6.2 speak well for the respondents - the chairmen of these councils. They mainly stress substantive assistance because this is the assistance they need the most. They are aware that many members are inadequately prepared to work in the council. Research shows that only about 40% of the members of the council are well or very well prepared to work on the council. It is reported that the vast majority of council members are not participating in the relevant courses or training. Figure 6.2 also shows that what the councils lack the most is knowledge of labor law; such training could help to build a knowledge base. Councils also have the opportunity to engage consultants, but they fail to do it (Wratny, Towalski, & Porter, 2011).

Councils also lack the contacts and cooperation with other councils (28%) which, as mentioned, could help them in solving emerging problems. This type of support may also indicate the need to create a nationwide system modelled on union structures. It is worth emphasizing that among the expected support, the need for funds ranked quite low (16%). This is a bit surprising since the costs borne by employers related to the functioning of councils are relatively small, or none. Only 8% of councils have their own budget and only these councils can therefore plan their activities and thus their spending autonomously. In most councils, the employer, after previous consultation, covers the running costs of the council. In approximately a quarter of the surveyed enterprises, the employer did not finance activities of the council. In light of the above information, one may wonder why there were relatively few indications of financial support for councils. The conclusion is that the lack of financial resources does not pose any special difficulties for the activities of the council, but maybe also because in a large percentage of councils, such activities that require financing are virtually non-existent.

Conclusions

In light of the foregoing considerations, it can be stated that the Polish works councils differ quite substantially from works councils in Western Europe (Skorupińska, 2009). The latter, although differentiated in particular countries, have decades of experience and an established position in many areas of the companies' operations. The broadest powers in this regard reside with councils in Germany and the Netherlands. In these countries, they enjoy the support of trade unions and this support determines to a large extent their strong position. It is precisely this cooperation with trade unions, beneficial for both parties, that plays an important role in their activities, because councils take advantage of the unions' facilities, their experiences, information, and research etc. The unions in turn can report to councils the problems, which they are not able to solve on their own, for presentation at the council's meeting and during negotiations with the employer.

The Polish works councils are only at the beginning of their operation and it is difficult to predict their further development. They operate in a difficult environment which limits their development opportunities. Despite the apparent decline in the negative attitude of trade unions towards councils, at least in those companies where councils currently operate, the clear support for councils from trade unions is still insufficient. The attitudes of Polish employers towards councils are not fundamentally different from those of employers in Western countries. They respect the powers of councils as far as necessary, and more specifically, as far as councils are able to enforce the respect. The weakness of Polish councils presented in this study indicates the modest role of these institutions in Polish industrial relations.

Hope for their further development should be seen in the general revision of the unions' attitude towards councils. Such a revision could be supported by the accumulated experience from the cooperation of the currently existing councils with the trade unions. In the vast majority of companies in which councils currently exist, there are also trade unions whose members are usually also members of councils. Both the councils and the unions should see mutual benefits for each other in such cooperation. The unions must be convinced that the strong position of councils is in their interest since it helps them to fulfill their union demands (Gardawski, 2011).

The development of councils also depends on many other factors. First of all, they need substantive support from the central authorities, mainly the Ministry of Labor and Social Policy. The Ministry should monitor their development including compliance with existing legislation, create structures to support this development, and keep under review the existing legislation on the subject, etc. The development of councils depends also on appropriate preparation of their members for such work. Such preparation should be taken into account already during the elections to the council. Council members should systematically improve their skills by participating in courses or training, both at the enterprise level and at higher levels. If possible, this should be a common training for council members and trade unionists.

Acknowledgements

The works of authors have been supported by the Polish National Science Centre funds allocated with the decision DEC-2013/11/B/HS4/00474.

References

Balsam, K. (2008). Rady pracowników w praktyce [Works councils in practice]. In A. Sobczyk (ed.) *Informowanie i konsultacja pracowników w polskim prawie pracy [Informing and consulting employees in the Polish labor law]* (pp. 237-242). Cracow, Poland: Friedrich Ebert Stiftung.

The European Parliament and the Council of the European Union. (2002). Directive of the European Parliament and of the Council of 11 March 2002 establishing a general framework for informing and consulting employees in the European Community. *Official Journal of the European Communities.* (Directive No. 2002/14/EC). Retrieved from http://www.mlsi.gov.cy/mlsi/dlr/dlr.nsf/All/3A0563DD26A11701C2257A3E003A3B53/$file/Directive%202002-14-EC.pdf?OpenElement.

Fulton, L. (2013). Worker representation in Europe. Labor Research Department and ETUI. Retrieved from http://www.worker-participation.eu/National-Industrial-Relations/Countries.

Gardawski, J. (2011). Partnerstwo społeczne oraz dialog w Europie i w Polsce [Partnership and social dialogue in Europe and in Poland.] In K. Jasiecki (Ed.) *Grupy interesu i lobbing. Polskie doświadczenia w unijnym kontekście [Interest groups and lobbying. Polish experience in the EU context].* Warsaw, Poland: Wydawnictwo IFIS PAN.

Gardawski, J. (1999). *Rozpad bastionu? Związki zawodowe w gospodarce prywatnej [The fall of the bastion? Trade unions in the private economy].* Warsaw, Poland: Instytut Spraw Publicznych.

Kohl, H. and Platzer, H. (2004). *Industrial relations in Central and Eastern Europe: Transformation and integration: a comparison of the eight new EU member states.* Brussels: European Trade Union Institute.

Rudolf, S. (2006). Partycypacja pracownicza – szansa dla przedsiębiorstw i pracodawców [Employee participation - An opportunity for enterprises and employers] In I. Dryll (Ed.) *Partycypacja w formie konsultacji czy informacji. Szanse czy zagrożenia [Participation in the form of consultation or information. Opportunities or threats]* (pp.9-12). Warsaw, Poland: Centrum Partnerstwa Społecznego Dialog.

Rudolf, S. (2007). Pośrednie formy partycypacji pracowniczej w nowych krajach UE [Indirect forms of employee participation in the new EU countries]. In: S. Rudolf (Ed.) *Perspektywy rozwoju partycypacji pracowniczej w Polsce w warunkach Unii Europejskiej [Prospects for the development of employee participation in Poland in conditions of the European Union]* (pp. 279-295). Lodz, Poland: Wydawnictwo Uniwersytetu Łódzkiego.

Skorupińska, K. (2009). *Rola rad zakładowych w krajowych i transnarodowych przedsiębiorstwach europejskich [The role of works councils in national and transnational European companies].* Lodz, Poland: Wydawnictwo Uniwersytetu Łódzkiego.

Skorupińska, K. (2015a). Towards a Europeanization of indirect employee participation: Polish experiences. *Economic and Industrial Democracy,* 1-21. Retrieved from http://citeseerx.ist.psu.edu/viewdoc/download?doi=10.1.1.970.50&rep=rep1&type=pdf.

Skorupińska, K. (2015b). The impact of globalization on the changes in industrial relations and development of employee participation – Evidence from Poland. *Eurasian Journal of Business and Management, 3*(1), 20-29. Retrieved from https://eurasianpublications.com/Eurasian-Journal-of-Business-and-Management/Vol.3-No.1-2015-3.pdf.

The Act of 22 May 2009 amending the law on informing employees and conducting consultations with them. (2009). *Journal of Laws, 97* (805).

The Act on employee self-government in state-owned enterprises of 25 September 1981. (1981). *Journal of Laws, 24*(123).

The Act on informing employees and conducting consultations with them of 7 April 2006. (2006). *Journal of Laws, 79*(550).

Wratny, J. (2006). Prawo pracowników do informacji i konsultacji w świetle Dyrektywy 2002/14 Wspólnoty Europejskiej Europejskiej [The right to information and consultation in the light of Directive 2002/14 of the European Community]. *Praca i Zabezpieczenie Społeczne,* (6 s 49).

Wratny, J., Towalski, R., & Porter, S. (Eds.). (2011). *Rola ekspertów w działalności rad pracowników [The role of experts in the activities of works councils].* Warsaw, Poland: Instytut Pracy i Spraw Socjalnych.

Chapter 7

Determinants of Transnational Regulatory Regimes

George Morgan[11] and Mark Thorum[12]

Abstract

A conceptual framework for cross-country regulatory regimes is modeled through the interplay between the private sector, government, and civil society. Our goal is to provide a baseline economic foundation for discussions of transnational regulation. A cross-country or transnational regulatory apparatus is demanded by some parties based on cost and benefits while other parties may meet the demand by supplying regulation based on cost and benefits. One of the contributions of the paper is an economic classification of the drivers that assists in identifying sources of conflicts between the different parties as well as identifying the factors causing divergence between public and private optimum levels of regulation. It also clarifies why some efforts at transnational regulatory regimes fail while others succeed. A graphical model shows how the interaction between demand and supply as seen from the perspective of private financial firms, government (and the public from which their power is derived), and civil society establishes the optimal level of transnational regulation. We analyze the emergence of various regulatory structures as a result of the interaction of supply of and demand for regulation. We further assess the effects of changes in the drivers that cause shifts in the demand and supply curves for regulation that make the creation of transnational regulation more or less likely. Those include the evolution of a common currency and globalization of trade that changes the level of economic integration over time. The results of the model are applied to and used to discuss the evolution of regulatory processes related to the Markets In Financial Instruments Directive (MIFID) as a process of shifting demand and supply curves that moves the optimal solution. We address how the shifting characteristics of the political and macroeconomic

---

[11] gmorgan@vt.edu

[12] mark.thorum@exim.gov

environments, legacy national cultures, and attitudes toward the regulation of financial services and markets affected the path of MIFID.

Introduction

In recent decades, numerous efforts to establish cross-country regulatory regimes in financial markets have been undertaken especially in Europe. Those include Basel Capital Accords on banking, the Markets In Financial Instruments Directive (MIFID) on financial markets, and the creation of an EU banking authority, international financial stability councils, and others. The drivers for such regimes are not well-understood, and the conflicts between the different parties that can result in failures of such regimes have not been readily identified.

In this paper, we develop a conceptual framework for the successful establishment of cross-country regulatory regimes and model the interplay between the private sector, government, and the public to address the issues identified and analyzed in Thorum (2015). We start with the notion that a cross-country or transnational regulatory apparatus is demanded by some parties based on cost and benefits while other parties may meet the demand by supplying regulation. Cross-country-coordinated regulatory regimes (such as Basel and MIFID) have specific problems that must be overcome if the demand for such regulation is to be met. However, the costs of supplying the regulatory regime may be too high relative to the demand, and thus, some types of cross-country regulation are not successfully provided.

First, we examine the demand for regulation. Fragmented financial markets can be costly to navigate as firms operate across multiple regulatory jurisdictions. Therefore, there will be a private demand for cross-country if not coordinated regulation. In the absence of such regulation, firms may participate in financial activities to a lesser extent and thus constrain economic growth, employment, efficiency, and standards of living (see Rajan & Zingales, 1998, 2003; Acemoglu, Johnson, & Robenson, 2005).

There will be additional demand for regulation from "*civil society*" including the customers of financial institutions and the public owners of claims on financial institutions. Society will see broader implications of fragmented markets with fragmented regulation. Those include higher transactions costs, lower diversification, and greater risk of loss (deposit insurance schemes notwithstanding). Major crises can affect the perception of the risks of fragmented regulation.

The demand for a global regulatory framework for the international financial markets derives from the complex interaction of numerous factors: economic globalization and its attendant effects, the rapid growth of structured products and derivatives, the inability of national regulators to keep abreast of financial innovation, the increasing number of financial institutions with global reach and systemic importance, and the growing role played by less-regulated entities such as the structured investment vehicles (IMF, 2008). Political stability, transparency, and legal protections may also influence financial markets governance (Goodell & Aggarwal, 2009). Kwok and Tadesse (2006) argue that cultural dispositions toward risk can also influence the financial governance architecture. Finally, the significant cross-national variation in the regulation and supervision of financial sectors may also give rise to the need for a global governance framework.

Financial regulators differ in terms of their levels of independence, relations with regulated firms and political leaders, policy preferences, and statutory authority. Absent a global framework for the international markets, those differences may result in divergent policy outcomes, facilitate regulatory arbitrage, and contribute to systemic risks (Mosely & Singer, 2011). A more defined regulatory regime at the international level would allow regulators to identify, measure, and deal more effectively with global systemic risks. However, the homogeneity induced by a transnational regulatory regime increases the probability of risks being systemic and creating contagion.

Next, we examine the "*supply*" or provision of regulatory services. A transnational regulatory regime requires coordination across the various states. Coordination is assumed to be a costly enterprise that is related to the number of countries involved, the breadth of cultural differences, and the level of financial and economic integration across the countries spanned by the regulatory regime. The cost of regulation is reasonably modeled as increasing at the margin as the number of countries rises and as the extent to which their economies become more unlinked and de-integrated. In addition, because de-linking of regulatory regimes and of economies exposes economies to costs generated by actions such as regulatory arbitrage, the level of de-linking also plays a role in the supply.

Government will also incur a cost of supplying regulation as well as produce a benefit from regulation. The cost of supplying regulation is the cost of operating a regulatory agency with employees' wages, rental and lease expenses on facilities, subsidies, and contingent claims. The marginal benefit that government will see is a reduction in costs of operating the government and electoral support from the voting public. As the stringency (that is, the degree of conformance with a centralized menu of requirements) of regulation is increased, the marginal benefit will decrease.

We develop a graphical model interacting (and intersecting) demand and supply as seen from the perspective of private financial firms, government, and civil society (similar in nature to the Santomero and Watson (1977) model for bank capital regulation). Our goal is to provide a baseline economic foundation for discussions of transnational regulation. The drivers of demand

and supply will establish the optimal level of transnational regulation as seen by each of the parties from an economic perspective. One of the contributions of our paper is the classification and organization of the drivers from an economic perspective. Using Simmons' (2001) framework, we classify the appropriate regulatory regimes according to the cost of coordination and the externalities of de-linked financial markets and regulation as shown in Table 7.1. Centralized/Transnational regulation, decentralized/national regulation, and various ad hoc regulatory schemes can be described within that taxonomy as in Thorum (2015). That will help to explain why there are conflicts between the different parties, what factors are causing the divergence between public and private optimum levels of regulation, and why some efforts at transnational regulatory regimes fail while others succeed. In this paper, we analyze the emergence of the various regulatory structures as a result of the supply and demand for regulation. We further assess (using "*comparative statics*" analysis) the effects of changes in the drivers that cause shifts in the demand and supply curves for regulation that make the creation of transnational regulation more or less likely. Those include the evolution of a common currency and globalization of trade that serve to increase over time the level of economic integration. We argue that effects on marginal costs/benefits are the relevant issue not on total costs and benefits.

Table 7.1: Taxonomy of International Financial Regulatory Models

FRAMEWORK	CHARACTERISTICS
Super Regulator (Centralized) Model	A global super regulator either using an existing entity or creating a new entity that is less prone to political interference from member countries. A "*WTO*" analogy for the international capital markets.
Regulatory Harmonization (Decentralized) Model	A new multilateral regulatory framework resulting in a partial loss of sovereignty for national regulators. Harmonization of national regulatory practices as common, agreed-upon regulations are incorporated into the national legal framework of each member. (See Anderson, 1994.) Enforcement occurs at both national and international level. National regulators remain the central actors. Recent examples include (i) the EU initiative to coordinate the European securities industries, MIFID, and (ii) the Basel Accords that proscribe regulations on capital, market and operational risks.
Event/Issue Driven (ad hoc) Model	Fragmented global financial leadership fragmented where regulatory coordination is top down and issue-specific. The primary actors are the national regulators from G-7/G20 countries.

Source: Thorum (2015)

The results of the model are applied to and used to discuss the evolution of regulatory processes related to MIFID as a process of shifting demand and supply curves that move the "*optimal*" solution from the bottom of Table 7.1 toward the top. The taxonomy is the basis for a continuous spectrum of the level of coordination/centralization in a demand and supply of transnational regulation. We address how success or failure of that "*upward*" movement changes over time depending on the various characteristics of the political and macro-economic environments as well as legacy national cultures and attitudes toward the regulation of financial services and markets.

Evolution of European regulation – An example of multinational interactions

MIFID's protracted history and nine-year implementation process (See Appendix 7.1) give rise to a basic question: If EU policy emphasizes the importance of financial markets integration, why are member states unsuccessful in coordinating their respective policies? One contributing factor for the phenomenon may lie with the asymmetrical distribution of power in the international financial markets. Regulatory harmonization reflects more of a top-down scenario than a multilateral approach (Simmons, 2001). Rather than implementing a pan-European approach, EU member states are often comfortable following Anglo-American practice and British regulators exercise their own interests to maintain the existing regime. Second, divergent models of state involvement in the domestic economy can affect the demand for regulation. Third, member governments may be loath to supply a new regime that would disadvantage their national firms and/or lead to a flight of capital to less regulated countries, and fourth, the increased economic and political linkages over time within the EU altered the conditions of demand and supply of regulation. As economic integration with a common currency and political arrangements such as the Schengen agreement have brought European countries closer, the question of financial market integration has only recently emerged.

The global crisis of 2008 and the more recent European sovereign debt crisis exposed the systemic weaknesses of the EU's regulatory architecture with national governments stepping in to fill the void. The fact that the efforts by individual members can be counter-productive when others adopt similar policies highlights the value of a coordinated effort. For example, the Irish government's decision to guarantee the deposits of its troubled banks prompted a flow of capital away from the UK that stimulated the UK government to follow suit with comparable depositor protections. In response to integration, the EU refocused its strategic priorities from the liberalization and harmonization of securities regulation to macro supervision as the costs of the existing regime and the perceived benefits to society of a more centralized regime increased leading to the promulgation of MIFID II and the Markets in Financial Instruments Regulation ("*MIFIR*")[13], for example.

Policy diffusion/transmission and financial markets governance

The study of policy diffusion offers insight into the processes through which the regulatory policies adopted by a select group of countries or institutions spread or "*diffuse*" to the peripheral countries. A diffusion perspective on financial markets governance argues that the regulatory order and market's best practices are first implemented by a select group of hegemonic states or market leaders and subsequently diffused to the remaining market participants. We argue below that the process is one of shifting supply and demand curves for regulation based on such factors as coordination costs, economic integration, financial linkages, expanding scope, expanding number of members, and a common currency.

Diffusion of policies and practices can be defined as "the process by which the adoption of innovation by members of a social system is communicated through certain channels over time and triggers mechanisms that increase the probability of its adoption by other members who have not yet adopted it" (Levi-Faur, 2005). The policy diffusion concept builds on the empirical observation that nations choose similar institutions over a period of time resulting in both temporal and spatial clusters of policy reform. Zachary Elkins and Beth Simmons (2005) observe that such "clustered policy making" is often coordinated by a hegemonic power or international organization through coercion or learning. David Levi-Faur and Jacit Jordana (2005) posit that diffusion should not be viewed as a smooth, mechanistic process because aspects of policies may converge and diverge at the same time. Viewed graphically, that causes the demand and supply curves to oscillate.

Policy diffusion literature distinguishes between three approaches to diffusion: horizontal, top-down, and bottom up. Horizontal refers to an interdependent decision process wherein the decision to adopt financial markets reform is taken collectively by an interdependent group of regulators.

---

[13] The scope of MIFID II expanded to include additional financial firms, authorized regulatory authority over certain financial products and derivatives trading, and increases pre- and post-trade transparency. MIFIR makes policies of four new bodies (including the ECB) with enhanced legal status superseding national regulators. See Thorum (2015) and more information at http://www.consilium.europa.eu/uedocs/cms_Data/docs/pressdata/en/ec/131388.pdf.

Typically, they face similar incentives to cooperate and are influenced by the actions of the others. Successful policy reform in one sector increases the likelihood that similar policy measures will be replicated by other nations' regulators. The bottom up explanation reflects a domestic dialogue among different interest groups and national regulators. Finally, the top-down approach explains national regulatory reform as a response to exogenous pressures. Similar to hegemonic stability theory, top down policy diffusion gives prominence to the asymmetrical power relationship between the "*market leader*" in the core and the "*market follower*" in the periphery.

Beth Simmons (2001) contributes to the debate by constructing a conceptual framework to explain the interaction between the financial hegemon and the financial regulators of other countries on the issue of regulatory reform. She posits that Neoliberal institutional theory and other economic theories such as "*racing to the bottom*" are less effective in explaining the outcomes of this interaction. Simmons remarks that, according to the tenets of liberal institutionalism, the international capital markets would have made a good candidate for institutionalization. However, there is no established organization that could serve as the WTO equivalent of the capital markets. She proposes, therefore, to focus on the mechanisms of harmonization instead and provides a four-quadrant taxonomy that incorporates the concepts of externalities and incentives to emulate. According to Simmons, the financial hegemon enacts financial regulatory reform based on the needs of its domestic political economy, not the needs of the other states. By virtue of being hegemonic, it would be costlier to change its market policy to suit other countries. It must, however, always deal with the consequences of enacting reform given its leadership position in the international system. Policy reform can have three outcomes: (i) incentives to other countries to emulate the reform, (ii) incentives for other states to diverge from this policy—typically as a result of the perceived cost, and (iii) no incentives to act. The hegemon will adopt the most cost efficient method.

In Simmons' quadrant one, there are high incentives for the others to emulate the financial innovation of the hegemon and high externalities for the hegemon if the policy is not implemented. As such, the hegemon leads by enacting the innovation first. Then, there is typically a lot of following the leader on the issues, implicitly cooperating with the hegemon without formal coordination. Simmons includes capital adequacy in the quadrant, arguing that non-hegemons had a significant interest to emulate the innovation to keep their banks on a level playing field with the hegemon banks. Not to do so would make the non-hegemon banks appear riskier than the hegemon banks and put them at a competitive disadvantage (despite the appearance of an advantage from their lower overall cost of capital). The high externalities of that particular example derive from the systemic risk of a weaker bank becoming insolvent and dragging down banks in another country.

Quadrant two reflects a "*high externalities but low incentive to emulate*" scenario. The author places anti-money laundering in this quadrant as it is more important to the U.S. than many other countries that may not have similar legislation. In that scenario, there is an underlying lower desire to cooperate between the hegemon and other states as the costs may appear to outweigh the benefits of compliance. As a result, the hegemon typically seeks formal coordination through a political solution and exerts influence through an international organization/regime structure. Quadrant three reflects low incentives to cooperate and low externalities, while quadrant four reflects high incentives to emulate with low externalities. In the last quadrant, the hegemon may not bother pressuring other states toward compliance as the issue is less important to the hegemon. Other nations should follow as it is in their interest to do so. Simmons puts the adoption of international accounting standards in quadrant four.

Adopting Simmons' style of categorization, the most appropriate regulatory structure depends on the interaction between the different factors as shown in the two-dimensional table below. In this paper, we will analyze the emergence of the various regulatory structures as a result of the supply and demand for regulation.

Table 7.2: Factors That Promote Various Regulatory Structures

Coordination Costs	(Externality) Cost of Delinking Markets	
	Low Cost	**High Cost**
Low Costs	Loosely Centralized (MIFID)	Highly Centralized (WTO Style)
High Costs	No Coordination or Integration	Ad Hoc or Follow- the Leader Coordination (EU pre-MIFID)

Source: Authors' adaptation of Simmons (2005)

Braun and Gilardi (2006) provide a similar description of the different diffusion mechanisms: coercion, competitive interdependence, and interaction among policy actors that engenders common norms of action and policy choices.

Fabrizio Gilardi (2005) studies the widespread establishment of independent regulatory agencies (IRAs) throughout European countries and in various sectors during the 1990s. He views those institutions as a core feature of the governance structure for regulatory capitalism. Gilardi attributes the diffusion to several factors: the creation of IRAs was an attempt to demonstrate commitment to policy reform and to enhance governance; second, the EU agenda called for creation of independent regulators; and third, policy decisions by states are interdependent. He concludes that the widespread establishment of IRAs reflects the diffusion process and that individual state decisions have been interdependent.

All of the cases of diffusion mechanisms describe the methods by which shifts in demand or supply of regulation occur. Next we address that framework.

A model of demand and supply of regulation

We develop a stylized model of demand and supply of regulation based on the concept that there are benefits and costs that vary as the level of national freedom to establish policies is reduced. We focus on the extent to which the regulatory regimes are coordinated and even centralized. At one extreme, one central authority creates the rules that must be followed by all the member states. At the other extreme, each state is free to set its own configuration of regulations as it sees fit but certainly taking account of the rules used by other member states against which it competes. There is assumed to be a spectrum of independence and coordination between those two extremes. The parties determine what level of coordination/centralization of rules is optimal. The locations of their demand and supply curves depend, in part, on the tradeoffs between the costs of coordination and the benefits of linking policies.

To keep the analysis tractable, we divide the economy into two sectors, private industry and public. The public sector includes individuals and their representative government. We incorporate six main aspects of the costs and benefits discussed in the literature: 1) compliance costs and their reduction related to increase coordination, 2) the sub-optimality of adopting rules created elsewhere that do not allow reaching first best business decisions domestically, 3) increased efficiencies associated with a commonly adopted set of rules, 4) the cost of lost sovereignty and national pride, 5) expected costs of systemic risks and contagions, and 6) operating costs associated with supplying regulation by national supervisors.

We adopt the standard economic perspectives on costs and benefits (with some exceptions where marginal costs may be decreasing and marginal benefits, at least at first, may be increasing) that are necessary to produce an optimal solution (or in some cases corner solutions – solutions that bump against the constraints rather than being on the interior of the feasible set of possible solutions). At least over some ranges, marginal benefits will diminish with increasing doses of the prescribed activity (coordination in this case) and marginal costs will grow with increasing doses as discussed below with some exceptions possible over some ranges. Because we are interested in the extent to which formal coordination (such as MIFID) is implemented across numerous state players, we first start with a fixed number of such players and examine the costs and benefits. For concreteness, it is often helpful to employ the number of regulations or regulatory areas from 0 to m (perhaps thousands of regulations or thousands of pages of regulations) as a proxy for the level of coordination that is formally implemented. We can then consider the incremental addition of coordination in "*one more*" regulatory area to the status quo. As discussed below, the status quo could be a state of highly independent states with no links or a tacit cooperative network without formal rules of coordination.

Private industry

The industry realizes that there are benefits to regulation. It is better if everyone plays by the same rules and if there is an "*enforcer*" that holds firms accountable. Customers perceive a benefit to dealing with firms that must comply with a known set of rules and regulations. Thus, firms have an incentive to support a regulatory environment for their domestic and international operations. Even at high levels of national freedom and independence (i.e., low levels of coordination), there is a cost associated with operations in the status quo regulatory environment. As the increment to the level of coordination increases from 0 toward m, benefits are reaped through the reduction in the costs of operating across the breadth of states due to less need to track and comply with a smaller and smaller variety of regulatory reporting jurisdictions. Cost of operating across the multiple jurisdictions may decrease in total, but at some point, adding measures to the coordination regime means that the amount of the benefit decreases with each incremental increase in coordination and with the resulting increased homogeneity. Furthermore, the firms' customers will perceive a benefit to coordination as their costs of doing business with firms decreases, but the benefits to increased coordination will decrease with each increment of coordination and centralization. The demand for the firm's services reflects that benefit conveyed by customers but with decreasing marginal benefits to the firms. The benefits of coordination are experienced by the firm on net as decreasingly beneficial at the margin.

Similarly, at low levels of coordination, there is an operating cost of adhering to regulations borne by the private sector that causes business decisions to deviate from the uncoordinated decisions. Those costs may be quite high even at low levels of coordination across multiple jurisdictions in the status quo. As the level of coordination increases, there is more likelihood that the regulations will be less-suited to the domestic situation thereby increasing the (opportunity) costs associated with a coordinated environment. Regulations that do not conform to the domestic market impose costs on the firms due to deviations from what would otherwise be their domestic optimum (the status quo). Such deviations from the private domestically optimal regulation reduce economic well-being (otherwise, that level of regulation would have been adopted in the status quo). The incremental costs of coordination increase as more and more "*externalities*" are imposed by the coordinated regime due to deviations from the domestic optimum. In addition, the investment required to successfully coordinate across multiple countries and cultures can be significant. That shifts the cost curve upward and increases the slope as incrementally including more countries in the coordinated regime will be increasingly costly.

The tradeoff of the benefits against the costs establishes for the country's private sector that an optimum level of coordination can be illustrated by a standard supply and demand curve. Downward sloping marginal benefits derived from lower marginal compliance costs as coordination increases intersect with increasing marginal costs of regulation due to domestic sub-optimality as coordination increases. An optimal level of regulatory coordination results.

Analysis of private sector optimum

The location of the marginal benefit and marginal cost curves depends on the circumstances and changes over time.

The larger the number of states/cultures/regions spanned by the business's operations, the costlier it is to operate transnationally. A larger number of states and more diversity of the cultures across those states mean more fragmentation at any given level of coordination, so the costs of tracking, monitoring, and reporting shift the total cost curve upward with added numbers of markets in the region of operation. However, the marginal cost may be unaffected if incremental coordination occurs across a fixed number of markets (independent of the total). The marginal cost could decrease for coordination measures because the cost savings to a more-widely (as a percent of the total) adopted rule are greater. International scope creates an opportunity for cost savings with coordination at each marginal step. So, the cost savings from each increment of coordination, i.e., the benefits curve, will be higher the greater the number, n, of prospective participants. That will mean an optimum that is, other things equal, higher on the coordination spectrum for greater numbers of states or more diversity of states and cultures.

In financial markets, particularly the London-based banks will see a benefit to coordination in reducing their costs corresponding to a shift right in the private demand by the industry leader. For a bank operating in a situation with many participants, for every increase in the scope of the bank's operations, the greater is the benefit of coordination. For the followers, there may be no shift related to the scope of operations or at least the shift would be much smaller.

Although maintenance costs of complying with a regime after it is agreed upon may not be directly related to the number of parties, cost increases as the cultural diversity becomes wider and as the needs of the various parties are more divergent (say developed vs. developing countries). So, as a first approximation, compliance costs are also viewed as increasing in number of participants and marginal benefits to coordination higher (cost savings are higher).

The opportunity costs due to deviation from the uncoordinated optimum are unaffected by the number of participants. The sub-optimality loss is not related to the number of participants but to the effect of the rule adopted. Only to the extent that more participants might make the rule more burdensome would it affect the sub-optimality or business decision costs.

Coordination is costlier in terms of the externalities because coordination increases statistical dependence and correlation across countries. Tail risk in one region is transmitted to another region when the regions have common regulatory practices as opposed to being independent. That is a source of domestic "*sub-optimality*" that would shift the cost curve upward, and to the extent that the marginal cost is increased, it would push the optimum level of coordination to the left.

In contrast, the existence of a common currency provides a level of integration that already has reduced the compliance costs of coordination and increases the level of shared response to events in one region relative to another. That is, we view the common currency's effect on the private sector as a substitute for regulatory coordination efforts.[14] As such, the incremental cost of additional coordination is essentially moved along the curves further making the increment to compliance cost smaller and the opportunity cost higher than when there is not a common currency. Thus, both curves shift to the left.

---

14 In this case, complementarity does not seem consistent with decreasing marginal benefits and increasing marginal cost. If more integration has dimensions that reflect an implicit coordination, then assuming that increases benefits at the margin contradicts decreasing marginal benefits.

We note that integration in political, cultural, commercial (trade), and financial dimensions can have different implications for the costs and benefits of coordinated regulation (in financial markets). Nonetheless, we base our analysis on the concept of substitutability of existing integration for further coordination, decreasing marginal benefits and increasing marginal domestic opportunity costs that apply across levels of existing integration consistent with the above recognition of the shape of the benefits and cost curves. The size of the effects may differ depending on whether the integration is political (affecting particularly the administrative or operating cost savings) or financial (affecting the opportunity cost and level of externalities already borne). A higher level of integration is analogous to moving the starting point for the coordinated regulation increments down the benefits curve and up the opportunity cost curve, i.e., equivalent to shifting the curves to the left.

In particular, globalization can increase economic integration. As with a common currency, that increases the common "*culture*" and economic foundation from which the benefits of a coordinated regulatory regime are initiated. But that also makes the potential for events and policies to deviate from a domestic optimum greater as it does with increasing marginal costs. As economic globalization increases over time, the benefits curve will shift down and become less steeply sloped while the cost curve will shift upward pushing the optimal level of coordination to the left. That occurs in part due to the fact that integration (and economic coordination) is occurring through other mechanisms (substitutes), and the benefit to coordinated regulation of financial markets contributes less.

In cases where one state serves as the industry leader by virtue of its history, continuity, or ability to attract industry to its shores, the location of the curves will be affected. For the leader, the benefits of reduced cost of operating across multiple jurisdictions will be positive but smaller than for other countries, especially when the degree of diffusion is already high. (When the initial level of diffusion is low, the leader could use coordination to "*force*" diffusion of its rules into other markets thereby increasing the benefits to harmonization.) The opportunity costs for the leader will be substantially higher as that state has certainly chosen its configuration of regulation to meet its internal needs and desires from others to "*coordinate*" are based on desire to deviate from the leader's established regime (as mentioned earlier in Simmon's categorization). Thus, for the leader, the optimum level of formal coordination is very low. Its leadership position substitutes for formal regulation. Again, substitution implies that the curve shifts to the left relative to what it would be for a leaderless group. If that leadership role is acknowledged within the group of countries, then the costs of compliance with the regulation could be high for deviations from the status quo, but the marginal benefit to increased formal coordination is very low. When other states already follow the leader, the benefit in terms of reduction of compliance costs becomes deminimus quickly because of the level of diffusion that has already happened. The benefits curve thus rapidly becomes inelastic. The cost of sub-optimality for the followers may currently be high, but the cost is not changed much for each incremental addition of formal coordination for the followers. We could represent that as a flatter sloped curve at a high level for the cost curve versus the highly inelastic benefits curve. The intersection occurs at low levels of coordination.

Public sector

While private industry assesses tradeoffs to coordinated regulation, customers and societal institutions also make their assessment. Here, we include government as a supplier of regulation as representing the needs of its constituents in the public. In particular, taxpayers support the government's budget and dictate its policies.

Customers experience some benefit from regulation and must consider the value of increasing coordination across member states. The benefits from coordination can be significant to the extent that customers can execute transactions at known costs common across various jurisdictions with known and common rules on disclosures, practices, and procedures. Consumers can benefit from efficiencies in trade and finance due to fewer frictions such as transactions costs. Again, despite the size of the benefits, the consideration of the optimal regime depends on the incremental benefits from increased coordination. As the level of coordination increases from zero, the marginal benefit of each additional increment is initially high but eventually becomes smaller. Initially, the benefit from more integrated markets is significant due to the reduced fragmentation of markets and ability to trade in multiple environments more freely (more liquidity, less transactions costs, lower information costs). But the increments' benefits dissipate at the margin. In part, the imposition of rules from other parties may cause deviations from the domestically (culturally) desirable set of rules and create costs to consumers of the services in terms of restrictions on availability and concerns such as privacy and security (either too loose or too stringent). Although the benefits associated with reductions of the costs associated with systemic risks belong in the benefits curve, we defer discussion to the assessment of the net cost of harmonization because of the convolution of costs and probabilities of contagions.

The government produces the regulation with the taxpayers' funds and decides based on the marginal benefits versus the costs on the optimal level of coordinated regulation. The cost of implementing a coordinated regulatory regime may not be significant, but we model it here as an increasing function of the level of coordination. Initially, going from an independent domestic regulatory regime to the first steps of coordination add minimal costs to achieve common rules in specific narrow areas (say the first $m/2$ of the m regulations); however, at some point, the costs of coordinating with other states and cultures as well as negotiating the specifics of the wide range of regulatory rules increase at the margin. Those reach a peak because, in the extreme, the local cost of a regulatory regime dictated elsewhere is very small because all the decisions are made in some other jurisdiction (e.g., Brussels in the EU). Thus, ultimately, the marginal cost curve drops. That could produce a second local optimum at the extreme of completely centralized regulation, but that is unlikely to be a global optimum. Another factor that increases the cost of more coordination is the cost of lost sovereignty over one's affairs. A psychological cost and loss of national pride, while difficult to measure, should be factored into the cost curve and may offset most of the decrease in costs from a centralized regulatory regime.

In addition, harmonization can be linked to the extent to which international systemic risks are significant. To the extent that international systemic risks are significant, regulators who see fragmented regulation could desire greater ability to identify, measure, and deal more effectively with global systemic risks through a harmonized or centralized regulatory regime. However, we note that sharing of information does not require more regulation or even harmonization. Nonetheless, harmonization can promote better information sharing.

The expected cost of contagion across states can be expressed as the product of two components: the expected cost conditional on contagion events (CCC) and the probability of a systemic crisis or contagion (PSC). Harmonizing and collaborating ahead of the crisis familiarizes the different countries' authorities with practices in other countries and makes it easier to collaborate and reduce CCC in the event of a crisis. At first, coordination efforts are beneficial by reducing CCC. They allow regulators to track spillover risks more effectively. But, the benefit of incremental harmonizing gets smaller and smaller possibly becoming zero. It does not take much harmonization to gain familiarity with the authorities in other countries so that when a crisis occurs there is greater collaboration in reducing the costs. Harmonization beyond some limit provides little to no incremental gains in terms of benefits (reduced CCC) in some future crisis. The PSC component, on the other hand, increases in harmonization, and ultimately, a fully centralized authority achieves a maximum level of homogeneity across states that enhances the probability of global systemic effects. As the regime moves toward more rules being dictated by a centralized entity, the practices of the regulated firms become more *homogeneous*. If one bank or country is heavily involved in lending to subprime (housing, auto, student loans, etc.), then they all will be (or a greater percentage will be) compared to the situation when individual states have more autonomy. As it is for securities in a portfolio, as they approach being perfectly correlated, the risk of the portfolio becomes greater. Adding one more measure on which harmony is achieved gives the individual states one less degree of freedom to operate differently. Systemic risk, therefore, increases and the cost of harmonization increases at an increasing rate. At first, the CCC effect is a net benefit relative to the effect on PSC. However, at some limited level of harmonization, the benefits dissipate and the increasingly costly effect on PSC dominates. The *net* expected cost of contagion then contributes an upward pressure on the marginal cost curve beyond some limited amount of harmonization.

The tradeoff of consumers and government (representing consumers) is illustrated below in Figure 7.1.

Figure 7.1: Consumer and Government Tradeoff of Benefits vs. Costs of Coordinated Regulation

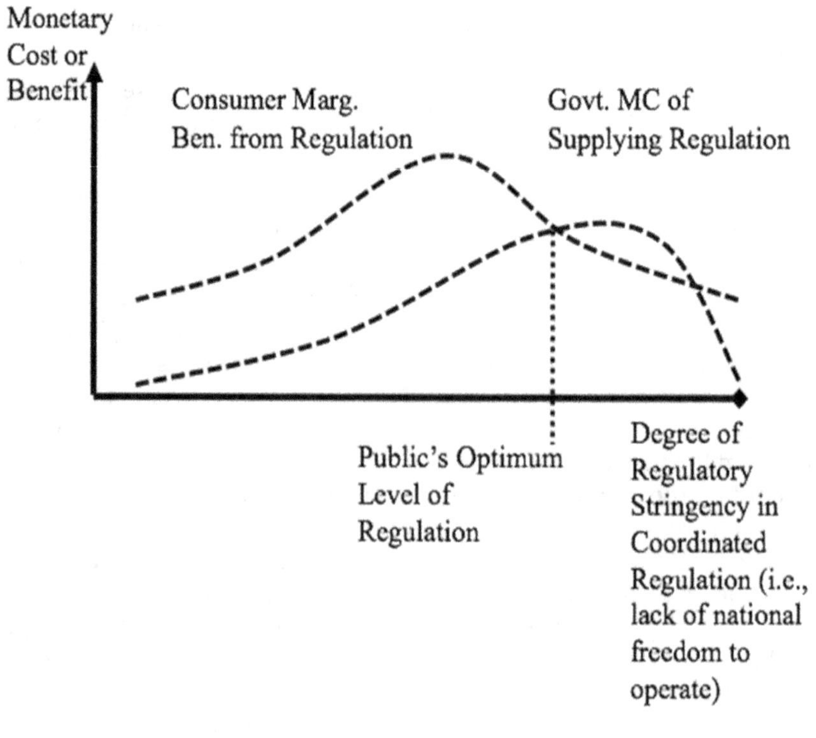

Analysis of the provision of regulation

The larger the number of jurisdictions and the greater the fragmentation of the markets, the greater the benefits that consumers see to increased coordination. More cultural diversity across the member states thus shifts the benefits curve up and pushes the optimum to the right. Greater diversity across the members may not have an initial effect on the marginal cost of supplying regulation, but at levels where the negotiations become more involved and require agreement among a more diverse set of parties on larger numbers of issues, the marginal costs may shift (twist) upward. The two effects could be offsetting in terms of the optimal level when there is a more diverse set of players. Economists may see a large shift in the benefits curve, whereas the patriotic consumer and resource-conscious national supervisor may see a larger shift in the cost curve when diversity of members is increased. So, it is not clear whether increasing diversity results in an increased level of formal coordination across the more diverse set of participants as it does for the private sector. At worst, greater diversity could increase convergence between public and private sector analysis of the optimum level of coordination, and that could produce a consensus on action for "*reforms.*"

The stronger the leadership role of a dominant state (i.e., the more other states naturally take the role of "*followers*" and emulators), the lower the marginal benefit would be to a formal effort to coordinate regulation depending on the dominant state's determination of the externalities. With low incentives for emulation wherein there is less ability for a state to exert a leader-follower relationship (as in Simmons' Quadrant 2), that weaker leadership role produces more incentive for formal coordination. For example, the benefits to an "*open market*" in goods to a leading exporter of goods in a group of countries, say Germany relative to the rest of Europe, inspires the country to work toward coordination within a free trade zone when other countries do not have incentives to naturally emulate and follow trade policies. But where leadership/followership is more pronounced, as with London in financial markets, less effort toward formal coordination will result. The marginal cost of supply might also be low for the acknowledged market leader, but it is reasonable to expect that the optimum level of coordination would not shift further to the right, and the status quo would remain more likely to persist with little formal coordination and the more informal follow-the-leader regime would remain.

The greater the span or scope (geopolitical) of the regulated entities, the greater may be the benefit that the regulators see to reducing the cost of contagion conditional on systemic risks arising. To the extent that harmonization facilitates information flow, harmonization can reduce the CCC and thus allow better control of the spillover and systemic risks. The cost curve shifts down until the point at which the marginal effect of harmonization on information flow dissipates. That is not to say that there is not some total benefit to harmonization, but only that the marginal benefit eventually becomes zero. The probability of systemic crisis (PSC), on the other hand, increases with more harmonization and, with a centralized regime, crises are almost guaranteed to become a systemic problem. Greater scope may have no effect on PSC or by virtue of adding more sources of possible origins of a crisis, may increase the probability, but the effect of incremental harmonization may be negligible especially at levels near to centralization.

At levels of harmonization that are very low, the marginal advantage of the next level of coordination is larger when the span or scope of the institutions is greater to the extent that the costs of systemic risks are greater. That shifts the left section of the cost curve to the right and the public-sector optimum toward more harmonization from a low base. Evaluated where there is already an extensive level of harmonization, i.e., closer to a centralized regime, then more of the same will likely not change the optimum or at worst push toward less centralization in an effort to short-circuit the systemic effects (and mistakes) of a centralized rule-making body.

For the government, we argue that globalization and a common currency either have no effect on costs, or act as complementary factors toward coordination. A common currency may provide countries with increased integration at the government level. That would smooth the way for further coordination in other spheres such as financial markets. Thus, rather than moving along the cost curves, regulatory coordination costs would be reduced due to familiarity with other governments through the process of managing a common currency. But in many cases, the monetary authorities are separate agencies and often independent agencies from the regulatory. Furthermore, a common currency would be controlled by a central bank for the currency union and not through coordination of various national central banks. So, familiarity and complementarity of costs may not prevail. In situations where the financial regulator and monetary authority are the same organization, costs of coordination may be reduced in situations of a common currency.

Globalization could likewise be viewed in this sector as complementary to coordinated regulation. Governments and consumers would be comfortable dealing across borders with the common currency providing for increased familiarity. The benefits to coordination that reduces contagion and spillover could also be greater. Substantial ability to coordinate trade and commerce would also reduce implementation costs at least initially. The marginal costs of added coordinated regulations after the first several would still likely remain as in a lesser globalized context. So, the left part of the cost curve would shift down but would eventually rise to join the original marginal cost curve. Nonetheless, that may result in a shift to the right of the optimum level of coordinated regulation. It is unclear whether the cost of lost sovereignty would be viewed as higher or lower in general as a result of globalization, but applying the concept of increasing marginal cost, globalization would increase the marginal cost and increase tensions against more coordination from the public sector arising from the sovereignty source.

Optimum solutions for the economy

By combining the private industry tradeoff analysis of marginal costs and benefits and the public tradeoff illustrated in Figure 7.1, we obtain Figure 7.2, showing the optimum from a macro perspective. A divergence between the private industry optimum (the leftmost intersect) and the public interest optimum (the rightmost intersect) means that there is not agreement on how the economy should be constructed and regulated. In Figure 7.2, we assume that equal weight is given to the private and public sectors (a euro of net benefit by one party is the same as a euro net benefit of any other party, so the simple sum is the net social benefit shown as the solid lines in Figure 7.2 and producing the "*social*" optimum), but that is not necessarily the political solution to the disagreement. Nonetheless, as the optimums evaluated by the private and public sectors converge, the "*social*" optimum, generally in between the other two as shown in Figure 7.2, will also converge to that agreement. A narrowing of the discrepancy fosters an environment of agreement on the outcome. A divergence, as illustrated in Figure 7.2, between the two optimums likely inhibits a solution from being implemented. Then, the status quo may prevail, or the minimum amount of coordinated regulation could be implemented. Shifts in the curves over time that serve to create convergence will likely produce an implementation that is socially acceptable.

We should note that there is a configuration where a corner solution arises for the public sector. If the cost curve does not rise fast enough or the benefits curve rises significantly, the optimum solution for the private sector is a centralized regulatory regime. In that instance, legislation or other means of changing the regulations could be implemented, thus giving less weight to the private sector optimum and establishing "*convergence*" with the public sector's desire for a centralized or highly "*coordinated*" regulatory regime.

Figure 7.2: Social Optimum of Demand for and Supply of Coordinated Regulation

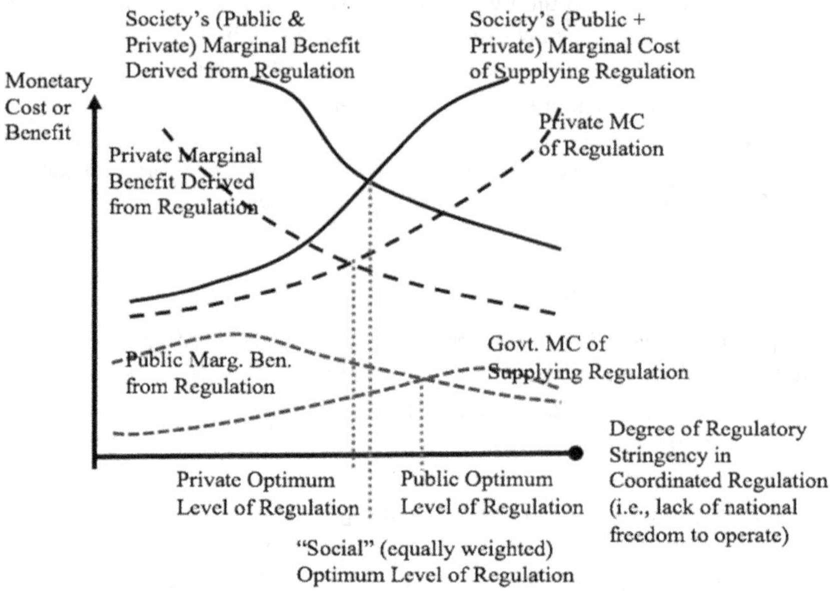

The effects of globalization, increased diversity, and a common currency on the divergence of the sector optimums are similar but not identical. Globalization (a characteristic of the degree of economic linkages between countries as opposed to harmonization or coordination of regulatory policies in a particular sector such as financial firms) results in a shift to the left of the industry/private sector optimum while the public optimum may move to the right (unless sovereignty issues dominate). If the starting position is, as we assume, that the private sector's optimum is for a less coordinated, less-centralized regime, then globalization increases the divergence and conflict between the two sectors. Because the two sectors move in opposite directions, it is unclear whether the social optimum (equally weighted) increases or decreases as it depends on the relative sizes of the movements. However, one suspects that the increased divergence would make it more difficult to reach the social optimum as a consensus and probably more difficult to increase the level of coordination (e.g., leading to delaying or dilution of a MIFID-like regime). A common currency also increases divergence between the perceived optimum as seen by public and private sectors based on the shifts identified in the previous sections, but it is a more reasonable possibility that the level of optimal coordination falls as there is little effect on the public-sector optimum. Again, the increased divergence may make it politically difficult to implement changes to the status quo especially a decrease in coordination if there was already some coordination in place. Certainly, an increase in coordination would not be foreseen.

If there was an increase in diversity of the members, there could be increased coordination as both the private and public sector optimums could move to the right and/or converge. The public-sector optimum may be less inclined to move right because the national supervisors' cost of managing negotiations and coordination with an increasingly diverse set of members may be large. We suggest that such an effect may be small relative to the other factors. But even if it is not, increased diversity appears to lead to increased convergence and a stronger consensus that would likely produce a movement toward more coordination and harmonization. However, we note that such an increase in numbers could increase the concentration of a specific type of culture or political regime thereby decreasing diversity and causing shifts in the opposite directions.

The primary conclusions of the analysis of the supply and demand of coordinated regulation are summarized in Table 7.3.

Table 7.3: Effects of Characteristics of the Group's Membership on the Location of Optimum Coordination

Characteristics of the Group	Private Sector Optimum	Public Sector Optimum	Optimums Converge/ Diverge?
Increased Diversity	More Coordination Benefits Shift Up	Ambiguous: More Coordination Possible (If Supply Costs Not Large)	Increases Convergence & Likely Increases Socially Optimal Coordination Levels
Increased Scope of Business	More Coordination Benefits Shift Up	More Coordination (At Low Levels), No Change (At High Levels)	Increases Convergence

Increased Global/ Economic Integration	Less Coordination. Substitutability Of Integration Benefits Shift Left	More Coordination. Complementarity of Integration Costs Shift Right (Except: Sovereignty Issues)	Increases Divergence (Unless Corner Solution) & Ambiguous Effect on Social Optimum Level of Coordination
Common Currency	Less Coordination	More Coordination. But No Effect on Supply Costs When Monetary Authority Is Not Supervisor	Increases Divergence & Decrease in Socially Optimal Coordination If Monetary Authority Is Separate Entity
Hegemonic Structure	Less Formal Coordination	Less Formal Coordination	Increased Convergence & Decrease in Socially Optimal Coordination

The political economy of MIFID

In this section, we provide a more detailed description of the evolution of MIFID and tie the progress or lack of progress to the above analysis of coordinated regulation.

When evaluating the implementation of the EU's financial regulatory agenda, it must be borne in mind that the EU is primarily a political union of sovereign states. In many respects, it is a unique phenomenon marked by the complex interaction of supranational agencies, committees, national governments, and pan-European interest groups. Indeed, as the EU grows in size with an increasingly diverse group of countries, further progress towards regulatory unification may be frustrated by the resurgence of national agendas.

MIFID requires member states to surrender a degree of sovereignty with respect to regulatory practice and supervision. To begin with, common principles and standards are adopted by each member state and are codified into the national legal system of each member. As such, national regulations converge toward a common platform. Second, regulatory supervision is now largely the responsibility of the home country regulator—not the jurisdiction where the securities activity takes place. For example, a UK domiciled firm would be largely regulated by the Financial Services Authority (2003), irrespective of where its foreign subsidiaries conduct business in the MIFID zone. To control cheating and the inevitable "*race to the bottom,*" MIFID created a structure to supervise the activities of its members. That function was shared among the Council of Economic Securities Regulators, member state regulators and other EU entities (European Commission, 2006). See Boyfield (2007) regarding the discretion allowed for countries.

MIFID requires its members to focus on longer term absolute gains, rather than short term relative gains. The underlying rationale for MIFID is to create pan-European capital markets with a common regulatory platform. Potential absolute gains include stronger financial governance, deeper and more efficient, competitive markets, lower transaction costs, greater transparency, and larger market share, among other things. (Romero & Torrijos, 2013; European Commission, 2010) Relative gains abandoned by members under MIFID include the loss of each member's domestic monopoly on equity trading as the market concentration rules allowed under the former ISD have been eliminated. Second, the consolidation of the financial sector has resulted in the loss of small to medium-size national firms that can no longer compete. Third, national exchanges have lost revenue and experienced declining margins resulting in consolidation (European Commission, 2011a, b).

MIFID's protracted history and nine-year implementation process give rise to a basic question: If EU policy emphasized the importance of financial markets integration, why were member states unsuccessful in coordinating their respective policies? One explanation for the phenomenon may lie with the asymmetrical distribution of power in the international financial markets. Both the international debt and equity markets have historically been dominated by two countries—the United States and the United Kingdom. By virtue of their respective market shares, internationalization of markets, and well-developed regulatory regimes, London and New York are the recognized global leaders in international finance and have traditionally defined "*best practices*" in the industry (LSE, 2013; NYSE, 2013).

Reflecting the hegemonic power of those two financial centers, regulatory harmonization reflects more of a top-down scenario than a multilateral approach (Simmons, 2001). Rather than implementing a pan-European approach, EU member states often adopted an Anglo-American practice. A case in point was London's liberalization of its financial markets, the "*Big Bang*," in 1986, which was followed by the French "*le petit big bang*" in 1988. MIFID supports the current asymmetric distribution of power in the financial markets. It does not call for the establishment of a super regulator that might conflict with the roles of the two hegemonic powers, the UK and the US. It requires further harmonization of regulatory practices, but those practices have already been largely established by the two financial centers. In essence, the MIFID regime provides a vehicle for the financial hegemons to implement "*best practices*" on a pan-European basis which is more important as the number of member countries and diversity of cultures increases and as the scope of operations of the UK institutions expands into central and eastern Europe.

A second explanation for the lack of European regulatory harmonization can be attributed to divergent models of state involvement in the domestic economy. The variation in the views of state involvement increases the coordination costs of the supply of regulation and may affect the level of private demand as well. The demand for financial regulation reflects the specific concerns of a member state's economic policies, rather than the broader EU agenda. Indeed, both France and Germany operate coordinated market economies with a tradition of government intervention dating back to the post-war era. As Christopher Anderson (1995) argues, during the post-war period a consensus as to the role of the state in managing the economy developed throughout West European democracies. The practice of state intervention has varied considerably among European countries. France, for example, nationalized several of its large banks and played an active role in credit allocation, monetary policy, and the capital markets (Story & Walter, 1997). Although this practice has waned over the past two decades, the belief that the government is to play an important role in managing the economy remains today. Other members of the European community do not have such an attachment to government intervention. Thus, in a wider EU, the demand is lower and the costs of coordination become larger.

A third explanation posits that member governments' lower demand for regulation arises because they may not have viewed rule harmonization to be in the best interest of their respective financial markets. Financial regulation and the regulatory function are matters of national sovereignty. National regulators are charged with the difficult task of safeguarding both the stability and competitiveness of their financial institutions. They must carefully assess the perceived costs and benefits of new regulation and anticipate the reaction of their financial institutions. As such, they are loath to implement rules that would disadvantage their national firms or lead to a flight of capital to less regulated countries. In this instance, governments are reflecting the private demand for regulation not the societal demand. Financial regulation can also be viewed as a regime of "*taxes*" and "*subsidies*" on the operations of financial intermediaries operating within a certain regulatory framework (Kane, 1987). Although the former increases the costs of financial intermediation and may make a firm less competitive, the latter serves to decrease the cost of financial intermediation. The difference between the regulatory subsidies and taxes to a particular type of financial institution in any given jurisdiction is defined as the net regulatory burden (NRB), a primary determinant of the private demand for regulation.

Conclusions

The process of EU financial integration will continue as a protracted negotiation among EU institutions and member states. When evaluating the implementation of EU legislation, it must be borne in mind that the EU is primarily a political union of sovereign states. As the EU grows in size with an increasingly diverse group of countries, further progress towards unification may be frustrated by increasing costs of coordination and supply of regulation that have resulted in the resurgence of national agendas, protectionism, and divergent patterns of state involvement. The nine-year implementation process of MIFID only confirms this premise. Proponents argue that MIFID provides numerous benefits to issuers and investors ranging from greater transparency to better execution. The demand from investors and companies for regulation is readily apparent. Moreover, they argue that it will promote further regulatory reform in the financial sector and stimulate economic growth. Society's demand based on such benefits is equally strong. On the other hand, the onerous costs associated with supplying regulation such as MIFID reflected in the greater administrative requirements and sheer complexity have inhibited the development of a MIFID regime until recently. Those EU members with less established capital markets and smaller firms continue to lose domestic market share to the larger, more-established financial centers, namely London and Frankfurt.

An analysis of MIFID may also provide valuable insight from the perspective of International Relations (IR) theory and, within that, a neo-realist perspective. In exercising its mandate, the EU Directive requires member states to bear the costs of the loss of sovereignty with regards to the regulation and supervision of certain financial intermediaries. MIFID's protracted evolution highlights the role of such costs in the struggle between principles of liberal institutionalism and the neo-realist behavior of member states with its focus on relative gains. It illustrates how the EU's demand for a common framework of regulatory governance was frustrated by a less than commensurate supply of that derived from competing national agendas, protectionism, and divergent patterns of state involvement in the financial sector. In striking a political consensus among member countries, the EU sought the lowest common denominator. The negotiated agreement weakened the EU Directive and resulted in 71 optional amendments that raise the level of complexity and costs of compliance for member states while avoiding the costs of lost sovereignty.

What would happen if a MIFID-type of effort was made globally? To the extent that systemic risks could be better managed, the demand by the public sector may be far enough to the right to encourage global coordination. The variation of different cultures and views on sovereignty (and associated perspectives on the increased systemic linkages and risk) and appropriate roles for regulators would increase the costs of supplying regulation substantially relative to Europe. Countries are not even bound together by a common currency as in the Eurozone. Europe has a lot more homogeneous culture than US, Europe, Asia, and Africa do. So, is such a global initiative doomed to fail for reasons that are highlighted by the MIFID experience (despite its appearance of some success)? Is the demand for regulation sufficiently high to justify bearing the costs? The Greek debt crisis highlights a relationship between Germany and Greece that would not exist in a broader global context among the 192 or so countries. The Brexit vote in 2016 highlights some of the obstacles to greater harmonization even within the EU. One cannot expect the interaction of demand and supply of regulation to result in a MIFID-type of outcome in a broader global context. The coordination costs are too high, heterogeneity too broad, and maintenance costs too high to produce an optimum that would be further along the axis of increased regulatory oversight.

Acknowledgements

We are grateful to David Bieri for his comments, questions, and suggestions and to the editors Linda Winkler and Harold Codrington for helping to improve our analysis.

References

Acemoglu, D., Johnson, S., & Robenson, J. A. (2005). Institutions as a fundamental cause of long run growth. In Aghion, P. and Durlauf, S. (Eds.). *Handbook of economic growth* (1A, pp. 386-472). Amsterdam: Elsevier B.V.

Anderson, C. (1995). *Blaming the government: Citizens and the economy in five European democracies.* London: M.E. Sharpe.

Benston, G. J. (1994). International harmonization of banking regulation cooperation among national regulators: An assessment. *Journal of Financial Services Research, 8,* 205–225.

Boyfield, K. (2007, February). Deeply unsatisfactory. [State of the Union Column]. *The Wall Street Journal Europe.* (Factiva No. WSJE000020070219e32j0001k).

Braun, D. & Gilardi, F. (2006). Taking 'Galton's problem' seriously towards a theory of policy diffusion. *Journal of Theoretical Politics, 18*(3), 298-322. Retrieved from http://www.fabriziogilardi.org/resources/papers/Braun-Gilardi-JTP-2006.pdf.

Elkins, Z. & Simmons, B. (2005). On waves, clusters, and diffusion: A conceptual framework. *Annals of the American Academy of Political and Social Science, 598*(1), 33-51.

European Commission. (2006). Commission directive 2006/73/EC. Retrieved from http://eur-lex.europa.eu/LexUriServ/LexUriServ.do?uri=OJ:L:2006:241:0026:0058:EN:PDF.

European Commission. (2010). Review of the markets in financial instruments directive. Retrieved from http://ec.europa.eu/finance/consultations/2010/mifid/docs/consultation_paper_en.pdf.

European Commission. (2011a). New rules for more efficient, resilient and transparent financial markets in Europe. Retrieved from http://europa.eu/rapid/press-release_IP-11-1219_en.htm.

European Commission. (2011b). Proposal for a directive of the European parliament and of the council on markets in financial instruments repealing directive 2004/39/EC of the European parliament and of the council. Retrieved from http://ec.europa.eu/internal_market/securities/docs/isd/mifid/COM_2011_656_en.pdf.

Gilardi, Fabrizi. (2005). The institutional foundations of regulatory capitalism: The diffusion of independent regulatory agencies in Western Europe. *Annals of the American Academy of Political and Social Science, 598*(1), 84-101.

Financial Services Authority. (2003). UK HM Treasury, Bank of England. In The EU financial services action plan: A guide. *Financial Times* (2007).

Goodell, J. & Aggarwal, R. (2010). Financial markets versus institutions in European countries: Influence of culture and other national characteristics. *International Business Review, 19*(5), 502-520.

IMF. (2008). Global financial stability report: Containing systemic risks and restoring financial stability. Retrieved from http://www.imf.org/External/Pubs/FT/GFSR/2008/01/index.htm.

Kane, E. (1987). Competitive financial reregulation: An international perspective. In R. Portes and A. Swoboda. (Eds.) *Threats to international financial stability* (pp. 111-45). Cambridge, Massachusetts: Cambridge University Press.

Kwok, C., and Tadesse, S. (2006). National culture and financial systems. *Journal of International Business Studies, 37*, 227-247.

Levi-Faur, D. (2005). The global diffusion of regulatory capitalism. *Annals of the American Academy of Political and Social Science, 60*, 12-32.

Levi-Faur, D. & Jordana, J. (2005). Regulatory capitalism: Policy irritants and convergent divergence. *Annals of the American Academy of Political and Social Science, 60*, 191-197.

LSE. (2013). Company overview London Stock Exchange. Retrieved from http://www.londonstockexchange.com/home/homepage.htm.

Mosley, L. & Singer, D. David. (2011). The global financial crisis: Lessons and opportunities for international political economy. In Phillips, N. & Weaver, C. (Eds.) *International political economy: Debating the past, present and future* (pp. 420-429). New York, New York: Routledge.

NYSE. (2013). About NYSE Euronext. Retrieved March 10, 2013. www.nyse.com/home.html

Rajan, R. & Zingales, L. (1998). Financial dependence and growth. *The American Economic Review, 88*(3), 559-586.

Rajan, R. & Zingales, L. (2003). The great reversals: The politics of financial development in the twentieth century. *The Journal of Financial Economics, 69*, 5–50.

Romero de Avila, D. & Torrijos, D. (2013). Finance and growth in the E.U.: New evidence from the liberalisation and harmonization of the banking industry. (Working Paper No. 266).

Simmons, B. (2001). The international politics of harmonization: The case of capital market regulation. *International Organization*, 55, 589-620.

Santomero, A. and Watson, R. (1977). Determining an optimal capital standard for the banking industry, *Journal of Finance, 32* (12), 67- 82.

Story, J. and Walter, I. (1997). *The political economy of financial integration in Europe: The battle of the systems.* Cambridge, Massachusetts: MIT Press.

Thorum, M. (2015). *Essays in international financial governance.* (Doctoral dissertation, Virginia Polytechnic Institute and State University). (Embargoed until 2017).

Appendix 7.1: Background on MFID

The European Commission formulated its Financial Services Action Plan (FSAP) in 1999. The plan sought to establish a single market for both retail and wholesale financial services over the 2002-2005 period. FSAP proposed an ambitious agenda and incorporated a broad range of reforms:

- Create a single wholesale market, enabling corporate issuers to raise debt and equity financing on competitive terms throughout the EU
- Provide investors unfettered access to all EU financial markets from a single entry
- Provide a sound legal environment for the sales, trading and settlement of securities
- Create a transparent and sound retail market with appropriate safeguards for individual investors
- Promote efficient cross border retail financial services
- Prudent regulatory supervision on a pan-European basis.

Faced with a three-year time frame to implement FSAP provisions and the lack of cooperation among certain EU members, the European Council decided it would streamline procedures for implementation. In 2001 it adopted an innovative regulatory process created for EU securities legislation called the "*Lamfalussy Process.*" [15]

The Lamfalussy Process eventually proved fruitful and gave rise to the new Markets in Financial Instrument Directive (MIFID). It was adopted in April 2004 by the European Council and the European Parliament, but took over three years for members' states to finalize the draft EU Directive. Contributing to the delay was the initial unwillingness of certain countries including France, Spain, and Italy to drop the domestic monopoly of their national exchanges (Boyfield, 2007).

---

[15] The Lamfalussy Process provides several benefits over traditional lawmaking, including a more-consistent interpretation and convergence in national supervisory practices. It consists of four levels, each focusing on a specific stage of the implementation of legislation (Financial Services Authority, 2003).

Chapter 8

The Death of the Social Contract and the Misery of XXI Century Interventionism

Miron Wolnicki [16]

Abstract

This paper addresses the relationship between the rise of the sovereign debt in the most developed market economies (G20) and the collapse of the social contract. The author argues that economic policies in the G20 increase the risk of chain debt defaults and political and economic instability leading to a populist backlash. The root cause of the mounting G20 sovereign debt lies in the demand deficiency originating in the cumulative effect of lagging wage rises relative to labor productivity gains. To stop expansion of sovereign debt, the developed democracies should abandon social devaluation policies, bring in line workers' income with productivity gains, and promote job creation in regions affected by globalization. G20 governments should restore overall fairness in the social contract between labor and capital. The real solution for the sovereign debt is not in deficit spending and privatized Keynesianism but in labor participation, in fair wages, and in arresting concentration of capital. The analysis of monetary policies in G20 shows that debt and near zero interest rates are far from being a lasting solution for demand deficiency. Such solution lies in restoring equilibrium between labor and capital. This equilibrium has been distorted by offshoring by multinational corporations to low cost countries and social devaluation at home. Economic fairness between capital and labor is the foundation of lasting social contract, balanced economy and liberal democracy. We are on the verge losing all of the above.

Introduction

The social contract in the developed market economies is dead. Not since the industrial revolution have labor wages in western economies lagged so much behind the rise of productivity as they do today. The gap between wages and

[16] miron.wolnicki@villanova.edu

productivity is becoming a major growth issue, forcing the governments of industrial economies to use deficit spending and sovereign debt to make up for missing labor consumption demand. Since the 2008 financial crisis, the lag between the wage increases and productivity has accounted for at least 75% of the $25 trillion new government debt in the OECD countries. The public and household debt in Japan reached 400% of GDP, in France 280%, in Spain 313%, in Greece 317% of GDP, and in the USA 233% of GDP (Dobbs et al., 2015; OECD, 2017). It would be easy to blame few fiscally irresponsible governments for the rising debt as suggested by the World Bank (Stefania & Ashoka, 2006; von Hagen, 1996, 2010). However, the problem is much more fundamental. In the last two decades, developed market democracies failed to address the social contract between labor and capital leaving a gaping hole in their consumption demands. The policy makers somehow disregarded the fact that growth originates not only in corporate investments but also in workers' consumption demand.

The anatomy of the failure

Even before the Chinese growth burnout in 2016, the US, the Eurozone, Japan and the UK have run out of ideas on how to cope with the chronic demand deficiency. More precisely, the G20 private sector and consumers have failed to spend enough to bring output anywhere close to a potential GDP. Slow growth has been accepted as a new normal. Democratic states are reluctant to address not only the wages but also broader labor policy issues, such as the replacement of permanent by part time labor contracts, weakening of the collective bargaining and rising unemployment among young educated workers. In the last two decades, the relations between labor and capital have become deeply dysfunctional and call for decisive action on the part of the G20. Putting off resolution of labor issues and jobs is raising the possibility not only widespread populism and trade protectionism, but also financial crises because of a massive leveraging of the industrial economies by sovereign debt.

The real causes of the 2008 great recession started well before the bogus securitization of substandard mortgages. The crisis began when undercompensated labor failed to deliver consumption demand without more household debt. Instead of promoting wage increases, the US government resorted to privatized Keynesianism, or relaxing lending regulations to artificially boost housing market and consumer demand. Between 1979 and 1990 in 34 leading OECD market economies, productivity rose annually by an average of 1.4% while compensation averaged increases by of only 0.5%. The 1990s were even worse. Productivity gains accelerated to 2.1% yearly and compensation only by 1.5%. But because compensation grew at less than three-quarters the rate of productivity, the gap continued to widen. Since 2000, annual productivity gains have increased to 2.3% per year, compensation rose by only 0.9%, and the gap widened still more. In 2012 (the last year for which data have been released), labor received only 58% of total output, the lowest by far in the entire postwar period (OECD, 2012; Galston, 2014).

The evidence of the last 15 years from the OECD G20 countries demonstrates that whenever technology increases productivity, the labor loses jobs and wages, and capital increases its profits (Table 8.1). The fundamental paradigm of the post-World War (WWII) growth model has been that workers are consumers and that corporate profits depend on worker income and consumption. This link is lost when capital offers workers cheap imports in exchange for their jobs and rising wages. Assuring for the economies' consumption, demand is left to costly government deficit spending and expansion of the often unaffordable welfare state. The politicians in the USA choose new debt over adjusting workers' income. Political expediency of politicians to appease capital and obtain election funding wins over the economic rationale that more debt means slower growth in the decades to come and further concentration of capital. Studies by Oxfam and by Thomas Picketty prove the existence of the historic underpayment of labor, and the alarming capital and wealth concentration. (Oxfam, 2015; Picketty, 2014).

Figure 8.1: Real Wage and Productivity Index in the G20

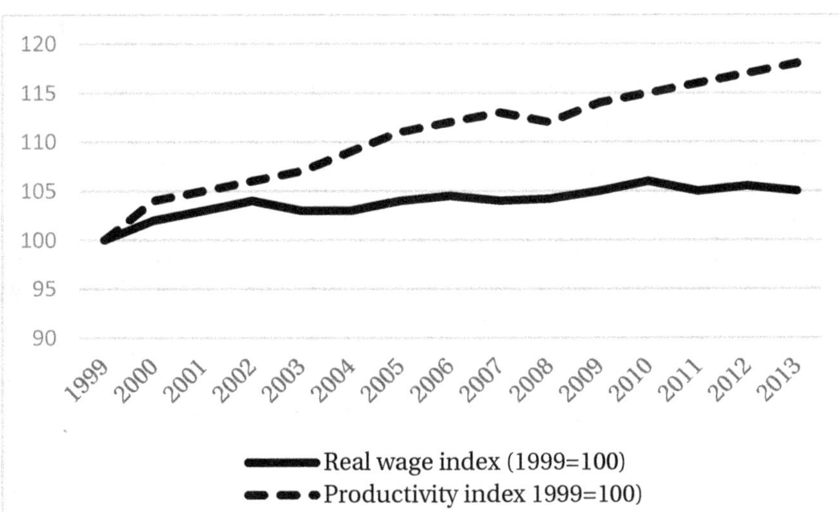

Source: OECD (2014)

The problems with the social contract in the EU and Japan

The commonly circulated hypothesis about the lingering recession after 2008 is that the EU ran out of ideas on how to face aging population, labor saving robotics, deindustrialization, and offshoring of jobs. In desperation, the central banks began to use two monetary remedies. One, quantitative easing (QE) or channeling public money into commercial banks, and two, negative interest rates or penalizing those banks with negative interest rates if they did not lend. Neither one worked as expected.

How did the EU address the missing labor demand in the past? The policy was based on two principles which assured continuous internal and external demand expansion. The first was "*deepening the EU integration.*" That is, the introduction of the single market and single currency. The second was the "*widening of the EU integration*" or periodical admissions of new members to the club. In the 1980s, the admission of Greece, Spain and Portugal was fundamental for the "*old EU*" to gain access to the new markets of Europe's southern flank. Germany, France, and Great Britain expanded export and became eager financiers for the region. The European economic powerhouse, Germany, after the unification with East Germany in 1990, squeezed wages and undertook tough reforms needed to ensure competitiveness. None of the above was possible in the low productivity countries of Greece, Spain, Italy and Portugal, so they chose debt since they could not devalue their currencies as the members of the Eurozone. Sovereign debt became the best default solution. The socialist governments in Greece and Spain were permitted to use EU subsidies and sovereign debt to finance oversized welfare state, expand the public sector and delay privatization of transportation and utilities.

In the middle of the 2004 recession, the EU opened the door to nine countries of Eastern Europe. German manufacturers gained a chance to break traditionally strong German unions' collective bargaining and relocate their production to low cost Hungary, Poland and the Czech Republic. The EU businesses gained zero tariff access to approximately 90 million new buyers and 30 million new workers who experienced a 50% wage discount and were physically closer than China. Eastern Europeans bought EU-made cars and apartments with EU mortgages and developed roads and infrastructure with EU cohesion funding (Dainkov, 2015). The EU expansion to the East Central Europe was de facto one of the world's most effective demand-side interventionism ever undertaken by industrial democracies. The EU growth more than doubled from 1.5% in 2003 to 3.2% in 2006.

However, in 2004, the EU had to close the list of possible new EU candidates. Admitting Ukraine and Turkey to the EU represented unacceptable strategic and immigrant risk. After the 2008 Great Financial Crisis, the use of *EU widening and deepening* became less attractive. The lending markets dried out and government spending was put on hold in Eastern and Southern Europe.

Today, the EU's fundamental problem is one of demographic disadvantage and immigration. The EU immigration issue is unlike the illegal immigration issues present in the US. The EU's immigration has been, until the collapse of Syria, relatively well controlled and very costly to government budgets. In France, the Netherlands, the Benelux countries, Switzerland, and the Nordic states, where immigrants are provided quite generous state-funded welfare, the first-generation immigrants become accustomed to welfare paychecks and have ever increasing expectations of the providing state. When the support programs end, many of them are angry at being abandoned by the system. Unable to integrate fully, they are left to live in ethnic and religious ghettos. Germany, France, and Belgium are trying to replenish it's their low-end job markets without building a socially inclusive society. As a result, the labor market is further destabilized.

Unlike the EU, Japan is practically isolated in Asia due to longstanding policy choices. It does not have a viable option of creating a Single Market or a Monetary Union with its neighbors. In the early 1990's, government deficit spending steroids proved ineffective as an antidote for imported US deflation. Until then, the Japanese liberal democratic government authorized spending trillions of yens to keep their workers on the job employed when the technology exports to the US did not materialize. The Bank of Japan, under full government control, allowed the Keiretsu banks to ignore non-performing loans, fund wages to underemployed workers and maintain cartel pricing at home. The democratic liberal government failed to see the need for competition therapy. Japanese cultural isolation, preserved their national identity, but also prevented them from adapting to rising low cost technology manufacturing at their doorstep in South Korea, China, Singapore and Malaysia. Instead of reforming labor markets and industrial organization to force more competition, the government increased borrowing, thereby pushing the debt to 519% of the GDP. The subsidies paid from the government-controlled pension funds dug the economy into a liquidity trap for two and a half decades. Japan has become a case study of misguided government interventionism. Finally, after 25 years of bailing out uncompetitive keiretsus, Abe's government began debt reduction, reformed competition and immigration policy, and pushed for defense spending to stop the decline.

The failures of the demand management models happen in liberal democracies, which, in principle, have representative mechanisms to address fundamental long-term challenges. Ideally, the voters, assuming their collective interest, should be able to resolve the causes of declining real wages, and unemployment, job training. Specifically, they should be able to defend employment and wages by making it easier to ease the adaptation to adapt to the changing technology, by offshoring and outsourcing production to low cost markets, and through economic integration, rising costs of living, and imported recessions. This does not happen.

The most glaring proof of the death of the XXI century social contract is rising debt of the richest economies. On one side, there are the cash-rich capital owners and the multinationals which do not need to borrow more or can borrow at a very low cost. On the other side, there are workers and the middle class which are either in debt or cannot borrow more because their incomes are too low. In the center of this are the central banks which seek remedies in supplying low cost money to the governments. The problem is that central banks control money supply and interest rates, but they do not control wages. They prefer to listen to neoliberal economists who see the growth as a business investment issue not the middle class income issue. The truly effective interventionism is not in paying unemployment benefits and debt as advised by the traditional Keynesian cookbook but to more effectively reward those who still work. The policy objective of G20 economies today assure that wages are closely linked to the rise of productivity, that a minimum wage is a living wage, and that employers are legally bound to share their profits with the workers. This is not advice from the socialist manifesto, but a survival kit for market economies locked in a "*doom loop.*"

The rise of populism in smaller countries like Austria, Poland, and Hungary but also in France, Germany and the USA should be a wakeup call for all who believe in the distributional effects of the market mechanism. We have to abandon the neoliberal belief that the distributional fairness is given in liberal democracies. It is not. In modern elected democracies, the political power of capital by far exceeds the collective power of labor and taxes on capital are effectively blocked by capital. Economic realism is pointing towards using democratic mechanisms to defend the income of the middle class. This is a last-defense frontier of the market economies against the abyss of populism, nationalism and protectionism.

The death of the US social contract

Consumption demand is far more important in the US than in any of the industrial democracies because it represents more than 70% of country's massive $17 trillion GDP. Also, Americans households are far much more involved in the labor markets than the Europeans with almost 54% of the population available for work.

Until the 1970's, growth in the U.S. was fostered by post-war reconstruction, rising education levels, higher workforce participation rates, and a resurgence in restored global trade. Increased investment and mass consumption were fueled by cheap energy and strong unions which that protected workers' income. But by the late 1970s, the government understood that it was unable to deliver on their promises of the Great Society, such as higher union pension hikes and old-age health-care for public-sector workers. To meet their obligations, government needed growth and debt. Owing to the 1970s oil price shocks and inflation, the Reagan era was marked by tax cuts and interest rate hikes which appreciated the dollar, thereby opening the gate to cheap imports and a pressure to raise nominal wages.

The most important demand management discovery came in the mid 1980's - public debt and tax reduction, which came straight from the Keynesian playbook. Public debt turned out to be a convenient substitute for inflation. It enabled the government to satisfy demands for social distribution. In the absence of domestic savings, the Treasury resorted to a massive bond selloff to foreign investors and sovereign wealth funds. During the second Clinton administration (1996-2000) the debt relief came from the "*dotcom*" revolution. The Republican Congress introduced austerity measures to cut public spending which increased income inequality. This prompted the Clinton administration to deregulate the financial sector (Steeck, 2011).

Deregulation of the financial markets and mortgage markets marks a switch to a "*privatized Keynesianism*" which, in effect, means replacement of public with private debt (Crouch, 2009). This time rather than the government borrowing money to fund social programs such as cheap housing and education, it is now individual citizens who, under a relaxed borrowing regime are allowed to take out loans at their own risk. The budget has a basic surplus and the top income earners were spared higher taxes. The relaxed regulatory regime allows financial services to promote itself to become U.S.'s prime industry, the leading economic sector in the US, with profits many times higher profits than in manufacturing. The burdens and the risks of demand adjustment are shifted from the government to working class borrowers. The problem is, however, that many of the borrowers lost jobs as some 16,000 enterprises closed nationwide in early 2000's due to "*offshoring*" and "*outsourcing*".

The U.S. social contract died with the introduction of privatized Keynesianism. Financial liberalization replaced social policy, private debt replaced public debt, real estate appreciation replaced wage increases, and the financial sector replaced domestic manufacturing as country's main industry. The bailout of the financial sector and households which followed the subprime mortgage crisis, in fact, was billed back to the U.S. government and world savings. It should be noted, that more than 40% of the post 2008 bailout was funded by foreign savings.

Many G20 governments decided to imitate the U.S. quantitative easing as well and sold off their sovereign debt as a default solution. As a result, Japan is today holding displaying the debt level of a developing country. The European Central Bank (ECB), instead of developing a viable plan to deleverage Southern Europe, and insists on austerity measures that are deepening the debt crisis. The ECB has no plan or resources to deleverage debtors or face chain defaults.

A new social contract as a debt crisis solution

In 2014, the average world debt as a share of GDP reached the WWII level and is rising (Dobbs et al., 2015). For selected economies: - Australia, Canada, France, Germany, Italy, Japan, Korea, Spain, United Kingdom and the United States, - the GDP ppp-weighted average government debt ratio reached around 116% of GDP in 2013, the same level as in the 1940's (Figure 8.2). The acceptable external debt limits are not known. According to an IMF study over the last 60 years, there were 633 cases of sovereign debt restructuring in 95 countries (Udaipur, Papaioannou, & Trebesch, 2012). A total of 447, the restructurings were in the framework of the Paris Club, while only 186 cases were with private creditors. Restructurings are not uncommon; however, because of the size of the debt, extreme reductions in interest rates, weak bank capital controls, and currency devaluations, the probability of orderly restructuring is increasingly doubtful (Feibelman, 2015).

Figure 8.2: Gross Public Debt of Selected Countries 1880-2015*

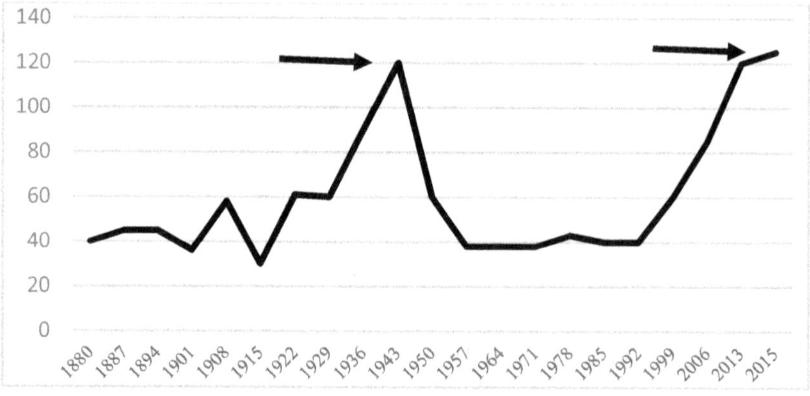

Notes: Historical debt levels, GDP-weighted average. *Includes Australia, Canada, France, Germany, Italy, Japan, Korea, Spain, United Kingdom and United States.

Source: Developed by author using data from IMF (2010); OECD (2013); Udaipur et al., 2012

Since the debt cycle is unstoppable and deleveraging is not in sight, an option, the probability a G20 sovereign debt crisis is very likely. The real long – term solution of the debt should address demand deficiency, increase labor participation and wages, or basically, introduce a new social contract between labor and capital.

The position of the New Left is that the social contract completely broke up years ago and, with it, the hope to reform the political system. Western capitalism, they claim, favors owners of capital and exploits workers (Steeck, 2011). The mainstream studies by the Economic Policy Institute blame governments for not siding with the labor in collective bargaining (Bivens et al., 2014). The theoretical models of social contract argue that the ongoing global diffusion of technology "*exports inequality*" across borders and makes it difficult for nations to maintain distinct institutions and social structures (Benabou, 2005).

This brings us to a fundamental question of whether there is a theoretical or a practical, alternative scheme of social distribution which could deliver both growth to the economy and social justice to the workers. Has, for example, Chinese state capitalism created such a system as some economists claim (Moyo, 2011)? After all, one may say, that pragmatic communist autocrats in China have succeeded in moving 300 million peasants out of poverty and, until last year, achieved stellar growth rates for the country. Social science with all its limitations may, if it does its work well, provide some facts and plausible interpretations. As long predicted, China is entering a middle-income trap. Cheap labor reserves are exhausted, demand by the western consumers are slacking, and so does the capital inflows. The Chinese economy is heading towards 7% real growth rates and its debt-to-GDP ratio is already reaching approaching the 300% mark (Dobbs et al., 2015).

Contemporary experimental behavioral economists, following Adam Smith's observation, argue that animal spirits and greed are the most reliable foundations of human behavior. The rising numbers of billionaires among the Central Committee of the Chinese Communist Party members suggest that there is a deep gap between the communist ideological narrative and the real motivation of the Chinese governing elite (Pei, 2016). Since China is lacking mechanisms to mitigate the social costs of growth as well as independent labor representation, it can hardly meet the requirements of an optimal participatory model of social distribution. According to Fukuyama, China does not operate under the constitutional "*Rule of Law*" but instead the "*Law of the Rules*" arbitrarily imposed by autocrats whose ultimate objective is to stay in power. Such a system does not guarantee either a fair social contract or even the social order in the long run (Fukuyama, 2011). Thus, a question as to if there is a better alternative to democratic capitalism remains open.

Conclusions

In the first dozen years of the XXI Century we observed the rise of particularly unconstructive, polarizing, populist, self-serving breed of politicians who tend to undermine the very foundations of liberal democracies. They promise growth, low taxes, protectionism, nationalism, or use anti-immigrant rhetoric to explain the dysfunctional labor-capital relations at home. If this path continues, liberal democracies risk falling into to the abyss of authoritarianism and dangerous nationalism. The underlying issue is that globalization overturned traditional framework of the nation-state social contract.

First, there is a reason why the old social contract does not fit the modern globalized economy. For all the practical reasons, in the XXI century, capital has become truly global while labor still remains bound to nation-state borders because of the nature of reproduction, family, borders, language, and cultural identification. Marginal productivity of globally mobile capital will always be higher than that of labor unless all borders are removed which will never be the case. In this sense, the return to labor (or profits, if you will) will be lower than the return to capital. Dealing with this systemic inequality falls on the redistributive function of the states and their governments, not multinational corporations.

Second, capital by itself does not produce value. It is the mix of labor and capital that does it. In modern production, labor input become intangible and dispersed. Today almost half of employees are TVC's or temporary workers, vendors and contract workers, who lose job security, benefits, bargaining power and compete today with low-cost workers in the developing countries and tomorrow will compete with artificial intelligence bots. We need new ground rules or social contract to allow independent labor, inventors, programmers and sophisticated machine operators to share the profits generated in the economy. The profit participation schemes should be mandatory for all kinds of labor contracts. Under the present social contract, in case of the failure labor loses income, while capital gets bailed out.

Third, we need new ground rules, or social contract for the millions of workers which will be in the underpaid service sector, those eliminated by the bots and import competition. The old social contract assumes that profit represents compensation for risk and since workers do not participate in risk-taking, they are not entitled to anything more than contractual wages. This logic does not fit the reality of nation-state economies. The post-labor manufacturing economies, as we may call them, the labor- sellers (workers) will need to find the source of living wage. In simple terms, underpaid workers must be able to buy the goods and services which the economy will produce or import. We cannot return to late XIX Century social contract and army of the unemployed or underemployed which the new economy promises today.

Fourth, there is deep imbalance in the world flow of world capital and savings. In the later part of the XX century, the rich nations became importers of capital, or savings of the poorer nations. Net exporters from Asia and resource exporters have purchased the debt of the G20. This may be rational in terms of building their reserves but exposes them to the risk of currency fluctuations or catastrophic collapse of the Eurozone which may never occur but it can. In the developmental sense, these savings would have done a better job building infrastructure in the developing nations then financing the debt of the rich countries.

Fifth, the fate of national labor is neither of concern to globe-trotting multinationals nor underfunded governments which cannot tax their profits kept in tax havens. As a result of budgetary crunch, governments resorted to creative monetary policy such as quantitative easing and sovereign debt. The quantitative easing (QE) schemes are not a substitute for responsible long – term monetary and income policies. QE may debase leading world currencies and destroy fragile demand in the long run.

What can policy makers do? The solutions are country specific. For the U.S., for example, it could be a serious long-term infrastructure program to raise productivity and the economic efficiency of labor. It could involve better access to education, reduction of the high-school dropout rate, high-quality technical training, and expanding basic research to create new products and industries. Generally, the G20 average households must be allowed to have a share in the benefits of growth through various contractual algorithms linking wages and productivity. The new economic policies must bring about not only new minimum wage standards but also formulas of profit sharing between better educated labor and capital. Treating labor as an easily disposable factor of production does is not commensurate with the need to maintain a macroeconomic stability which, in turn, defines capital profits.

Whatever philosophical, economic or moral arguments the developed Western societies use to explain concentration of capital, they still need to understand that capital is an enabler, not the inheritable right to economic and political power. Taxes on capital profits are not penalties and should commensurate with the opportunities that the free democratic societies create for the entrepreneurs, such as the rule of law, education, safety, and individual freedoms. It is discouraging that such common truths must be restated in developed Western democracies which often lose the appreciation of values they have created over centuries and look at state capitalism as acceptable alternative solution.

Excessive wealth concentration and underpayment of labor is socially disruptive and without exception leads to socio-political destabilization. That is why predictable inheritance tax should be regarded as a necessary social justice equalizer. The inheritance tax is consistent with our expectation that wealth should improve the quality of life of future generations rather than creating the entitlement to good life to a narrow, self-perpetuating oligarchy.

There has been lot of confusion created by neoliberal economists and politicians about the value of the social contract and taxes. The neoliberal narrative that taxes kill entrepreneurship, growth, and competition is worth as much as the stories about communist egalitarianism. Free-wheeling American multinationals who keep their profits in tax havens need to understand that they do owe something to their country of origin. Democracies which breed and boast of the rising number of rich at the top will stagnate. The birth of the sharing economy, (Bitcoins, Crowdfunding, Crowdsourcing, Uber, and Air B&B) is showing the new tendency of labor to shake off dependency on capital in the market place. Also, grassroots initiatives and reforms are needed in democratic capitalism.

References

Benabou, R. (2005). Inequality, technology and social contract. In Aghhion, P. & Durlauf, S. (Eds.). *Handbook of economic growth*, (1st ed., Vol. 1, pp. 595–616.). Retrieved from http://www.sciencedirect.com/science/article/B7P5F-4HP4N1N-G/2/34b1c3fa603b4707f139552f9917428f.

Bivens, J., Gould, E., Mishel, L., & Shierholz, H. (2014). *Raising America's Pay: Why It's Our Central Economic Policy Challenge.* (Economic Policy Institute Briefing Paper No. 378). Washington DC.

Crouch, C. (2009). Privatized Keynesianism: An unacknowledged policy regime. *The British Journal of Politics and International Relations, 11*, 382–399.

Dainkov, S. (2015). Is foreign ownership of banks problematic for Eastern Europe. *Peterson Institute for International Economics.* Retrieved from http://blogs.piie.com/realtime/?p=4751.

Dobbs, R., Lund, S., Woetzel, J., & Mutafchieva, M. (2015). Debt and (not much) deleveraging. *McKinsey Global Institute.* Retrieved from http://www.mckinsey.com/global-themes/employment-and-growth/debt-and-not-much-deleveraging.

Feibelman, A. (2015). The IMF and regulation of cross-border capital flows. *Chicago Journal of International Law, 15*(2), 409-451.

Fukuyama, F. (2011). *The origins of the political order.* New York, NY: Farrar, Straus and Giroux.

Galston, W. A. (2014, February). The U.S. needs a new social contract. *The Wall Street Journal.* Retrieved from https://www.wsj.com/articles/SB10001424052702304558804579375290378927928.

IMF. (2010). A historical public debt Database. (Working Paper No. 10/245, International Monetary Fund). Retrieved from https://www.imf.org/external/pubs/cat/longres.aspx?sk=24332.0.

Moyo, D. (2011). *How the West was lost: Fifty years of economic folly--and the stark choices ahead.* New York, NY: Farrar, Strauss and Groux.

OECD. (2012). Labor losing to capital. In *OECD Employment Outlook 2012,* 109-161. Retrieved from http://www.oecd.org/els/emp/EMO%202012%20Eng_Chapter%203.pdf.

OECD. (2013). OECD economic outlook 94 database. Retrieved from https://stats.oecd.org/Index.aspx?DataSetCode=EO94_INTERNET.

OECD. (2014). G20 labor markets: Outlook, key challenges and policy response. *International Labor Ministerial Meeting.* Melbourne, Australia. Retrieved from https://www.oecd.org/g20/topics/employment-and-social-policy/G20-labour-markets-outlook-key-challenges-and-policy-responses.pdf.

OECD (2017), National Accounts of OECD Countries, General Government Accounts 2016. Paris: OECD Press. DOI: http://dx.doi.org/10.1787/na_gga-2017-en

Oxfam. (2015). Wealth: Having it all and wanting more. Retrieved from https://www.oxfam.org/en/research/wealth-having-it-all-and-wanting-more.

Pei, M. (2016). *China's crony capitalism: The dynamics of the regime decay.* Cambridge, Massachusetts: Harvard University Press.

Piketty, T. (2014). *Capital in the Twenty-First Century.* Goldhammer, A. (Trans.). Cambridge, Massachusetts: Harvard University Press.

Steeck, W. (2011). The crisis of democratic capitalism. *The New Left Review, 71.* Retrieved from https://newleftreview.org/II/71/wolfgang-streeck-the-crises-of-democratic-capitalism.

Stefania, F. & Ashoka, M. (2006). Can budget institutions counteract political indiscipline? (Working Paper, International Monetary Fund). Retrieved from https://www.imf.org/external/pubs/ft/wp/2006/wp06123.pdf.

Udaipur S., Papaioannou, M, & Trebesch, C. (2012). Sovereign debt restructurings 1950–2010: Literature survey, data, and stylized facts. (Working Paper No. 12/203, International Monetary Fund). Retrieved from https://www.imf.org/external/pubs/cat/longres.aspx?sk=26190.0.

von Hagen, J. (2010). Sticking to fiscal plans: The role of institutions. *Public Choice 144*(3-4), 487-503.

von Hagen, J. & Harden, J. (1996). Budget process and commitment to fiscal discipline. (Working Paper No. 96/78, International Monetary Fund).

Chapter 9

Ukraine in a Transformation Period: An Assessment of Ukraine's Investment Climate by Foreign Direct Investors

Ewa Bojar[17], Andrij Razhyk[18], and Jakub Bis[19]

Abstract

This paper presents an assessment of the investment climate in Ukraine by foreign direct investors and the main motives driving their decisions in choosing Ukraine as a place of investment. The paper is structured by presenting the definition of foreign direct investment and the concept of investment climate. This is followed by presentation of Ukraine's performance in various independent international rankings. The second part of the paper discusses the research findings of the study carried out on a sample of 52 enterprises with foreign capital. According to this study, weak competition, labor costs, access to cheap raw materials, and opportunities to gain the above-average profits are the most common reasons for investing in Ukraine as declared by the owners and managers of surveyed enterprises. On the other hand, the scale of corruption is the main barrier which hamper foreign investors from entering the Ukrainian market. Most respondents declare that they regard the investment climate in Ukraine as neutral.

Introduction

Globalization processes in the world economy, including the rapid development of the global capital market, create new conditions for the economic development of countries and provide governments with new instruments for effective implementation of economic policies and achieving social goals. In modern conditions of economic transformation and world

17 e.bojar@pollub.pl

18 wz.sekretariat@pollub.pl

19 j.bis@pollub.pl

integration, a country's development is closely connected with the dynamics of occurring investment processes. It is beyond question, that one of the most interesting economic processes observed in recent years, is the process of internationalization of economic activity. This consists of the creation of various links between local and foreign enterprises. Companies search for the most effective and efficient ways of entering foreign markets. Investing in the form of foreign direct investments (FDIs) is just one of many possible options for business expansion. Hence, elucidating determinants affecting investors' decisions concerning selection of investment locations is very important.

For most countries, the effective use of foreign investments is the crucial factor of their economic development. Foreign direct investment contributes immensely to integration with the world economy. With these investments, countries can markedly accelerate their access to global financial and commodity markets. Investors continuously look for the best investment options in the effort to multiply their profits and outpace the competition. On the other hand, the governments and regional authorities continuously compete for investors. It is commonly understood that foreign direct investments are a carrier of innovation. Therefore, they contribute to the strengthening of competitive advantages of host economies.

This is particularly important in the case of developing countries which suffer from lack of their own financial resources. Therefore, the role of foreign capital is increasingly important. Foreign direct investments generate jobs in local economies and automatically include local and regional economies into the network of global linkages. Moreover, FDIs are long-term investments which are usually involved in the relations with local and regional authorities, as well as with local communities. However, in conditions of market economy, developing countries are hampered in their efforts to attract foreign capital by the fact that investors pursuing their business development strategies look for the most optimal investment locations. Thus investors more frequently choose more developed countries instead of developing economies.

This paper presents the study of FDIs in Ukraine, including the assessment of the country's investment attractiveness and the evaluation of its investment climate by foreign investors.

Definition of foreign direct investments

The term investment derives from the Latin word "*investire*" meaning to "*clothe,*" "*surround,*" or to "*cover.*" Many contemporary languages have borrowed this term from the Latin: in German, "*investition;*" in Russian, "*investicija;*" in French, "*investissement;*" and in English, "*investment*". According to Polish *"Dictionary of Foreign Terms"* (Sobol et al., 1997), the

Polish term "*inwestycja,*" borrowed from the German language means the transfer of financial means in order to increase or restore the assets, or to purchase securities. However, according to the definition contained in *"Encyclopedia of Business"* (Pomykało, 1995), the investment is defined as the conversion of financial means for tangible goods, services, usufruct, and patents. The investment generates fixed assets capable of producing more profit or savingt costs in the future (Pomykało, 1995).

In the last decade, along with a tendency to differentiate an approach to foreign direct investments, there are trends to develop a uniform definition of FDIs. The origins of this process derive from the need to develop a uniform system responsible for collecting and processing data on foreign investments in the world. Such a system, if developed, would enable the comparison of the flows of foreign direct investments in different countries. Therefore, it would facilitate a better understanding of this phenomenon. In the forefront of these unification efforts are the Organization for Economic Co-operation and Development and the International Monetary Fund (IMF). The first version of benchmark definition of foreign direct investment was published by OECD in 1983.[20]

According to the OECD's definition of foreign direct investments, a direct investment is a category of cross-border investment made by a resident in one economy (called the direct investor) with the objective of establishing a lasting interest in an enterprise (the direct investment enterprise) that is resident in an economy other than that of the direct investor.

Foreign direct investors are characterized by a strategic approach and their motivations relate to long-term objectives. The foreign direct investor must have a significant influence on the management of the direct investment enterprise. Therefore, foreign direct investments are regarded as only those investments where the investor owns or acquires at least 10% or regular shares in this enterprise, or at least 10% of the vote at the general assembly of shareholders (OECD, 2008). The OECD's benchmark definition of foreign direct investments has gained a widespread consensus and is widely used for statistical purposes. The OECD is of the opinion that a 10% share in the direct investment enterprise is sufficient to maintain a lasting influence on its management, operations, and performance. At the same time, the OECD states that this threshold should be strictly upheld.

---

[20] Upon several years of extensive international consultations, in April 2008 the OECD Council adopted the 4th edition of the benchmark definition of foreign direct investments.

In Europe, the threshold of shares owned by foreign investors in the direct investment enterprise was decreased from 20% to 10% of the nominal capital at the end of the 1990s under the influence of the OECD (for example in Germany and France). In the final stage of work on the fourth edition of the benchmark definition of foreign direct investment, the OECD experts considered increasing the threshold of shares or vote up to 20% in line with the new International Accounting Standards (IAS) and common practice in the USA. However, experts failed to reach consensus and the 10% threshold remained. The position of the OECD is questioned by many authors and FDI experts who rightly argue that a 10% or even a 20% threshold should not be the only valid criterion. They claim that this strictly set limit does not always reflect the diversity and complexity of real-life situations. They argue that there are many examples of enterprises, where owners, despite having a 10% share or more, have rather insignificant influence on the management of owned enterprises. They also give examples of enterprises, where owners have quite a significant influence on its management and decision-making process, although their share in the enterprise is less than 10%. A minority shareholder may have a considerable influence on appointments of the board of directors and the supervisory board members, as well as on decisions concerning preferential long-term loans. These are situations, where the shareholder, despite having shares below the OECD's threshold, has lasting influence on enterprise management.

The concept of investment climate

In literature, investment climate is not seen as an unambiguous concept. Authors commonly use related terms such as *investment attractiveness, business environment,* and *national* or *regional competitive advantage* interchangeably resulting in a lack of conceptual precision. Due to the fact that basically all these designations include the same elements, it is very difficult to arrange them from the narrowest to the widest in terms of their meaning (Rymarczyk et al., 2008; Rosińska, 2005; Kłysik-Uryszek, 2010). The country's investment climate, also called investment environment, is understood as a set of features and phenomena important for investors. Generally, investment climate incorporates political, social, and economic conditions along with legal regulations. This can have a strong impact on foreign investors' decisions (Budner, 2004).

The most popular definition of investment climate is a broad definition proposed by L.C. Nehrt, who distinguishes investment climate components, as follows (Stępniak, 1996):

1. "*Economic climate A*" refers to the current and expected economic situation in the country of prospective investment, which influences the very decision on making FDI.
2. "*Economic climate B*" describes the state of existing material infrastructure (e.g. transport and telecommunication facilities, electric power distribution system) and anticipated long-term changes in the country's economic situation. These can affect foreign investors' decisions and thus shape the flows of foreign direct investments.
3. "*Social climate*" includes the current situation on the labor market, the social, cultural, and ecological conditions affecting the quality and stability of work (including labor market regulations such labor code, minimum wage regulations, trade unions regulations, trade union activity and policies), and the quality and credibility of workforce.
4. "*Administrative climate*" is the scope of interference of the state institutions on the country's economy (taxation policies, control of revenue transfers, profit transfer regulations, business set-up procedures, the status of foreign enterprises, accounting and financial regulations, capital market regulations).
5. "*Political climate*" includes the risk of an adverse change of government in the country of intended investment. As such, changes may result in nationalization. Political climate also encompass prevailing political views, particular aspirations of government circles and political factions, historical background of political decisions, and the role of private sector in the economy of receiving country.

E. Bojar argued that such factors as economic, political, and social situation in a country describe the state of its economy and the outlook for economic growth. The country's spatial organizational system and legal regulations create the legal framework for making foreign direct investments and therefore determine the country's investment climate (Bojar, 2001).

M. Przygoda rightly notes that development conditions, which have an essential influence on investment attractiveness of any given area, should be analyzed comprehensively (2014). As a result of progressing globalization and social and economic integration, investment conditions in different counties are now similar. On the other hand, investment climate to a large extent is shaped by policies adopted at the governmental and regional levels.

Ukraine's Performance in International Rankings

One of the simplest methods of assessing the country's competitive position in terms of its attractiveness for foreign capital consists of comparing this country with other economies in the region. This approach results from the very definition of the competitiveness of economy, which states that the competitiveness includes the ability to sell goods and services on international markets in desired quantities, as well as the ability to compete effectively on international production means markets for capital, labor, and technologies (Misala & Weresa, 2006). International rankings are a readily available and useful source of information for prospective international investors. The following table illustrates Ukraine's performance in major international rankings.

Table 9.1: Ukraine in International Rankings

Ranking	Score / Total classified	Year
Democracy Index	92 / 167	2014
E-Readiness	81 / 148	2014
Freedom in the World	Partly Free	2014
Global Competitiveness Index (GCI)	76 / 144	2014
Global Peace Index	111 / 162	2014
Globalization Index	44 / 191	2014
Bertelsmann Transformation Index, BTI – Management Index	87 / 129	2014
Bertelsmann Transformation Index, BTI – Status Index	57 / 129	2014
Economic Freedom of the World Index	155 / 178	2014
International Property Rights Index (IPRI)	86 / 97	2014
Business Environment	72 / 82	2014
Ease of Paying Taxes	108 / 189	2014
Worldwide Press Freedom Index	127 / 180	2014
The World Competitiveness Scoreboard	49 / 60	2014
Quality of Life Index	57 / 67	2014
Business Competitiveness Index (BCI)	66 / 80	2014
Ease of Doing Business Index (EDBI)	112 / 178	2014
Corruption Perceptions Index (CPI)	142 / 175	2014
Human Development Index (HDI)	83 / 166	2014
Index of Economic Freedom	162 / 178	2014
Doing Business	96 / 189	2014

Sources: Assembled by authors from web-sites, see references

As shown in Table 9.1, Ukraine performs badly in many international rankings. In the best case, it is classified in the middle of the ranking. This results from its difficult geopolitical and economic situation. It is worth noting that in 2015, the Ukrainian government embarked on a massive program of reform concerning the legislative, executive, and judiciary areas. This may improve the country's performance in international rankings in the nearest future. In order to better illustrate Ukraine's investment attractiveness, Figure 9.1 presents its position in selected international rankings in 2014 in comparison to its neighboring countries.

Figure 9.1: Ukraine's Performance in Selected International Rankings in 2014 in Comparison with Neighboring Countries

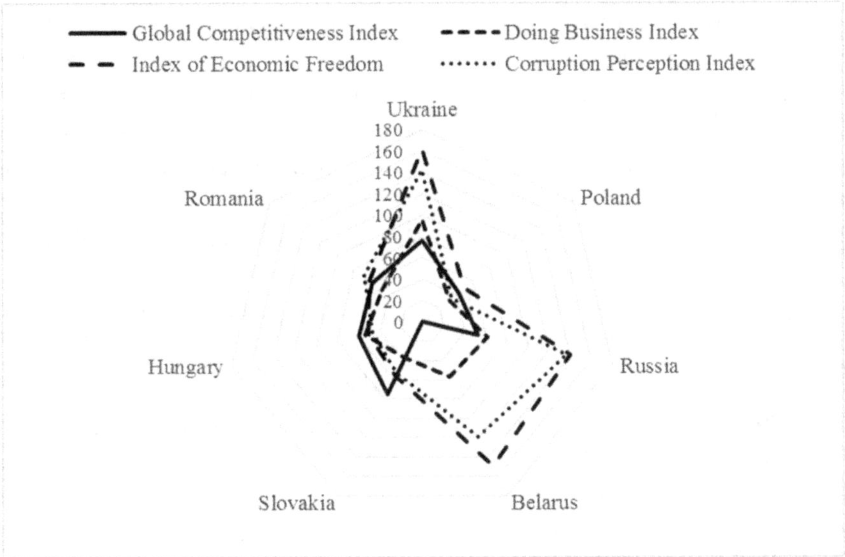

Source: Calculated from international rankings: World Economic Forum, World Bank Group, The Heritage Foundation, Transparency International

As shown in Figure 9.1, Poland wins the best positions, while Ukraine takes the worst positions in all analyzed international rankings. Romania, Hungary and Slovakia hold similar positions, and the worst performers among Ukraine's neighbors are Russia and Belarus.

Ukraine's performance in international rankings results from neglect and untapped opportunities over the last two decades. Recenly, it has been aggravated by the ongoing military conflict with Russia in the country's east. It should be noted that until 1991, the level of economic development in Ukraine was even higher than in Poland. According to data published by the

International Monetary Fund (IMF), in 1991, Ukraine's GDP per capita amounted to 6,700 international dollars[21], compared to 6,300 international dollars in Poland. In 2013, Ukraine's GDP per capita remained at the level of 9,100 international dollars whereas in Poland, it grew to 23,900 international dollars.

Unfortunately, Ukraine still is not taking advantage of its many strengths. With a total area of 603,500 sq. kilometers, Ukraine is the largest European country. The country contains four major international transport corridors. Its transport infrastructure includes over 22,000 kilometers of railways, approximately 170,000 kilometers of roads, and 2,000 kilometers of waterways. Only 29 countries have longer railways than Ukraine. Moreover, it has the fourth longest network of pipelines in the world. Ukraine also has well-developed agriculture: its percentage of cultivated land gives the country the eighth position in the world. It is worth noting that only two countries have more arable land than Ukraine. Ukraine is the world's thirteeth largest coal producer and eighteenth biggest producer of electricity. About 30% of black earth resources lie within Ukrainian territory. Thanks to fertile lands, the country is the world's biggest exporter of sunflower oil, barley, and maize, and the sixth biggest exporter of wheat. Ukraine's education system is ranked twenty-fifth in the world. In terms of the number of certified IT specialists, the country holds fifth, and, in terms of the number of engineers graduating each year, it holds the seventh position in the world.

After fourteen years of negotiations, Ukraine was admitted to the World Trade Organization (WTO) on May 16, 2008. In the course of negotiations, Ukraine pledged itself to a number of concessions, including the reduction of customs tariffs for agricultural and industrial commodities, cessation of setting minimum prices for imported goods, withdrawal from discriminatory haulage fees used in railway transport, opening of the country's internal market in all sectors and sub-sectors, free transit of goods, including energy, and the abolition of customs duties and gradual reduction of existing export duties over a time span of 5-10 years.

Although Ukraine is not a member of the Organization for Economic Co-operation and Development, it is granted a non-member observer status in

[21] The international dollar is a hypothetical unit of currency that has the same purchasing power parity that the U.S. dollar had in the United States at a given point in time. It is widely used in economics to compare Gross Domestic Product per capita according to purchasing power parity.

the OECD's Steel Committee, Working Group on Shipbuilding Industry, Working Group on Small and Medium Enterprises. In 2009, the OECD began the Eurasia Competitiveness Programme – Enhancing Investment Competitiveness and Private Sector Development. The main goal of this program is to increase the investment attractiveness of certain countries by providing them with expert advice and recommendations for their governments concerning necessary reforms. The Ukraine is also a member of other international and regional organizations, including ONZ, International Monetary Fund (IMF), World Bank, International Finance Corporation (IFC), FAO, UNICTAD, UNIDO, The GUAM Organization for Democracy and Economic Development (GUAM), and The Black Sea Economic Cooperation (BSEC).

The conditions of carrying out economic activity in Ukraine by foreign investors

The study was carried out on a sample of 320 enterprises with foreign capital operating in Ukraine by means of a specially designed web-based questionnaire published in the internet service Google Docs. The questionnaire was available only to the enterprises covered by the study and contained questions about the main reasons for choosing Ukraine as a location of their investment. Top-level managers of enterprises covered covered by the study were invited to fill out or to authorize competent persons to fill out the questionnaire via email. On average, for every six e-mails inviting managers to participate in the study, we received one completed questionnaire (a 16.25% feedback). Table 9.2 below presents the survey findings.

Table 9.2: The Most Important Reasons for Choosing Ukraine as a Place of Investment

The most important motives	Number of responses	%
Weak competition	24	46.20%
Cheap workforce	23	44.20%
Access to cheap raw materials & other production components	15	28.80%
Opportunities to yield above-average profits	14	26.90%

Special Economic Zones	11	21.20%
Logistics	11	21.20%
Low tax rates	9	17.30%
Special allowances available to foreign investors	8	15.40%
Lack of similar products on the Ukrainian market	7	13.50%
Ukraine's economic outlook	7	13.50%
Export opportunities to neighboring countries	6	11.50%
Presence of other foreign enterprises co operating with your enterprise	5	9.60%
Law protection & support offered to foreign investors	5	9.60%
Purchasing power of Ukraine's residents	5	9.60%
Inflation level	2	3.80%
Functioning of the Ukraine's banking sector	2	3.80%
Other reasons	1	1.90%
Total	52	-*

*Since respondents were allowed to give up to three answers, these values cannot be summed up to 52 and 100% respectively.

The most frequently indicated reason for choosing Ukraine as a place of investment is weak competition in the relevant sector of the economy (46.2%) and low labor cost (44.2%), followed by an access to cheap raw materials or production components (28.8%) and opportunities for the above-average profits (26.9%). Surveyed investors also indicate special economic zones (21.2%), logistics (21.2%), and low taxation (17.3%) as important decisive factors. The less important factors are low level of inflation (3.8%) and the functioning of the banking sector in Ukraine (3.8%).

The survey employes the main economic reasons driving foreign investors' decisions to expand business operations, proposed by J.H. Dunning (1994). See Figure 9.2 for survey results.

Figure 9.2: The Main Economic Reasons Driving Decisions of Foreign Investors to Expand Business Operations

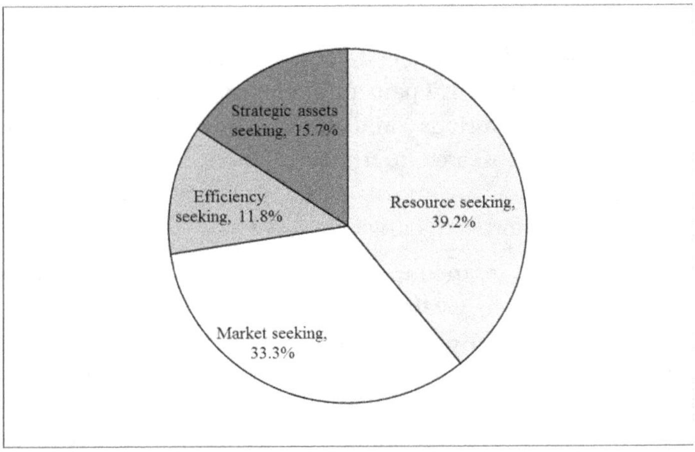

Source: From survey results

From the collected data, it is evident that foreign direct investors seek effective ways to reduce production costs. The survey reveals that as many as twenty enterprises included in the study seek cheap resources (39.2%). One-third of these enterprises point to market seeking as the main reason for choosing Ukraine as a destination of intended investment (33.3%). Only 11.8% of surveyed enterprises with foreign capital want to improve efficiency and 15.7% seek strategic assets.

The main aim of companies relative to resource seeking is acquiring particular types of resources which are not available in their countries or are available at lower cost elsewhere. For the market seeking companies, the most important role is played by demand-related factors such as market size, its characteristics, and development prospects. Efficiency seeking investors strive to rationalize their operational activity by changing the structure of business, introducing organizational improvements, and better utilization of available resources. Strategic asset seeking is characteristic of companies operating in capital-intensive and high-tech sectors. These aim at retaining or strengthening their competitive position on international markets by acquiring a new technological base rather than exploiting the existing assets.

The study also reveals that most surveyed enterprises spot the presence of other foreign investors – 33 out of 52 surveyed enterprises (64.71%) indicate that they perceive other enterprises with foreign capital operating in the same sector. Results show 35.29% of responding enterprises are unaware of the presence of competitors with foreign capital. Most enterprises (61.54%) declare that they do not cooperate with other enterprises with foreign capital operating in Ukraine.

The study also identifies the major areas of cooperation between enterprises with foreign capital. Eighty-five percent of enterprises cooperate in sales and distribution, 40.6% on various production quality improvement projects, 21.95% cooperate in research and development, and 21.9% in human resource management. The lowest areas of cooperation are in finance management (5.77%), and marketing (9.61%).

A competition study is an important part of this survey. The surveyed enterprises were asked to give estimates as to the number of their direct competitors being enterprises with foreign capital. In our results, 26.9% of respondents have 2-4 competitors, 19.2% of surveyed enterprises have 4-6 competitors, and 13.5% of enterprises have more than 11 competitors with foreign capital. Only 7.7% of respondents have 7-10 competitors. Only one enterprise indicated it has 1 competitor, and lack of competitors are reported by 34.6% of surveyed enterprises (Figure 9.3).

Figure 9.3: The Number of Direct Competitors

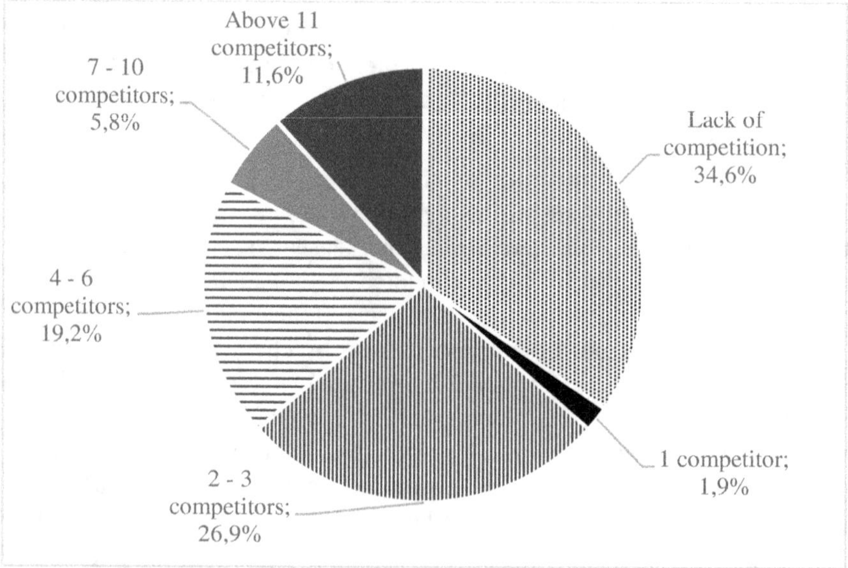

Source: From survey results

According to the views expressed by 44.2% of enterprises with foreign capital, corruption is the main barrier discouraging foreign investors from entering the Ukrainian market. Corruption is a serious problem typical of former USSR countries. Habib and Żurawiecki (2002) note that although the studies carried out by J. Hines, D. Wheeler and A. Mody have not confirmed any negative correlation between corruption and foreign direct investments, some other researchers e.g., S. Wei and L. Busse, and M. Habib and L. Zurawicki (in Habib and Żurawiecki) have found a significant correlation between corruption and the inflows of foreign direct investments (Habib & Żurawiecki, 2002).

This study shows that the second most important barrier discouraging foreign investors is government policy, indicated by 38.5% of respondents. Political stability is a variable extremely difficult to define precisely. Generally, one can expect that political instability in a country negatively affects the inflow of foreign direct investments. However, many empirical studies show that the relationship between political stability and FDIs is much more complex and controversial. For example, Jóźwik and Miłek explore opposing views about political stability with R.S. Basi and Y. Aharoni (in Jóźwik & Miłek, 2007) claiming that political stability plays a crucial role in the process of making investment decisions. On the other hand, J.R. Piper, P.T. Bennet, R.T. Green, and W.H. Cunningham (in Jóźwik & Miłek) argue that there is no significant relationship between political stability in a country of intended investment and foreign direct investments flowing into this country (Jóźwik & Miłek, 2007).

In this study, 30.8% of surveyed enterprises declare that the functioning of Ukraine's banking sector and its capital market plays an important role in choosing Ukraine for investment. A well-developed banking sector is capable of offering entrepreneurs a wide range of credit facilities meeting their needs, and other finance services supporting daily business operations, domestic and international. The state of development of the capital market is important from the viewpoint of seeking additional sources of financing for business activities. Our study reveals that the least important reasons for choosing Ukraine as an investment location are a level of inflation (1.9% of responses), low quality of goods offered on the Ukrainian market (7.7%), difficult access to raw materials (11.5%), and reputation of other players operating in the sector (17.3%).

The view that reputation is the most important instrument in the process of building competitive advantage on the market is mentioned by 42.3% of enterprises. Almost equally important is knowledge of the market and understanding the customers' needs (38.5% of enterprises). Less important is the quality of production (34.6%), followed by prices (30.8%), human capital (26.9%), brand (23.1%), production technologies (23.1%), and market knowledge (21.2%).

The research findings clearly demonstrate that the enterprises with foreign capital operating in Ukraine are not focused exclusively on the optimization of production costs in order to maximize their profits. They also try to gain the customers' trust, and thus build their competitive advantage.

M.E. Porter opts for a dynamic model of competition. He claims that the country can turn negative factors into its competitive advantage. Porter argues that the competitiveness of national economy first and foremost results from the ability of particular entities, especially enterprises, to create innovation and introduce improvements such as new techniques and new procedures, as well as from the ability of enterprises operating in a given area to use available resources efficiently to produce valuable goods and services (Porter, 2001). Foreign direct investments are particularly important for less developed countries where enterprises with foreign capital are often the key innovators. They are also very important for economies in a stage of transition. In countries like Ukraine, foreign direct investments supplement scarce domestic resources and help many local enterprises operating in key sectors of the Ukrainian economy, including small and medium-sized enterprises, to implement new technologies, improve production methods, increase efficiency, and thus build their international competitive advantage.

An assessment of investment climate in Ukraine by foreign direct investors

The simplest way to assess investment climate in Ukraine is to ask foreign investors already present there. Responses are not positive. Among polled investors, 63.46% express the view that investment climate in Ukraine is not conducive to foreign investors and is not meeting their needs and expectations. Only 36.54% of surveyed entrepreneurs are satisfied with investment climate. Undoubtedly, the most important reasons explaining this situation is the change of political power in 2014 and hostilities in the country's east, which result in financial instability. In order to get a more precise assessment of Ukraine's investment climate, the surveyed enterprises were asked to place their opinions on the scale ranging from 2 (good investment climate) to –2 (meaning bad investment climate). The findings are shown in Figure 9.4 below.

Figure 9.4: An Assessment of Ukraine's Investment Climate by Foreign Direct Investors

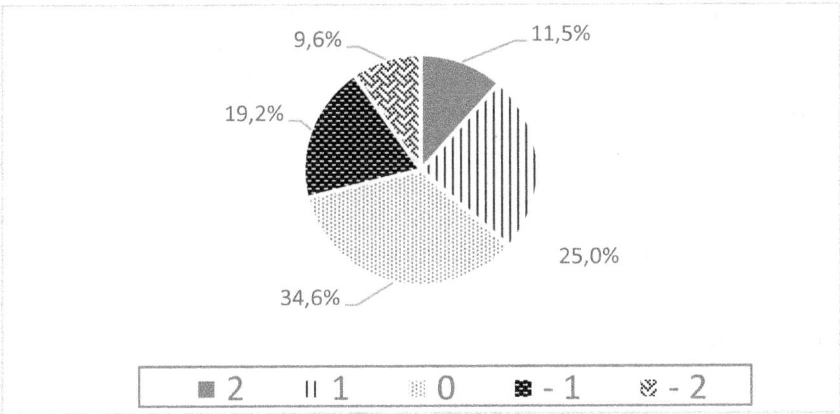

Source: Survey results

The largest group of surveyed enterprises assesses the investment climate in Ukraine as neutral (34.62%), 25% as neutral to good rated (score 1), while only 11.54% of respondents assess Ukraine's investment climate as good (score 2). Further, 19.23% of companies assess the investment climate as rather negative (score –1), while only 9.62% of surveyed enterprises with foreign capital view the investment climate in Ukraine as bad. Because of the complex and difficult economic situation in this country, these findings may be a little bit surprising. However, it seems apparent that foreign investors can adapt to difficult conditions in Ukraine, which can also be confirmed by the 2014 study of changes in investment climate in Ukraine (Figure 9.5).

Figure 9.5: Assessment of Changes in Ukraine's Investment Climate in 2014

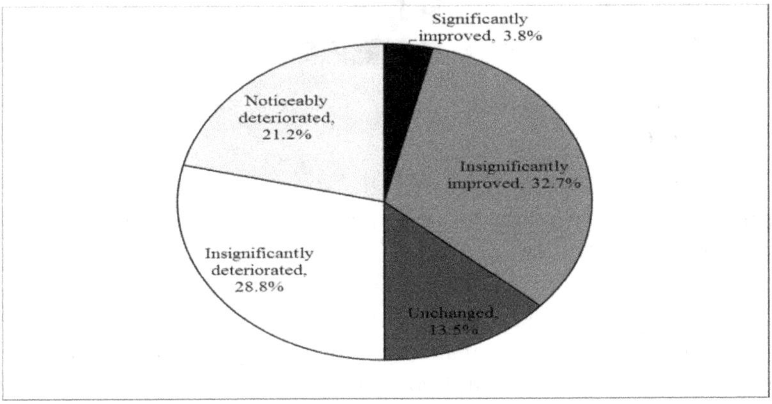

Source: Survey results

In 2014, almost 50% of surveyed enterprises with foreign capital observe the worsening of investment climate in Ukraine. However, according to the study findings, 3.8% of surveyed companies observe a distinct improvement in investment conditions in Ukraine's and 32.7% declare that the country's investment climate improved insignificantly. Considering extremely difficult political and economic situation in Ukraine in 2014, the lack of a drastic decline in the level of investors' confidence is undoubtedly a positive phenomenon.

In the next part of the study, foreign investors are asked to indicate the most significant negative phenomena occurring in the Ukraine's economy in 2014. Figure 9.6 below exhibits relevant findings.

Figure 9.6: Negative Changes in Ukraine's Investment Climate in 2014.

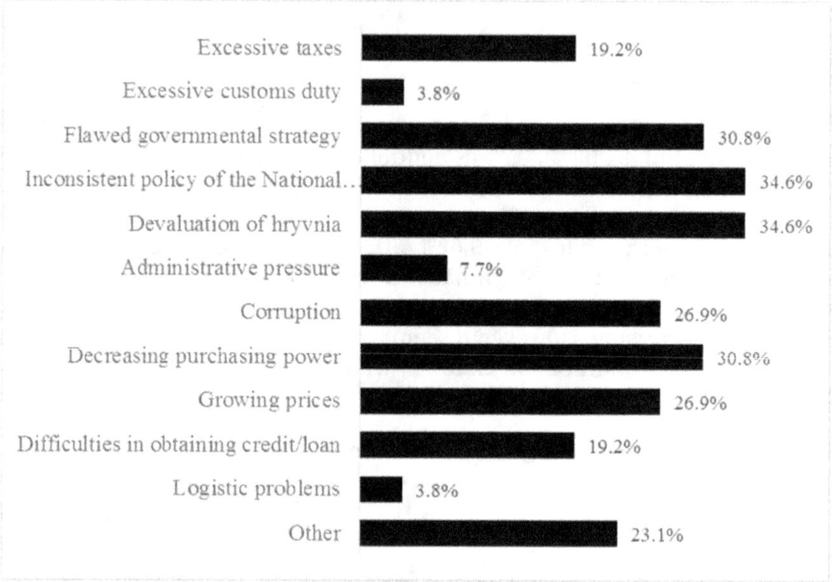

Source: Survey results

Pursuant to the views expressed by surveyed foreign investors, the devaluation of the Ukrainian currency, hryvnia, is the most significant factor which adversely affects the investment climate in Ukraine (34.6% of enterprises). Equally negative impact is caused by inconsistent policy pursued by the National Bank of Ukraine (34.6% of respondents). Moreover, significant problems for foreign investors result from decreasing purchasing power of the country's population (30.8%) and policy of the Ukrainian government (30.8% of respondents). Corruption (26.9%) and price increase (26.9% of responses) are also important factors contributing to negative assessment of the investment climate in Ukraine. For foreign investors, access to large markets, market growth dynamics, and purchasing power of the population as well as government policy and macroeconomic indicators are also very important factors affecting their investment decisions.

In a final part of the study, foreign investors were also asked to indicate the most positive changes observed in 2014 which positively affected the investors' opinions on Ukraine's investment climate. A majority of foreign investors points to an active fight against corruption (63.5%), followed by the deregulation of economy (42.3%), judiciary system reform (23.1%), currency exchange policy (15.4%), agricultural reform (13.5%), and improving access to raw materials (11.5%). In foreign investors' opinions, the most positive changes occurred in the Ukrainian political climate. However, they also express the view that a military conflict with Russia can only slow down the process of the country's reforms. Most surveyed foreign investors regard the Ukrainian market as a very attractive location for investing (64.7%). It is surprising that about 63% of foreign investors are dissatisfied with the state of investment climate in Ukraine, and almost 50% admit that they even observed the symptoms of its deterioration.

The resolution of the protracted military conflict in Ukraine's east is the first and most important step in improving the country's investment climate according to 53.8% of surveyed foreign investors. In investors' opinions, the following efforts can also contribute to the improvement in the investment climate in Ukraine: the acceleration of economic reforms, combating corruption (34.6%), stabilization of prices (30.8%), devolution of power (23.1%), judiciary system reform (21.2%), stabilization of finance sector (21.3%), deregulation of economy (17.3%), and tax system reform (15.4%).

Conclusions

This study shows that weak competition, labor costs, access to cheap raw materials, and opportunities to gain above-average profits are the most common motives for investing in the Ukraine. The scale of corruption is the main barrier discouraging foreign investors from investing, followed by government policy. Most respondents view investment climate in Ukraine as neutral.

According to the surveyed investors, Ukraine's investment climate deteriorates in 2014. They state that the devaluation of the hryvnia, government policy, and decreasing purchasing power of the population are the main reasons to blame for the worsening of investment conditions in Ukraine. The investors welcome an active fight against corruption, deregulation of economy, and reforms of the judicial system. About 63% of foreign investors declare that they are dissatisfied with Ukraine's investment climate, and almost 50% observe adverse changes in investment conditions. However, most respondents view the Ukrainian economy as an attractive investment destination. In their opinions, a resolution of the military conflict in the country's east is the first and the most important step to improve the investment climate.

Based on the research findings, in order to improve the investment conditions in Ukraine, the following measures are recommended:

1. develop a new system of allowances and incentives for foreign investors investing in selected sectors and regions;
2. adjust existing legal regulations to international standards;
3. introduce a simplified accounting and reporting system for small and medium-sized enterprises;
4. simplify business start-up registration procedures;
5. strengthen legal protection of property rights of both domestic and foreign entities;
6. simplify taxation system;
7. reform the education system in order to improve the quality of the work force.

The globalization and resultant global division of labor as well as the process of transformation of Ukraine's economy initiated over two decades ago create new opportunities for the country's economic development. In order to ensure an accelerated economic growth, Ukraine should improve its investment climate to attract more foreign direct investments. Although Ukraine's economy has a huge growth potential, it suffers from the scarcity of domestic capital. FDIs can have a multifarious influence on the development of the Ukrainian economy. They can supplement domestic financial resources, contribute to the production restructuring, generate new jobs, and bring in advanced technologies. Thus, they can contribute to increasing innovation and competitiveness of the Ukrainian economy on the global markets.

References

Bojar, E. (2001). *Bezpośrednie inwestycje zagraniczne w obszarach słabo rozwiniętych [Direct foreign investment in underdeveloped areas]*. Warsaw, Poland: PWN.

Budner, W. (2004). *Lokalizacja przedsiębiorstw [Business location]*. Poznań: Wydawnictwo AE.

Dunning, J. H. (1994). Re-evaluating the benefits of foreign direct investment. *Transnational Corporations*, 3(1), 23-51.

Habib, M. & Żurawiecki, L. (2002). Corruption and Foreign Direct Investment. *Journal of International Business Studies, 33*(2), 291–307.

Jóźwik, B. & Miłek, B. (2007). *Działalność inwestycyjna firm brytyjskich w Polsce [Investment activities of British companies in Poland]*. Lublin: Wydawnictwo KUL.

Kłysik-Uryszek, A. (2010). *Bezpośrednie inwestycje zagraniczne w gospodarce regionu. Teoria i praktyka [Direct foreign investment in the region's economy. Theory and practice]*. Warsaw, Poland: Wydawnictwa Fachowe CeDeWu.pl.

Misala, J. & Weresa, A. M. (Eds.) (2006). *Podstawowe problemy pomiaru międzynarodowej konkurencyjności gospodarki kraju [Basic problems measuring the international competitiveness of the country's economy]*. Warsaw, Poland: Wydawnictwo SGH.

Pomykało, W. (Ed.) (1995). *Encyklopedia biznesu [Business Encyclopedia]*. (Vol. 1). Warsaw, Poland: Fundacja Innowacja.

Porter, M. E. (2001). *Porter o konkurencji [Porter about competition]*. A. Ehrlich (Trans.) Warszawa, Poland: PWE.

Przygoda, M. (2014). *Atrakcyjność inwestowania w regionach słabo rozwiniętych [Attractiveness of investing in underdeveloped regions]*. Warsaw, Poland: Wydawnictwo Naukowe Wydziału Zarządzania Uniwersytetu Warszawskiego.

Rosińska, M. (2005). Stymulanty i destymulanty bezpośrednich inwestycji zagranicznych w warunkach globalizacji na przykładzie Polski [Stimulants and destimulants of foreign direct investment in the context of globalization on the example of Poland]. In Karaszewski, W. (Ed.). *Bezpośrednie inwestycje zagraniczne w podnoszeniu konkurencyjności polskiej gospodarki*. (pp.117-129). Toruń: Wydawnictwo UMK.

Rymarczyk, J., Błaszczyk, M., Michalski, B., Niemiec, M., Niemiec, W. & Wróblewski, M. (2008). *Klimat inwestycyjny Dolnego Śląska w ocenie bezpośrednich inwestorów zagranicznych [Investment climate of Lower Silesia in the opinion of direct foreign investors]*. Wrocław: Oficyna Wydawnicza Arboretum.

Sobol, E. et al. (1997). *Słownik wyrazów obcych*. (Wydanie nowe). *[Dictionary of foreign words*. (New edition)]. Warsaw: Wydawnictwo Naukowe PWN.

Stępniak, A. (1996). *Integracja i transfer kapitału. Inwestycje bezpośrednie w aspekcie klimatu inwestycyjnego w Unii Europejskiej [Integration and transfer of capital. Direct investment in the aspect of investment climate in the European Union]*. J. Tomidajewicz (Ed.) Gdańsk: Wydawnictwo Uniwersytetu Gdańskiego.

The Organization For Economic Co-operation And Development [OECD]. (2008). Benchmark Definition of Foreign Direct Investment. (4th Edition.) Paris, France: OECD. Retrieved from https://www.oecd.org/daf/inv/investmentstatisticsandanalysis/40193734.pdf.

Database Websites

Freedom House. Retieved from https://freedomhouse.org.

Human Development Report Office. Retrieved from http://hdr.undp.org.

Institute for Economics and Peace. Retrieved from http://economicsandpeace.org.

International Institute for Management Development. Retrieved from http://www.imd.org.

Numbeo doo. Retreieved from http://www.numbeo.com.

PricewaterhouseCoopers. Retrieved from http://www.pwc.com.

Reporter Without Borders. Retrieved from http://rsf.org.

Sudestada. Retrieved from http://www.sudestada.com.uy.

Swiss Economic Institute. Retrieved from http://globalization.kof.ethz.ch.

The Bertelsmann Stiftung. Retrieved from http://www.bti-project.org.

The Economist Intelligence Unit. Retrieved from http:// eiu.com.

The Heritage Foundation. Retrieved from http://www.heritage.org.

The Heritage Foundation. Retrieved from http://www.heritage.org/index/download.

Transparency International. Retreieved from http://www.transparency.org.

Transparency International. Retrieved from http://www.transparency.org/cpi2014/results/.

World Bank Group. Retrieved from http://www.doingbusiness.org/rankings.

World Economic Forum. Retrieved from http://www3.weforum.org/docs/WEF_GlobalCompetitivenessReport_2014-15.pdf

Chapter 10

Regional Growth and Poverty in Ukraine

Fyodor I. Kushnirsky[22] and Svitlana V. Maksymenko[23]

Abstract

To forecast Ukraine's regional growth and analyze persistent poverty there, we build an econometric model consisting of four blocks—industry, agriculture, construction, and services—as autoregressive distributed lag (ARDL (p, q)) models. We adjust a baseline 2015-2017 forecast for a structural break caused by a fall in production, and modify it based on exponential smoothing which assigns greater weights to more recent observations. Our analysis shows that the construction and service sectors will be advancing in all regions, although the gap in regional industrial and agricultural development will only widen. We also find that it is the agricultural, rather than industrial growth that could potentially lead to a poverty decline in economically lagging regions.

Introduction

After 25 years of independence, the situation in Ukraine is extensively discussed by politicians and scholars. Many scholars focus on the absence of real political and economic reforms, the persistence of corruption, and structural issues that prevail in the country (Kuzio, 2011; Korostelina, 2014; Myerson & Mylovanov, 2014; Nizalov, 2014). It is emphasized that a more efficient government would produce policy decisions closer to final beneficiaries (Sologub, 2014). Caution is also warranted on decentralization (Cai & Treisman, 2005) because it may let finances flow from poor to well-endowed regions, exacerbating the interregional inequality.

The Ukrainian public is quite skeptical about the flurry of activity for decentralization and economic reform in the country (Kushnirsky, 2014). People in provincial areas do not feel positive changes. On the contrary, prices and tariffs rise, living standards fall, infrastructure keeps crumbling, and

[22] fikush@temple.edu
[23] maks@pitt.edu

business is sagging under the pressure from punitive rules and regulations. Inflation and depreciation of the currency are the driving causes of rising poverty, especially among the middle class and retirees.

To research and forecast the performance of Ukraine's regional economy consisting of 24 oblasts, the Autonomous Republic of Crimea, and special-status cities of Kyiv and Sevastopol, we build an econometric model with variables in four economic sectors—industry, agriculture, construction, and service—by region. The estimation sample covers the 2000-2013 data, and the midterm forecast period is 2015-2017. Our analysis and forecast of the best and lagging regions in Ukraine is important for improving territorial economic efficiency and for smoothing the negative consequences of a projected reduction in the distributive function of the central government.

The paper organization includes a description of the data, the model, and the methodology in Section 2. In Section 3 an outline of a baseline forecast is provided and, because of a sharp decline in Ukraine's economic output in 2014, we design a nonlinear scenario for adjusting the baseline forecast. The regional discrepancies are considered in Section 4 and an analysis provided of how variation in industrial and agricultural growth leads to a persistent poverty in several territorial units.

The data, model, and methodology: The data and model

Our data originate from the State Statistics Service of Ukraine (Ukrstat) and cover the 2000-2013 timeframe. In some instances, we use our own estimates employing splicing time series based on growth rates and levels, interpolation, and short-term extrapolation. The Gross Regional Product (GRP) is used as an aggregate indicator of development in a region. The industry data give the sum of Gross Value Added (GVA) for three types of economic activities: mining, processing (manufacturing), and production and distribution of energy, gas, and water. Ukrstat reports GVA series in nominal prices so indices (growth percentages) are used to convert the series into 2007 constant prices. Since agricultural output is reported by Ukrstat in constant 2010 prices, it is converted into constant 2007 prices using regional price indices for 2008-2010. The GVA data in construction and services are the sum of output by type of economic activity.

A baseline regional forecast is produced for 2014-2017 followed by a separate 2014 forecast. The latter cannot be used for gauging the predictive ability of the model, due to a sharp decline in 2014 production, especially industrial. However, it plays an important role in constructing a nonlinear scenario for Ukraine's regional economy after testing the time series for structural break and employing exponential smoothing. Our equation estimation is based on the use of autoregressive distributed lag (*ARDL(p, q)*) model which contains lagged values of endogenous variable y and exogenous variables x:

Equation 10. 1

$$y_t = \alpha_0 + \alpha_1 y_{t-1} + \ldots + \alpha_p y_{t-p} + \beta_0 x_t + \beta_1 x_{t-1} + \ldots + \beta_q x_{t-q} + e_t$$

Theoretically, a sufficient number of lags of y and x is to be included to reduce serial correlation in error terms. In experimental trials, we find a two-period lag adequate for forecasting regional growth. Assuming that standard assumptions on the error term e hold, least squares are used for estimating parameters in (Equation 10.1). Altogether, there are over 340 equations in our model and about 50 identities. We use EViews for the estimation.

Methodology

In the extended 2000-2014 sample, there appears the likelihood of a structural break in the last observation resulting in two subsamples, 2000-2013 and 2014, with 14 and 1 observations, respectively. In this case, the Chow test for structural break cannot be applied because the number of observations in the second subsample is less than the number of parameters. Therefore, the predictive Chow test is used:

$$y_i = \begin{array}{ll} X_i\beta_1 + e_i & i \in (A) \\ X_i\beta_2 + e_i & i \in (B) \end{array}$$

where (A) and (B) are the two subsamples, the total number of observations is n ($n = n_1 + n_2$), and the number of parameters on the right side of each equation equals k. The null hypothesis is:

$$H_0 : \beta_1 = \beta_2 .$$

As $n_2 < k$, the Chow test statistic is:

Equation 10.2

$$F = \frac{(SSE - SSE_1)/n_2}{SSE_1/(n_1 - k)},$$

where *SSE* and SSE_1 are the sum of squared residuals in the full sample and larger subsample, respectively.

A typical response to a structural break is to use a dummy variable in a pooled time series. This is not a reasonable option in a one-observation subsample. Past statistics are still relevant, because they reflect the accumulated production capacities, but their weight is not decisive, as a greater emphasis should be placed on a new trend. For this reason, exponential smoothing (ES), which assigns greater weights to more recent observations, is appropriate. By producing a smoothed time series, ES helps harmonize the baseline forecast with the 2014 output. The basic recursive formula of ES is:

Equation 10.3

$$\hat{y}_t = \alpha y_t + (1-\alpha)\hat{y}_{t-1},$$

where $\hat{y}_t$ is a smoothed series of y_t, and $|\alpha| \leq 1$ is the smoothing parameter. Single smoothing (Equation 10.3) is used when there is no trend in the data; otherwise, it is included as a part of a more complicated smoothing. Out of several such methods, we choose the one that provides a smaller root mean square error (RMSE) conveniently reported by EView: $RMSE = \sqrt{\sum e_i^2 / n}$, where *e* is the difference between the actual and estimated values of the dependent variable.

Baseline forecast and nonlinear scenario: The production sectors

Industry's share in Ukraine's GDP equals 29% whereas service and agriculture account for 59% and 12% respectively (CIA, 2015). The main part of Ukraine's industry belongs to the so called "heavy group" (A) which makes capital goods. The group's output constitutes 70% of Ukraine's industrial output. A disproportionately smaller "light group" (B) produces consumer goods (Geography of Ukraine, 2015). Ukraine's industrial production is concentrated in four regional complexes: Donbas, Trans-Dnieper, Trans-Black Sea, and Trans-Carpathian (Nemec & Zavoloka, 2009).

Per our calculation, the mining industry accounts for 14.7% of Ukrainian industrial production in 2014. Based on mineral commodity summaries of the U.S. Geological Survey, more than 5% of the world reserves of iron ore constituting 46% of reserves of the former Soviet Union (FSU) is concentrated in Ukraine. While the deposits of oil and natural gas are insufficient, oil refining is well developed. Coal is the main fossil fuel of Ukraine. Ukraine's mining industry has been going through a process of restructuring, yet safety in many working mines remains below the standards of neighboring Poland, Russia, and Slovakia.

The processing (manufacturing) industry accounts for 67.6% of Ukrainian industrial production in 2014. The country's iron and steel production peaks at 43 million tons in 2007, but after the 2008 financial crisis declines to 30 million tons (Levine et al, 2010). The machine building (MB) complex in Ukraine has more than 3000 plants and factories, accounts for 20% in nation's exports, and sells its products to 54 countries (Nemec & Zavoloka, 2009). Ukraine's transport aircraft industry is particularly outstanding, with the Antonov Design Bureau producing a cargo plane An-140 and a military transport plane An-70, both of a potential interest to the EU air transportation industry.

Thermal and nuclear power stations supply 90% of energy. Ukraine has four active nuclear plants constructed in the Soviet period—Zaporizska, South-Ukrainian, Rivenska, and Khmelnytska. The Zaporizska nuclear plant, the largest in Europe, produces 20.4% of Ukraine's electricity (Zaporizska Nuclear Plant Website). The thermal power plants are the largest air and water polluters in the country.

Ukraine utilizes 69% of its land area for agricultural purposes, with arable land occupying over a half of the total (Bogovin, 2006). There are three agro-climatic zones: forest, forest-steppe, and steppe. Steppe, the most intensively cultivated area in Ukraine, claims one of the world largest areas of fertile black soil and accounts for 40% of Ukraine's territory. It is well-known for its rich harvests of wheat, sunflower, corn, and soybeans (Rogovska 2014). In a sign of structural change, agriculture produces 12% of Ukraine's GDP, down from 17% in 2001 (Ukrstat). Following the disintegration of the FSU, Ukraine's grain output falls but then improves to 60.5 million metric tons in 2014, surpassing a 2011 record of 57 million tons (Mykhailov 2014). Labor-intensive production of sugar beets remains a viable option for many small farms with limited access to agricultural machinery. In addition, meat production is responsible for a third of Ukraine's agricultural output. Household cattle farms are small, but they continue to supply 65% of milk to domestic market, often directly by producers. Inadequate dairy quality is an obstacle to compete on the EU markets (Bogovin, 2006).

By our estimation, Ukraine's construction sector accounts for 2.9% of country's value added in 2013. The majority of the provincial population is unaffected by new construction as close to a third of all funding flows to Kyiv, followed by Dnipropetrovsk, Donetsk, and Odesa. There are some modest gains in residential construction. An average housing space per inhabitant is 23.7 square meters, low in comparison to neighboring countries (PMR, 2014). According to Ukrstat, trade and repair, transportation and communications, and real estate contributed the most to the value added of the country's service sector in 2013—25.6%, 18.3%, and 11.4%, respectively. Country's exports in 2014 are estimated at 52.5 billion USD, imports at 60.4 billion USD (Ukrstat, 2015). Major export commodities are agricultural products, metals, and chemicals; top imports are energy, machinery, and equipment. Odesa accounts for 80% of cargo shipments by sea. Ground transportation is affected by poor road conditions. Communications is one of the fastest growing services in the country. About one-third of Ukraine's networks are digital.

Summary of the forecasts

Our baseline forecast covers the whole territory of Ukraine and is measured in million Ukraine's hryvni (UAH) in 2007 constant prices. Because the baseline forecast could not reflect a war-related slump in economic production in 2014, we use a novel methodology for an appropriate adjustment as explained below. We call the adjusted forecast a nonlinear scenario, and it incorporates territorial changes caused by the war conflict. In this process, we combine the in-sample data, Ukrstat 2014 statistics, and the baseline forecast by applying exponential smoothing after analyzing the volatile time series for a structural break.

After examining industry, agriculture, construction, and service blocks in the non-linear scenario, the first two are considered the most important from the analysis of regional disparities and poverty. Table 10.1 gives the non-linear scenario for Ukraine's industry forecast.

Table 10.1: Nonlinear Scenario: Ukraine's Industry Forecast

Region	2014 Actual	2015	2016	2017	2017/2014 Annual %
A1. Mining (Top 5 Regions)					
Dnipropetrovsk	8283	8584	8908	9014	2.86
Donetsk	5910	7271	7454	7579	8.64
Luhansk	NA	4612	4578	4564	NA
Poltava	3526	3528	3402	3356	-1.63
Zhytomyr	2182	2492	2656	3204	13.66
Ukraine	**26668**	**28649**	**30643**	**32007**	**6.27**
B1. Processing (Top 5 Regions)					
Donetsk	15005	17065	17517	17742	5.74
Dnipropetrovsk	13647	13453	14948	15335	3.96
Zaporizhia	7596	7414	8364	8789	4.98
Kharkiv	5573	5432	6092	6274	4.03
Kyiv City	4995	5299	6975	7158	12.74
B2. Processing (Bottom 5 Regions)					
Khmelnytsk	1397	1413	1404	1399	0.05
Ternopil	1500	1393	1417	1433	-1.51
Kherson	1255	1386	1368	1359	2.69
Volyn	1300	1158	1153	1151	-3.98
Chernivtsi	528	582	600	611	4.99
Ukraine	**102046**	**99176**	**109582**	**113462**	**3.60**
C1. Energy (Top 5 Regions)					
Donetsk	3520	3156	3185	3214	-2.99
Zaporizhia	2050	2246	2266	2285	3.68
Dnipropetrovsk	2213	1972	2000	2026	-2.90
Kharkiv	1513	1722	1737	1751	4.99
Kyiv City	NA	1417	1422	1426	NA
C2. Energy (Bottom 5 Regions)					
Ternopil	144	197	198	197	11.01
Zhytomyr	178	195	202	202	4.31
Volynnia	203	153	157	158	-8.01
Chernivtsi	143	139	149	146	0.69
Zakarpatia	117	117	120	121	1.13
Ukraine	**22151**	**22210**	**22326**	**22435**	**0.43**
D1. Industry Total (Top 5 Regions)					
Dnipropetrovsk	24618	24700	25763	26231	2.14
Donetsk	24021	22844	26987	28578	5.96
Zaporizhia	10226	9994	10767	11094	2.75
Poltava	8329	8485	9235	9409	4.15
Kharkiv	7896	7732	8491	8706	3.31
D2. Industry Total (Bottom 5 Regions)					
Zakarpatia	1945	1754	1710	1686	-4.65
Ternopil	1795	1677	1703	1720	-1.41
Kherson	1472	1623	1614	1605	2.93
Volynnia	1437	1337	1338	1339	-2.33
Chernivtsi	673	724	752	759	4.09
Ukraine	**148467**	**146150**	**161219**	**167865**	**4.18**

Section A of Table 10.1 predicts that out of top five oblasts in Ukraine's mining, the fastest growth takes place in Zhytomyr, at an average annual rate of 13.7%, followed by Donetsk with 8.6%. Overall, Ukraine's mining output grows by 6.3% annually. Ukraine's processing industry (Section B) grows at an average rate of 3.6%: All the five top regions show a respectable annual growth of at least 4%, with the best growth in the capital city. Of the bottom five regions, only Kherson and Chernivtsi exhibit a positive growth in processing, leading to a total industrial growth in these two oblasts (Section D). The rest continue to lag in position. Energy production (Section C) is the least efficient industry in Ukraine. Out of the top five regions in energy, the only two oblasts exhibiting growth are Kharkiv and Zaporizhia. Overall, Ukraine's total industrial production rises at an average 4.2% rate.

Table 10. 2: Nonlinear Scenario: Ukraine's Agriculture Forecast

Region	2014 Actual	2015	2016	2017	2017/2014 Annual %
A1. Agriculture Total (Top 5 Regions)					
Vinnytsia	14151	14662	14775	14712	1.30
Kyiv	10765	11302	10302	9960	-2.56
Poltava	10282	10784	9853	9305	-3.27
Cherkasy	9885	10382	10558	10697	2.67
Dnipropetrovsk	9256	10004	10296	10565	4.51
A2. Agriculture Total (Bottom 5 Regions)					
Volyn	4667	4463	4538	4627	-0.29
Ivano-Frankivsk	4098	4168	4340	4526	3.37
Luhansk	3482	3606	3571	3557	0.71
Chernivtsi	3347	3286	3349	3411	0.63
Zakarpatia	3130	2951	2937	2927	-2.21
Ukraine	**173476**	**172740**	**171064**	**170246**	**-0.62**
B1. Grain (Top 5 Regions)					
Poltava	4033	4293	4354	4294	2.11
Vinnytsia	4361	4273	4387	4456	0.72
Kharkiv	3754	3650	3781	3858	0.92
Sumy	3529	3545	3740	3868	3.10
Khmelnytsk	3164	3448	4184	4769	14.66
B2. Grain (Bottom 5 Regions)					
Luhansk	991	888	876	872	-4.17
Ivano-Frankivsk	702	720	781	846	6.42
Volyn	883	696	677	664	-9.06
Chernivtsi	539	539	555	571	1.94
Zakarpatia	305	277	275	274	-3.51
Ukraine	**53176**	**49871**	**51981**	**54027**	**0.53**
C1. Meat (Top 5 Regions)					
Cherkasy	2668	2661	3211	3274	7.06
Kyiv	2034	2133	2173	2191	2.51
Vinnytsia	2291	2101	1970	1904	-5.98
Dnipropetrovsk	1922	1942	2165	2273	5.75
Donetsk	1096	1177	1221	1260	4.76
C2. Meat (Bottom 5 Regions)					
Kirovograd	458	423	422	420	-2.85
Sumy	430	391	384	378	-4.21
Chernivtsi	509	389	379	370	-10.09
Odesa	401	386	382	379	-1.86
Mykolaiv	344	300	299	299	-4.57
Ukraine	**21611**	**19803**	**20767**	**21874**	**0.40**

As Table 10.2 indicates, the best agricultural growth is projected for the Dnipropetrovsk and Cherkasy oblasts (Section A) at respective annual rates of 4.5% and 2.7%. Of the bottom five oblasts, production declines in Volyn and Zakarpatia. There are two shining spots in grain production growth when comparing 2017 forecast with 2014 actual output: Khmelnytsk (14.7%) and Ivano-Frankivsk (6.4%). High growth in meat production is expected in Cherkasy and Dnipropetrovsk oblasts, but all five bottom oblasts have declining growth, because of falling animal herds.

Regional disparities

Table 10.3 gives the Ukraine's January 2016 average regional wage for five top and bottom regions. The average for Kyiv City, at the top of Table 10.3, is 63% higher than for the country as a whole (4,362 UAH or 166 USD), and Ternolil, at the bottom of the table, is 69% lower. Moreover, the top five regions (Kyiv City, Donetsk, Kyiv oblast, Dnipropetrovsk, and Zaporizhia) and the bottom five regions (Zhytomyr, Kirovograd, Kherson, Chernivtsi, and Ternopil) do not change their position from the beginning of this century.

Table 10.3: Ukraine's Average Wage by Region, UAH per Month

Region	January 2016
Top 5 Regions	
Kyiv City	7126
Donetsk	5142
Kyiv	4453
Dnipropetrovsk	4445
Zaporizhia	4341
Bottom 5 Regions	
Zhytomyr	3297
Kirovohrad	3286
Kherson	3249
Chernivtsi	3139
Ternopil	3008

Source: Ukrstat (2016)

The Millennium Development Goals of Ukraine (2015) give an estimate of 24.5% of the population below the national poverty line. The German Advisory Group on Economic Reform (2004) considers poverty across oblasts, with the lowest 3% for Donetsk and the highest 18% for Rivne. The 2013

Ukrstat data give much higher estimates for these two oblasts: 6% for Donetsk and 29% for Rivne.

Ukraine's government uses an officially approved subsistence minimum (SM) to calculate the poverty rate and eligibility for exemptions and subsidies. To determine eligibility, it calculates total income from a variety of sources such as monetary income, consumption from personal agricultural and nonagricultural production, exemptions and subsidies for municipal services, energy, heating, health care, transport, communications, and food help from relatives and other donors. Thus, the 2016 SM level for the working-age individual is 1,330 UAH (51 USD) and 1,074 UAH for the nonworking-age individual (41 USD). The minimum wage is 1,378 UAH (52 USD) (en.interfax.com; AiF-Moscow, 2015). Overall, the minimum gradually rises by an official inflation rate of 12.5% in 2016.

We divide all 24 oblasts of Ukraine in two groups, top and bottom, based on industry and agriculture performance. According to our calculations, the top 12 regions by industry GVA in 2013 are in descending order: Donetsk, Dnipropetrovsk, Luhansk, Zaporizzia, Kharkiv, Poltava, Kyiv, Lviv, Mykolaiv, Odesa, Zhytomyr, and Sumy. The bottom 12 regions are: Ivano-Frankivsk, Cherkasy, Vinnytsia, Rivne, Khmelnytsk, Kirivograd, Chernihiv, Zakarpatia, Kherson, Ternopil, Volyn, and Chernivtsi. The top 12 agriculture performers are: Vinnytsia, Kharkiv, Poltava, Kyiv, Cherkasy, Dnipropetrovsk, Kirovograd, Khmelnytsk, Donetsk, Odesa, Kherson, and Mykolaiv. The bottom 12 agriculture performers are: Zaporizzia, Chernihiv, Zhytomyr, Lviv, Ternopil, Sumy, Rivne, Volyn, Luhansk, Ivano-Frankivsk, Chernivtsi, and Zakarpatia.

This classification allows us to identify seven oblasts which are among top performers in both industry and agriculture and, similarly, seven oblasts which are among bottom performers in both categories. The former group consists of Donetsk, Dnipropetroovsk, Kharkiv, Poltava, Kyiv, Mykolaiv, and Odesa. The group at the bottom of both industrial and agricultural production includes Ivano-Frankivsk, Rivne, Chernihiv, Zakarpatia, Ternopil, Volyn, and Chernivtsi. Identifying the latter group is especially important because of the highest concentration of households at the SM in these oblasts. A major question is "What could become the driver out of poverty there?"

We regress the percent of regional poverty on industrial output and agricultural output from 2005 through 2013, with a special attention to the seven oblasts at the bottom of both industrial and agricultural production given above. Our results indicate that the coefficient multiplying industrial output variables are insignificant in six out of these seven oblasts, implying that the rise in industrial production does not likely affect the level of poverty there. On the other hand, the role of agricultural production in these oblasts is more in line with the expectation. In five out of the seven oblasts (Ivano-Frankivsk, Rivne, Zakarpatia, Volyn, and Chernivtsi), the coefficients of agricultural output are significant and negative, meaning that the rise in agricultural output indeed leads to a decline in poverty. Exception occurs for Chernihiv and Ternopil oblasts where the respective coefficients are insignificant.

Shifting production from agriculture to industry is generally a sign of structural change that results in productivity increase. Yet, given our regression findings, the issue is not so straightforward for Ukraine. As indicated, the country claims one of the world largest areas of fertile black soil, with agriculture producing 12% of Ukraine's GDP and generating a quarter of country's exports. The leading role of food production might rise in view of the 2016 implementation of a free trade zone with the European Union. This deal is expected theoretically to bring more competition, modernization, and foreign direct investment for Ukraine's agro-industrial producers.

Despite the abundance of agricultural land, there is no market for it in Ukraine. For over 15 years, the *Verkhovna Rada* has extended a ban (moratorium) on sale of agricultural land. Out of 42 million hectares of agricultural land, 22 million are used by agricultural enterprises which lease it from individual landholders (Nizalov 2014). Most of the latter have received a land parcel (*pai*) of 4-5 hectares during the privatization of state and collective farms in the 1990s. The legislature should stipulate who can buy the land, who has a priority (e.g., legal entities versus individual purchasers), the ceiling on the size, the participation of non-residents, and other pressing social and legal issues. However, the mutual mistrust of the ruling elites in Ukraine is so deep that they would rather not have a market at all than to face the land in possession of someone not to their liking.

The cooperation with the IMF might be helpful. When the IMF extends new credit for Ukraine's government, it sets criteria following its conditionality requirements: raising prices of natural gas and heating, increasing the pension age, privatization of coal mines, restructuring the energy companies, implementation of stress tests for major banks, changing state procurement rules, reducing the number of higher education institutions, and the like. It is hard to understand why the IMF cannot help Ukraine pursue strategic goals, rather than get involved in micromanagement tasks illustrated above.[24]

---

24 Foreign producers are interested and waiting. Thus, the US Cargill has already invested $100 million in the construction of a grain terminal in port Yuzhnyi (Odesa oblast), http://economics.lb.ua/business/2016/02/24/328707.

Conclusions

To analyze and forecast the economy of Ukraine's administrative regions, we build an econometric model consisting of four blocks—industry, agriculture, construction, and services—with over 340 equations. We produce two types of forecasts: baseline and its modified version called a nonlinear scenario. The forecasts identify both bright spots and problems in Ukraine's regional economy. The bright spots are mining and the service sector, e.g., gross regional product generated by the latter will rise at 12.6% per annum through 2017. On the other hand, energy production and agriculture may not recover from stagnation caused by a 2014 recession.

From the policy analysis perspective, we use our model to analyze Ukraine's regional disparities, to establish a link between the level of poverty, on the one hand, and industrial and agricultural growth, on the other, and to identify conditions for a reduction in rural poverty. After dividing all 24 oblasts of Ukraine in two groups based on industry and agriculture production and determining the top and bottom performers, we regress the percent of regional poverty on industrial and agricultural outputs, with particular attention to seven oblasts at the bottom of both industrial and agricultural production. Our analysis demonstrates that the rise in industrial production does not affect the level of poverty in the bottom regions. On the other hand, the role of agricultural production is found to be statistically significant for poverty reduction in the Ivano-Frankivsk, Rivne, Zakarpatia, Volyn, and Chernivtsi oblasts.

The finding that agricultural, not industrial production is significant for the reduction of poverty in the economically lagging oblasts of Ukraine is at the first glance surprising. However, for Ukraine, which claims one of the world largest areas of fertile black soil and whose agriculture generates a quarter of country's exports, agricultural sector may remain one of the important drivers out of poverty and a source of reducing regional disparities.

For the agricultural sector to succeed, the rural areas must become more attractive places to live. However, with few exceptions, Ukraine's rural towns and villages have no hospitals, with nurses and especially doctors unavailable in many villages. Clearly, Ukraine government's policy of abandoning investment in rural healthcare, education, cultural and recreational facilities is unacceptable.[25] Ukrainian agricultural experts estimate that the country's minimum annual investment in agricultural and non-agricultural rural development should amount to 50 billion UAH, whereas actual investment

[25] Thus, funding for rural social infrastructure fell fivefold from 2010 to 2014 (Azhaman 2014)

was 7.6 billion UAH in 2011 (Hylka 2015). Without new tax incentives and availability of low-interest loans for private domestic and foreign investors, calling for the appropriation of government funds for rural infrastructure remains just wishful thinking.

References

Azhaman, I. (2014). The funding peculiarities of social objects' construction in the rural areas of Ukraine. Retrieved from http://brtsbiblioteca.socionet.ru.

Bogovin, A. (2006). *Country pasture/forage resource profiles: Ukraine*. Food and Agriculture Organization of the United Nations. Retrieved from http://www.fao.org/ag/agp/agpc/doc/counprof/PDF%20files/Ukraine.pdf.

Cai, H. & Treisman, D. (2005). Does competition for capital discipline governments? Decentralization, globalization and public policy. *The American Economic Review*, 95 (3), 817-830.

CIA. (2015). World Factbook Ukraine. Retrieved from https://www.cia.gov/library/publications/the-world-factbook/geos/up.html.

Geography of Ukraine. (2015) Retrieved from http://shkolyar.in.ua/promyslovist.

German Advisory Group on Economic Reform. (2004). T25. Poverty in Ukraine, Kyiv.

Hylka, M. (2015). Prospects of Economic Development of Rural Areas of Ukraine. *International Journal of Economics and Society*, 1, 41-46.

Korostelina, K. (2014). Ukraine twenty years after independence: Concept models of the society. *Communist and Post-Communist Studies*, 46(1), 53–64.

Kushnirsky, F. (2014). Ukraine and the IMF: An Uneasy Cooperation. *International Journal of Business and Social Research*, 4 (4), 120-130.

Kuzio, T. (2011). Political culture and democracy: Ukraine as an immobile state. *East European Politics and Societies*, 25 (1), 88–113.

Levine, R., Brininstool, M. & Wallace, G. (2010). The Mineral Industry of Ukraine. In *2007 Mineral Yearbook*. United States Geological Survey.

Millennium Development Goals–Ukraine. (2015). United Nations Development Program.

Mykhailov, I. (2014, October 21). Ukraine grain exports to rise. Retrieved from *Agriculture.com*.

Myerson, R. & Mylovanov, T. (2014). Fixing Ukraine's Fundamental Flaw. *KyivPost*. March 7.

Nemec, L. & Zavoloka, U. (2009). *Economic and social geography of Ukraine*. Kharkiv: Educational-methodical complex

Nizalov, D. (2014, September 8). Land moratorium: Guess who benefits from the status quo? [*VoxUkraine*]. Retrieved from http://voxukraine.blogspot.com/2014/09/landmoratorium-guess-who-benefits-from.html

PMR. (2014). *Construction Sector in Ukraine: 120*. Retrieved from https://www.pmrpublications.com/product/Construction-sector-in-Ukraine-H2-2014.

Rogovska, N. (2014). Crop production in Ukraine. Presentation at Iowa State University, Ames Iowa.

Sologub, I. (2014). Decentralization Reform in Ukraine. Forum for Research on Eastern Europe and Emerging Economies. *Free Policy Brief Series*. October.

Retrieved from http://freepolicybriefs.org/2014/10/08/decentralization-reform-in-ukraine/.

Ukrstat. (2009, 2013, and 2014). *Statistical Publication on Regions of Ukraine.* Kyiv: State Statistics Committee of Ukraine.

www.en.interfax.com, AiF-Moscow 2015, Dec. 20, 2015. Retrieved on February 12, 2016 from www.en.interfax.com.

Zaporizska Nuclear Plant Website. Retrieved on November 21, 2015 from http://npp.zp.ua.

Chapter 11

TCB in India's New ICE Age: Lessons for BRICS

James P. West[26]

Abstract

Over the last quarter century, India has moved to privatize its economy. Unable to rely on natural resource exports or low cost manufacturing, India has focused its strategies on development of human capital and intellectual property. Three industry sectors: Information Systems, Communications and Entertainment, or ICE, are areas where India has succeeded. India's "ICE Age," as it is ironically called, has produced both individuals and companies securing its reputation as a leader in intellectual property-based businesses. In this acronym rich paper, the term TCB represents both the need for prudent public policy to 'Take Care of Business' but also to fend off the TCB (Taxes, Corruption and Bureaucracy) long endemic to India's political economy. These three maladies threaten the realization of a market-based economy. This paper investigates the extent of these maladies and explores the prospects for revitalizing the free enterprise economy both in India and abroad.

Introduction: India's new ICE age

> *'In capitalist reality as distinguished by its textbook picture, it is not the kind of (static) competition which counts, but the competition from the new commodity, the new technology, the new source of supply, the new type of organization"* Josef Schumpeter, 'Capitalism. Socialism and Democracy', 1942.

[26] westj@moravian.edu.

The idea that India is entering a new ICE age was proposed and discussed over a decade ago at a jointly held seminar offered by the United Nations and the London School of Economics in New Delhi (LSE/UNCTAD, 2004). The ICE Age was a clever acronym for three of India's biggest (though not only) growth sectors—Information, Communication and Entertainment. These three industries were proposed to be driving the Indian economy to modernism. Unlike China, India was projected to make its mark, not in low-cost manufacturing, but in high value-added intellectual property businesses.

I have lived and worked in India for several years and still travel there frequently. Without doubt, India has a wealth of cultural creativity along with an ever-increasing abundance of technological human capital. Over the last decade, the transformation of these ICE sectors of the Indian economy, especially in the liberalized market economy, is unmistakable.

Indian universities, like Indian Institute of Technology (IIT), rival the best technical universities in the world and a seemingly endless supply of talent to India industry and abroad. Technological centers like Bangalore (Bengaluru) are reminiscent of Silicon Valley and lead the country with an explosion of technological and information insourcing. Likewise, in communications, the ubiquitous cell phone has linked a country which a few short decades ago had one of the most basic, primitive telephone and switching systems. As an economist once indicated in the ironic phrase, "*the advantage of backwardness,*" countries like India are skipping several generations of communication innovation and going right to wireless or beyond.

Take also the example of Bollywood, the Indian Hollywood centered in Bombay, (now Mumbai) with its huge domestic and global market. For those unaware of Bollywood star power, the industry is nothing short of amazing. India loves its movies and has such a rich and diverse culture that its films find an audience not only with a big part of the billion-person domestic market but also with an export market in the Middle East, Africa and Southeast Asia. Bollywood, along with other regional filmmakers in Bengal, Karnataka, and other cities produce more films per year than Hollywood, their predecessor and counterpart.

In *The Economist* article "India's economy: A chance to fly", India's current potential and pitfalls are discussed. Per that article, "India possesses untold promise. Its people are entrepreneurial and roughly half of the 1.25 billion populations are under 25 years old. It is poor, so it has lots of scope for catch-up growth: GDP per person (at purchasing-power parity) was $5,500 in 2013, compared with $11,900 in China and $15,000 in Brazil. The economy has been balkanized by local taxes levied at state borders, but cross-party support for a national goods-and-services tax could create a true common market. The potential is there; the question has always been whether it can be unleashed" (India's economy..., 2015).

TCB: Taking care of business or taxes, corruption and bureaucracy

> *"The difference between what it costs a firm to hire a worker or employ a unit of capital and what the worker receives net of taxes is called the 'tax wedge'... Clearly it now pays for a firm to hire fewer workers and acquire less capital. On the supply side, an increase in the wedge reduces net wages received and the net yield savers retain. Again less work and savings will be supplied".*
> Arthur Laffer, (Miles, 2004).

The prediction of the role of the ICE Age is both promising and provocative and surely much has already changed since the Soviet Union collapse and the challenge to the reign of the India's left-leaning Congress Party (LSE/UNCTAD, 2004). Yet my own years of experience working and travelling in India gives me reason to question my enthusiasm for the seemingly triumphant inevitability of this prediction.

During the conference discussion mentioned above, I raised my hand, and, with the best of intentions, offered a second appropriate, in my opinion, acronym (LSE/UNCTAD, 2004). My contribution was "*TCB.*" Another participant guessed, "*Taking Care of Business?*" "*Yes,*" I responded, "*taking care of business' would be a needed public policy direction for ICE success; however, the 'TCB' I am referring to are actually: Taxes, Corruption, and Bureaucracy.*" It is these three institutional realities that have plagued Indian development in the past and threaten the future of ICE as well as other industries and initiatives.

The collapse of the Soviet Union, now almost three decades ago, generated at that time a global euphoric mood of high expectations. For the BRICS and other developing economies much went right—initially. Economic reform, technology diffusion, increases in foreign and domestic investment, an education explosion, and a new mobility of labor and capital led many millions out of poverty and created an energetic emerging class of entrepreneurs, who became the bulwark of the growing middle and very rich upper class.

Among the early academic optimists of these 1990s post-Soviet transformations is Francis Fukuyama, whose interpretation of world events led him to posit a triumphant philosophical consensus in his widely-read work, *'The End of History and the Last Man'.* In this book, Fukuyama sees the culmination of the Hegelian dialect into the Universalist manifestation of the ideal social philosophy, i.e., liberal democracy. Democratic governments and market driven economies would spread throughout the planet and countries one by one would be joined in self-interested, yet harmonious, relations (Fukuyama, 2002).

It is not long before this somewhat utopian scenario is deconstructed by the author Samuel Huntington, who looking beyond the unifying rationality, identifies the less rational, but nonetheless, convincing cultural markers that diversify, differentiate and too often divide the peoples of the planet. Cultural fault lines, particularly between religious perspectives, notably Christianity, Islam and the secular default, create liberal democratic believers and non-believers, with little prospect of reconciliation. Other prominent writers of the time, such as Daniel Kahneman (2003), throw into question assumptions, e.g., the market-based assumption of individual rationality, while the French writer Thomas Piketty (2014), in his book '*Capital,*' attacks the practice of free enterprise as perpetrating ever-widening inequality. Soon the Pope joins in with his encyclical '*Laudato Si'* and other writings.

While these writers and more are important in explaining the ups and downs of liberal democracy in this period, one author is of particular interest for this paper. That is the Peruvian economist Hernando de Soto, author of two very influential books, '*The Other Path'* and '*The Mystery of Capital'.*

In the '*The Mystery of Capital',* de Soto addresses the principal failing of newly market-oriented economies. De Soto cites an experiment he undertook while starting a garment business in Peru. He writes that his team "*spent six hours a day and until it finally registered as a business ---289 days later.*" The shop was to have only one worker and the registration costs were thirty-one times the monthly minimum wage. He further reports that to build a house on state-owned property, it "*took six years and eleven months, requiring 207 administrative steps, in fifty-two government offices.*" Similarly, a taxi driver faced twenty-six months of red tape to get official recognition of his route. He cites further examples in Venezuela, Haiti, Brazil, the Philippines and Egypt, where bureaucratic restrictions over property rights squashes entrepreneurship, retards economic development, and drives economic activity in to an illegal, unregulated, underground, yet productive 'black' economy. In his book, he cites the case of Brazilian '*favelas'* (or slums), where a revolt against rent control and the adoption of a U.S. dollar economy have created an attractive 'extralegal' shadow economy. In such an economy, public corruption and 'crony capitalism' become self-interested allies. As de Soto remarks, "*In every country we investigated, we found that it is very nearly as difficult to stay legal as to become legal. Inevitably migrants do not break the law as the law breaks them ---and they opt out of the system*" (de Soto, 2000).

De Soto goes on to show that the lack of clear property rights, not only retards and distorts growth of the legal economy (including the tax base), but prevents the development of financial capital. This is the central message of his book, '*The Mystery of Capital*'. He writes: "*Capital, like energy, is also a dormant value. Bringing it to life requires us to go beyond looking at our assets as they are to actively thinking about them as they could be.*" The energy of capital is not exclusive to the rich and powerful, but extends to the common homeowner. He states, "*the potential value locked up in a house can be revealed and transformed into active capital in the same way that potential energy is identified in a mountain lake and is then transformed into actual energy... Legal property thus gave the West the tools to produce surplus value over and above its physical assets*" (de Soto, 2000).

It is worth noting in these days of despair over the widening gap between rich and poor (the 'top 1%' and so on), that property rights extending clearly to the small land/house owner and business person, may well lie at the heart of remedying this situation. Public officials and 'crony capitalists' have far less difficulty defining and defending their property rights and therefore have full reign to enrich themselves through the 'mystery' of capital.

De Soto's analysis of property rights and capital formation resonates in the work of Indian economist, Arun Kumar, author of the book, *India's Black Economy* (Kumar, 2002). The lack of economic mobility, perhaps tracing to the caste system itself, has resulted in extreme inequality as the privileged sectors, with secure property rights, amass capital (much of it in Swiss banks), while the lack of property rights of the poor and only recently emerging middle class, has left them at the mercy of a black economy in India. Kumar's call to arms to fight the black economy has gained strength with the election of current Prime Minister Narendra Modi. A study of India's black economy and the path to reform will be instructive for the BRICS nations.

India's black economy

> *"What is well known but is not visible is surrounded by mystery. It excites the imagination and people spin yarns about it"*
> Arun Kumar 'The Black Economy of India', 2002.

The TCB (Taxes, Corruption and Bureaucracy) case in India parallels the anti-property malaise of the Peru and other countries featured in De Soto's work. One professor and author from Jawaharlal Nehru University (JNU) in New Delhi, investigates, analytically not anecdotally (in his words), the underground, extralegal economy that pervades and distorts India's development efforts. His results and assessment are found in the highly regarded book, "*The Black Economy in India*" published in 1999 and revised in 2002. The foreword, written by India's former Prime Minister V.P. Singh, focuses on the centrality and the difficulty of the issue: "*The problems India faces are uniquely its own and mostly a creation of the elite... in the short run the black economy may seem to benefit the elite, it also harms their long term interests so that it is in their self-interest to deal with this problem and solve it... the attempt to contain and eliminate black money is a fight to re-establish the rule of law, enabling all citizens to live in dignity. Indeed, it would be a fight to build a dynamic, a civilized society*" (Kumar, 2002).

Kumar begins by asserting that the black economy is all-pervasive in India, "be it the purchase of a house or a pin." He further dissents, "that while some say it (the black economy) promotes efficiency, it in fact creates economic and societal costs including higher costs due to corruption, poor quality of construction, and the 'black premium' including bribes that are attached to many transactions." The money cost, writes Kumar, is not the only cost; there are also the delays, harassment and tension affecting the clear majority of Indians, while a small minority percentage (he estimates 3%), are the primary beneficiaries as this minority accumulates wealth far beyond what they could do legally. He further provides evidence that this corruption lies both in the public and the private sectors and its wealth flow finds a home, less in productive savings and investment, but rather in less or unproductive assets, including gold, real estate, flight of capital and illegal activities.

The moral leadership to launch a successful battle against the black economy is also problematic, if not hopeless, in Kumar's mind. He remarks, "*As Buddha said, let the one who has done no wrong cast the first stone and no one could do so. Today, no section of society is able to provide leadership...the black economy and the erosion of the institutions of democracy are interlinked*" (Kumar, 2002).

Issues of excessive taxation are often said to be at the core of the rising 'black economy. Income tax rates in India have soared as high as 97.5 %, clearly illustrating the incentive to hide income and wealth. But although rates have now fallen to a high of 40% and later 30%, the essential motivation 'to earn extra profits by everyone, including teachers, doctors, businessmen and bureaucrats (taxed or not) drives the black economy. Even paying (some) taxes helps legitimize black money, but the 'triad' of businessmen, bureaucrats and politicians, assure that even the after-tax flows are substantial (Kumar 2002). Therefore, taxes, while a proximate driver of black money, are not the primary cause. The roots of the problems are endemic and complex.

In *The Economist* article referenced earlier, the tax complexity and possible reform are summarized, "The economy has been balkanized by local taxes levied at state borders, but cross-party support for a national goods-and-services tax could create a true common market. The potential is there; the question has always been whether it can be unleashed (India's economy..., 2015).

India and education

India has been labeled as a dual economy with a modernizing urban sector and a tradition bound less educated rural center. India is also a country whose largest social construct was the caste system and an attendant fatalism. While the caste system is now ostensibly illegal by Mahatma Gandhi's decree, and many Indians (increasingly secular) have chosen enterprise over fatalism, the pernicious nature of these social systems has had a lasting impact of elitism that has exacerbated income disparities in the country. James Tooley, inspired by Mahatma Gandhi's focus on private village schools, argues that statism in education, like other industries, stifles the creativity in 'The Beautiful Tree' (Tooley, 2009). Human capital development has been the strategy of India and increasingly relied on private sector initiatives to supplant or complement the burgeoning government sector. Reinvigorating free market beliefs and systems are one of the challenges facing India after many decades of socialism and crony capitalism that feeds the black economy. While India has nationwide public education, it allows encouraging flexibility to create private sector schools at the primary, secondary and higher education levels.

Policy prescriptions

The four P's (part 1): Production and property

The four 'Ps' as explored in earlier articles by this author (West, 2009; 2015) are at the heart of what Adam Smith called "*the system of natural liberty.*" Smith knew that private production, not the accumulation of wealth and power, is the driving force of prosperity. A system of property rights, prices, and profits would generate unparalleled production and prosperity. While Smith identifies many important roles for the government in the economy, he cautions that the system of natural liberty must be left free to work its magic. (West, 2009)

According to West, the essential 4 'Ps' that form the essence of the 'system of natural liberty' were implicit in the work of the famed Scotsman, Adam Smith, in "*The Wealth of Nations*" (Smith, 1776). These four P's, Production, Property, Prices and Profits, are often subtle and even counter intuitive aspects of a prosperous economy. India's move from socialism to capitalism required fundamental rethinking in each of these four areas.

> *Socialist regimes try to guarantee the value of things rather than the ownership of them. Thus they tend to destroy the value, which depends on dedicated ownership. In the United States however the government guarantees only the right to property, not the worth of it*
> (Gilder, 1992)

Property issues, raised earlier, in the context of de Soto's analysis are particularly critical for India, but in the case of the ICE industries, are even greater. Intellectual property is the essence of these industries. The use of legal property protection (patents, trademarks, copyrights) is increasingly asserted, as are private mechanisms of privacy protection. Nevertheless, the institutions of property rights cuts two ways. While we expect and assert that our property rights be protected, the failure to respect the property rights of others (particularly the disenfranchised) is pervasive in the black economy dynamics of India. The routine violations of property rights in technology, entertainment, pharmaceutical, and manufacturing industries undermine the assertion of property rights across the board to the point where the 'unusual becomes usual' as Arun Kumar, indicated earlier. Intellectual property theft, whether downloading a new Bollywood film or producing illegal 'knock-offs' or generics, becomes routine. In the BRIC nation of China, the Ali-Baba entrepreneur, Jack Ma, goes so far as doubting the inferiority of many counterfeit goods and initially showed little conflict in offering them for sale on his retail platform.

Unlike China, India's global focus is not on low cost production for export. India's years of import substitution protectionism, an upper caste disdain for manual labor, as well as Gandhi's legacy of 'homespun' cottage industry, helps to create a disinterest in manufacturing especially for export. India's focus on education and its English-speaking capacity leads to various forms of outsourcing /offshoring in call centers as a source of employment and foreign exchange. The attraction to education and private school development, coupled with these new tech enterprises, quickly led Indians to move from the low-end call centers to higher value added technology jobs. Likewise, India's family education ethic and global and democratic heritage motivate Indian youth to seek education and overseas employment opportunities abroad. Their relatively easy assimilation, intelligence, and drive leads to well-paid jobs, which allows repatriation of funds to family in India. Finally, due to the fall of the Soviet Union, India's allegiance to socialist policies begins to fade. The ICE industries feed into this model of development, and soon technology centers like Bangalore and top universities, like Indian Institute of Technology (the ITT), become the way forward for the Indian economy.

While the Indian model has yielded much success, the failure to develop a simultaneous effort in manufacturing centers is an opportunity lost and one that could have truly benefitted the lower income populations. The IT (Information Technology) sector in India has made impressive strides, but the more than 100 million poorly educated youth need these sorts of manufacturing jobs, not just for export (which was the initial error) but to support a growing middle class in need of consumer goods. James Tooley, an academic specializing in developing country education, finds that the bias toward government controlled schools (where the black economy plays a large role) is diminished, though has not halted, the dynamic recognized and non-recognized private school sector. Tooley concludes from case analysis in Delhi and Hyderabad, that "*in the vast majority of cases, types of private schools, recognized and unrecognized, were either superior to government schools in providing needed inputs (buildings, desks, chairs, fans, books, libraries, blackboards etc.) or there was no statistical difference between school types.*" (Tooley 2009). The private vs. public, rural vs. urban, the manual vs. intellectual labor are long-standing biases with which both India's society and economy wrestle. Moving forward on these fronts, especially in the areas of education would add a needed dynamism to the neglected poorer sectors in India.

The four 'Ps' (part 2): Prices and profits

Prices are such a common phenomenon that their origins and significance often go unappreciated. Prices at their root are a form of economic communication. Like the letters that make words, prices communicate information about the values buyers and sellers need to make beneficial decisions. The complex economy requires that this information be rapidly developed and disseminated. Prices generated by market processes create that information. We may not always like the prices we get, but the artificial manipulation of prices undermines the important communication function of businesses (West, 2009).

> *Price stability encourages economic growth and stability. With price stability, incentives are not distorted, resources are not wasted trying to anticipate the next up or down of inflation and inefficient utilization of machines relative to workers is avoided. In short, stable money makes life easier for all and allows individuals to focus on attaining their goals and fullest potential. Economic freedom is increased* (Miles, 2004).

Finally, 'Profits' are frequently the most demonized of all of the 'P' concepts. A prosperous, vibrant economy requires creativity and risk taking which profits encourage. Yet, critics complain about the very concept that encourages creative and sensible risk taking. Profits are a driving force of human creativity. Not all creativity, of course but a lot of it. Profits reward those who take risks to create new products, services and explore new frontiers. Suffering the consequences of the failure to make profits, i.e. bankruptcy, is likewise a part of healthy capitalism. The political desire to sustain unprofitable business is short-sighted, as are policies that discourage individuals and firms from making profits (West, 2015).

Conclusions: Lessons for the BRICS

"Emerging markets used to be a beacon of hope in the world economy, but now they are more often a source of gloom. China's economy is slowing. Brazil is mired in stagflation. Russia is in recession, battered by Western sanctions and the slump in the oil price; South Africa is plagued by inefficiency and corruption. Amid the disappointment, one big emerging market stands out: India". (India's economy..., 2015).

Brazil, Russia, India, China, and South Africa comprise the BRICS. They are seen as representative of the best opportunities for high profile successes of the post-Soviet global economy. As the above quotation from *The Economist* indicates, the writers have particular and continued confidence in the economy of India.

When I first moved to India in 1975, the country was frozen in traditionalist economics and laboring under both British and Soviet influenced socialism. Reflecting these socialist trends, the high school economic course textbook I used as a textbook contained no supply or demand curves, just a lot of five-year plans.

India's protectionist policies created Hindustan Motors with subsidized production and heavy tariffs on imported cars (e.g., 150%). Indians who wanted a car either waited years and paid the high tariff price for an import or bought one of the two unchanging models produced by Hindustan. As a result of this protection, the car industry never developed. Decades later, with virtually no innovations in the car style, the same old, sometimes 30-year-old, cars are on the road, and production is tiny, especially compared to the burgeoning population.

With the collapse of the Soviet Union and the socialist model generally, BRICS countries, like India, face many transition challenges. Socialism is no longer a viable alternative. Creating free enterprise institutions, and overcoming endemic problems of excessive taxation, corruption, and bloated bureaucracies become the immediate challenge. In the subsequent decades of transformation, market idealism frequently collides with reality. However, optimism for the BRICS and many other emerging markets lies not only with identifying growth sector industries but also with identifying objectively their institutional failures. In that regard, India's proactive policies may yet serve as a critical role model for the transitioning world.

References

De Soto, H. (2000). *The mystery of capital: why capitalism triumphs in the West and fails everywhere else.* New York: Basic Books, Perseus Books Group.

Fukuyama, F. (2002). *The end of history and the last man.* New York: Perennial.

Gilder, G. (1992). *Recapturing the spirit of free enterprise.* San Francisco: ICS Press.

India's economy: A chance to fly. (2015, February). *The Economist.* Retrieved from http://www.economist.com/news/leaders/21644145-india-has-rare-opportunity-become-worlds-most-dynamic-big-economy-chance-fly.

Khaneman, D. (2003). Maps of bounded rationality: psychology of behavioral economics. *American Economic Review,* 93(5), 1449-1475.

Kumar, A. (2002). *The black economy in India.* 2nd Edition. New Delhi: Penguin books.

Lal, D. (2013). *Poverty and progress: realities and myths about global poverty.* Cato Institute.

LSE/UNCTAD (2004, March). The new global trade paradigm. Symposium hosted by The London School of Economics and Political Science and the United Nations Conference on Trade and Development, New Delhi.

Miles, M. ed. (2004). *The road to prosperity: the 21st century approach to economic development.* Washington, D.C.: Heritage Books,

Piketty, T. (2014). *Capital in the twenty-first century.* Cambridge: Harvard University Press.

Rosenberg, N. & Birdzell Jr., L., (1986). *How the west grew rich: the economic transformation of the industrial world.* New York: Perseus Books.

Sen, Amartya. (1999). *Development as freedom.* New York: Alfred Knopf Publishers.

Schumpeter, J. (1942). *Capitalism, socialism and democracy.* New York: Harper & Row.

Smith, A. (1776). An inquiry into the nature and causes of the wealth of nations. 5th ed., London: Methuen & Co.

Tooley, J. (2009). *The beautiful tree: A personal journey into how the world's poorest people are educating themselves.* Cato Institute.

West, J. (2009, September 2). Pillars of prosperity: back to the basics. *Chicago Tribune, Morning Call* p. 16.

West, J. (2015). Rational, relational, reflective and constrained: the mindset of American capitalism. In I. Gorges (Ed.) *Global perspectives on sustainable regional development* (pp. 329-338). Hamburg: Verlag Dr. Kovac.

Chapter 12

Western Marketing and Economic Principles in the South Pacific and the Decline of Communal Values

Cristanna M. Cook[27]

Abstract

The cultures of the ocean states in the South Pacific are traditionally communal in nature, with strong traditional influence and communal land. Today, university students in the South Pacific are taught the value of western management and marketing concepts without any thought about the effects of western thinking on the wider traditional culture or how western macro-marketing affects the larger society. This paper discusses some of the impact of this dialogue between traditional and modern and the relevancy of various marketing approaches. Marketing messages sell foreign goods and services that have been imported, but the constant barrage of messages is having consequences beyond the marketplace. One such consequence is the decline of communal values and norms (i.e. the importance of the group) and the move to more individualistic thinking. While there exists a dual economy, with both global and traditional practices in existence, it is clear that the traditional economy is under siege from the marketing messages. The marketing methods found in the South Pacific are directed at the global sector but impact the traditional sector by diminishing the values that have directed behavior in the past. Government decisions are also beginning to reflect this individualism in the guise of inclusiveness. The move to a western individualistic philosophy has not solved the economic problems of these states. Since the resource base is limited, people live by subsistence agriculture, exports are largely agricultural, and almost all the economies depend on foreign aid and remittances from workers who have moved abroad.

[27] cookc@husson.edu

Introduction

Marketing is presented to students as the only functional area of a business that generates revenue. All other functional areas are cost centers so that without marketing, there would likely be limited revenue for the companies. Therefore, marketing must provide value to the business or organization. Foreign markets are increasingly important as businesses look for new markets abroad. Slumping demand in the home economy is a motivator for entering foreign markets, but learning how to enter these markets requires extensive knowledge. Such global marketing knowledge is valuable and is taught in undergraduate and graduate marketing programs. However, examples offered in marketing programs in places like the South Pacific may relate mostly to foreign companies located in that area.

Business Schools in developed countries do not question the value that the knowledge of marketing offers students. It is obvious from training and daily experiences in the world around us that marketing principles are at work. However, this experience and training we take for granted in developed economies should not necessarily be of value elsewhere. Emphasis on the values of the western marketing principles should not necessarily be accepted everywhere without critical review. Foreign students see the conflict of such theory within their own culture.

One student in the Fiji Islands speaks eloquently of the conflict between what she is being taught in marketing management and the communal values of her way of life with the emphasis on personal communication. She notes that in most of the smaller islands of the South Pacific, land is owned in common and not all goods can be sold on the open market. Therefore, marketing does not facilitate the exchange of all goods. Such interaction with South Pacific students underscores the need to re-assess the marketing concepts being taught in the South Pacific and elsewhere. The relevancy of these principles on the society should be documented. It is not that these concepts have no value; in fact, in the western world, these concepts are very useful. However, they need to be reviewed and one should be careful when teaching such concepts in non-western environments. The principles of marketing should be viewed skeptically in non-western societies and their impact on the society should be documented. At the very least, we should try to understand how western marketing principles work in the South Pacific context.

Theory

There have been several ways to categorize the marketing discipline. Some of these point out the need for an understanding of the social context in which production and marketing take place. Sheth, Gardner, and Garrett (1988) provide a way to identify marketing perspectives or schools that are more appropriate for non-western cultures since they emphasize the importance of the social interaction that explain human behavior.

Marketing schools are divided into interactive vs. non-interactive and economic vs. non-economic types. Non-interactive economic schools include the commodity, functional, and regional perspectives. In contrast, the institutional, functionalist (not the same as functional) and the managerial are interactive economic schools. The buyer behavior, activist, and macro-marketing views comprise the non-interactive non-economic schools whereas the organizational dynamics, systems, and social exchange models are interactive non-economic. As will be discussed below, theories which stress the importance of social and cultural ties are more applicable to non-western nations including the ocean states of the South Pacific. Other theories are more useful to the understanding of urban markets but do not apply to what we could call the substantive or traditional segment of the large ocean states.

The different marketing approaches and their relevancy to the South Pacific Large Ocean States

Non-interactive economic approaches

Within the *non-interactive economic approaches,* the commodity school is concerned with the movement of goods from producers to consumers. The emphasis is on the products rather than the human interactions that move the products. The development of product classification systems is a key principle of this school. There are several different ways to classify goods. Melvin Copeland (1923) offers a classification that today is used in most marketing texts: convenience, shopping, and specialty goods. Other classification systems include those suggested by Holbrook and Howard (1977), Aspinwall (1958), and Enis and Roering (1980). These classifications are not very helpful in understanding marketing in the context of the South Pacific. In some areas of the South Pacific, retailing is a major part of the urban economy but not much of an influence in the traditional sector. There are strategies that are associated with durable, non-durable, convenience, shopping, and specialty goods. However, these strategies would be immediately understood by marketers, and there is not much need for further clarification. A classifying of the different retailing options may be useful in explaining the major types of retailing formats. For example, off-price retailers as we understand this format in the western world do not exist in the South

Pacific. Overstocked, branded merchandise is not often seen there, and accordingly, no reason exists to sell branded goods cheaply. Foreign brands are often sold in the second-hand market only. The dollar store format exists in the South Pacific in the form of small Chinese-owned shops.

The functional school divides marketing into activities that occur in a business. This approach is the forerunner of the 4 Ps of marketing popularized by McCarthy (1960): product, price, place (distribution), and promotion. McQuarrie lists contractual, merchandising, pricing, propaganda, and physical distribution and termination functions. In order to fulfill the needs of customers, functions have to be performed (Lewis & Erickson, 1969). This approach is relevant more in the urban sector of the South Pacific as products have to be priced, distributed, and promoted, especially in the global markets. This approach also applies where traditional markets exist.

The regional school might be applicable in environments where transportation is limited and the environment acts to retard movement of products and people. However, this seems to emphasize the location of retail stores and the tendency of a consumer to visit one store location or another based on distance of the store, population size, and trade area analysis. This particular view is not helpful in large ocean states that have very few towns or cities and limited retailing to begin with.

Interactive economic approaches

Within the interactive economic approaches, the institutional school combines the functional with the commodity schools by tying them together through the institutions that carry out the functions which enable the movement of goods from producer to consumer. The role of marketing channel members is shown to be critical to the movement of goods from the producer to consumer. The intermediaries play important marketing functions that cannot be fulfilled by producers. Decisions are made largely on grounds of efficiency and other factors are not considered important. Various kinds of middlemen are available throughout the South Pacific in both the urban and rural sectors. In these islands, where relationships and kinship ties are important in all aspects of life, the theoretical approach has to be modified in order to understand the working of intermediaries.

The functionalist school is similar but places emphasis on the system within which the distribution takes place. Pioneered by Alderson (1965), this approach teaches that one can achieve a great deal more though interaction with others in a system than trying to function alone. People interacting within a system act together to ensure joint survival. This approach can be seen in traditional systems in the South Pacific where there is the extended family or clan.

In the managerial school, the emphasis is on the consumer, not the producer, and on using economic theory to help make efficient managerial decisions. The concepts of marketing mix and market segmentation are introduced and thought to be helpful to the development of marketing plans which can aid decision making (McCarthy, 1960; Smith, 1956). While this point of view is most important in societies that are large enough to have segments for which different marketing mixes can be developed, the approach does have relevancy in both urban and rural parts of non-western societies. All people have needs that can be met effectively by the concern of responsive business. In fact, societies with large government bureaucracies, as is true throughout the South Pacific, may benefit from a service orientation focused on consumer needs.

Non-interactive non-economic approaches

In the *non-interactive non-economic approaches*, the buyer behavior school looks at why people behave as they do in the market place. This approach uses explanations from human psychology and sociology to explain market behavior and is more quantitative than earlier schools. Some of the early writers in this area are Rodgers (1983), Katz and Lazarsfeld (1955), Katona (1953) and Festinger (1957). However, the results of this school are contradictory and inconclusive (Kassarjian, 1971). This approach identifies reference groups that can influence purchase behavior. Katz and Lasarsfeld demonstrate that mass media is less important than personal influence in making choices (Sheth, Gardner, & Garrett, 1988). This is particularly true in non-western societies. More recently, there is an emphasis of applying consumer buying theory to non-profit organizations (Sheth, Gardner, & Garrett, 1988). This can be very useful in the South Pacific as these societies are aided by non-governmental non-profits and many aspects of the economy are under the control of the government, also considered a non-profit institution. As religion is very important in South Pacific society, more recent emphasis on religion and consumer behavior can be useful (Hirschman, 1983).

The activist school looks at consumer welfare and satisfaction. This approach should be useful in the South Pacific because when people interact with the urban market, they are not equipped to deal with a superimposed western consumer model. In addition, the urban market is often monopolistic and individuals have little recourse but to pay the high prices they face. Government controls certain industries such as communications and, thus, prices are often high for services such as basic land lines and cell phone services. In fact, a consumer movement per se is lacking in the South Pacific or very rudimentary at best. The governments are seen as more responsible for controlling nefarious business behavior than any grass roots consumer movement.

The macro-marketing school views the effect of marketing on society and relates feedback. Holloway and Hancock (1964) outline the sociological, political, economic, legal, ethical, competitive and technological forces that marketing can influence. This school could be very applicable to the South Pacific as rural society becomes subject to urban sector forces of marketing. To this extent, it is a very important approach. Since many South Pacific economic sectors are governmentally controlled, marketing is influenced by politics. Kotler (1986) states that marketing is becoming more political and could be used to influence governments. He also argues that beyond the 4 Ps, power and public relations should be included in the marketing mix in order to reach the desired markets by influencing gatekeepers such as governments. Governments can also lessen the tendency toward the destruction of communal society from the influx of western capitalistic values or they can be used to further the destruction of communal society.

Interactive non-economic approach

Within the interactive non-economic approach, the organizational dynamics approach comes from the institutional school. But where the institutional school emphasizes economic efficiency affecting a particular distribution structure, this school emphasizes the competitive interaction among the members of a distribution channel. The channel of distribution is a system with powerful members but also with conflict. So, this approach stresses the importance of the bargaining process through the channel of distribution. This approach is applicable to South Pacific societies as power and conflict exist in traditional channels of distribution as well as urban channels of distribution.

The system school of thought in marketing organizes marketing entities into systems where all parts of the system are integrated. Marketing systems such as social systems are made up of norms, roles, and statuses. There is emphasis on how marketing systems can survive by gathering information from the environment and using that information to make necessary system changes (Katz & Kahn, 1966). This approach is more important to urban markets where more formal methods of gathering information include information technology and database creation.

The social exchange school's focus is on the transaction between buyer and seller and the motivation for that transaction. Alderson and Martin (1965) develop the law of exchange to explain why two parties will enter any transaction. Basically, there must be enough difference between the goods exchanged to warrant the transaction. Plus, the partners in the exchange must want what each other has more than they want another good from anyone else based upon their perceptions of what is available in the market. Bagozzi (1975) stresses that transactions are social and are affected by social factors such as similarity and prestige. As social factors are primary motivators in non-western society, this approach is most appealing to understand exchanges in both rural and urban non-western societies.

Other marketing views

While marketing is basically associated with free-market western economies, non-western societies have utilized other approaches to produce, distribute, and consume. These represent alternative ways of fulfilling these functions not based upon markets. Some non-western societies have markets, but many depend on other possibilities for acquiring goods and services. These include reciprocity, redistribution, self-sufficiency and trade (Dalton, 1968). Anthropologists describe these different production and distribution systems worldwide which determine who consumes what.

Reciprocity is a distributional system where economic needs are met through exchange where one partner receives immediate value in the exchange. The other partner can expect reciprocal value at some point in time. It often takes the form of some kind of gift-giving or economic remuneration to help the individual or family in need. Sahlins (1972) lists three kinds of reciprocity: generalized, balanced, and negative. Generalized is gift-giving (such as funds for school fees) without expectation of immediate return although there is an expectation of future return of some kind. Balanced reciprocity means an even exchange of goods or services. Negative reciprocity occurs when one partner in the exchange gets more from the exchange than the other partner. Negative exchange commonly happens in trade when each party in an exchange is out for their own self-interest within the legal parameters of the society. The transaction may be even outside those legal parameters if one party can get away with uneven exchange which may be illegal but not easily proven. Trade is a form of exchange which does not necessarily need so-called free markets. People who exchange establish an equivalent value for the goods to be exchanged. However, the equivalency or price at which one good exchanges for another is not found necessarily through a self-regulating free market.

Redistribution is a distributional system where goods are accumulated by a central authority which distributes the goods but not necessarily equally. Chiefdom systems in the South Pacific are redistribution systems. These systems exist today, although in some areas such as Fiji, the power of the chiefs is under stress because of an unsympathetic government.

Self-sufficiency involves production of goods for one's own use or for family (often the extended family) use. This is the common form of production today among rural people in the South Pacific together with resource control by chiefs.

It is possible for any of the above alterative exchange systems to co-exist with markets as they currently do in islands of the South Pacific.

Economic theory, markets, and marketing

When one reads development theorists or economic anthropologists, it is clear that there has been an economic evolution from pre-history through the industrial revolution. This evolution is usually viewed in stages that include hunting and gathering to "*advanced*" societies based on service economies. Under this evolution, it seems that the move to a self-regulating market is inevitable. It is the creation of the western illusion of human nature (Sahlins, 2008). This illusion includes the belief that humans are completely rational in economic decision, making doing the best for oneself at the expense of others if necessity dictates. Sahlins shows this economic rationality to be an illusion as this total competitive self-interest does not exist in all other societies. As a result, the view of man as Homo Economicus is mostly applicable to capitalistic societies. In addition, as economic anthropologists foresaw, this view of economic man brings with it negatives resulting from the move to make land, labor, and capital market commodities. The many differences between western and non-western society have been characterized as the *substantive* versus the *formal* view of the economic institutions of cultures. These differences illustrate the importance of non-economic factors which create the framework in which an economy develops.

Substantive versus formative definition of economy

Karl Polyani (1957) first identifies substantive and formative economies. Substantive is applied mostly to societies based on more "*primitive*" economic systems. The formal or formative is applied to those based upon laissez-faire self-regulating economic system. The substantive economy includes methods and institutions that people develop to solve the basic economic needs of production, consumption, and distribution. The economy is embedded in culture and cannot be separated (Dalton, 1968). The culture and society determine (within limits of the environment) the economy, not the other way around. As such, the economy is a by-product of political, familial, and religious obligations (Dalton, 1968). For example, in many non-western societies, land and labor are not bought and sold but allocated according to needs by mostly hereditary leaders or chiefs. One's economic existence is assured and one does not individually face tough economic times. There are others – kinsmen for example - there to help. In many parts of the South Pacific, land and labor are still allocated by hereditary chiefs. This reality makes these societies very different from what is experienced by consumers in western societies or those who live and function in the cities of the South Pacific where the formative or formal definition of economy predominates.

The formative or formal economy is synonymous with what is taught in a basic economics course. Within this definition, the economy is the determining factor for that society or culture. The formal definition lists land, labor, and capital as factors of production. These factors are viewed as separate from society and can be manipulated and used in the most efficient way possible to create goods and services for the self-regulating market. Markets exist in non-western societies, but these markets are not defining characteristic of these economies. The fear of individual deprivation and the desire for individual gain over one's relatives and friends are not the motivating factors in non-western societies like those in the South Pacific.

Analysts of market systems argue that rising incomes make the market superior to other "*primitive*" economic systems. It is the view that people will be paid their marginal product and that exploitation does not widely exist where the market system operates. People are paid what they are worth in the form of wages. Economic anthropologists that advocate for the formative or formal view propose that people would be a lot worse off if they did not sell their labor to the market. That may be true where land and labor are fully market inputs and there is enough capital to integrate land, labor and capital efficiently. Land and labor are not alienated in the South Pacific as they are in western society. As Polyani (1944, 1957) points out, the market system divorces the economy from social relationships and obligations (Dalton, 1968). Surprisingly, Polyani (ibid) does not dwell upon exploitation but mentions the degradation of the human condition that results from the separation of the economy from the society and culture. A hallmark of this degradation is the loss of the norms, values, and beliefs that formerly held society and culture together.

There is no lack of anthropological literature on the effects of a foreign market system on the breakdown of society and culture. One only has to look at the cities and slums of Australia, Papua New Guinea, and Africa to see the result. Humans are not necessarily innately desirous of gain, nor are their lives determined totally by economic principle. Those who lose their old ways of living and suffer a self-regulating economy may not be equipped to deal with the new rules of survival. Some may be able to integrate, but many cannot. The state then steps in with well-meaning welfare or assistance that robs people of self-esteem and purpose. Or even worse, there is NO social welfare solution as is common in most large ocean states in the South Pacific. Poverty that results from a market-system is not addressed though social welfare here, but people do have a traditional way of life and control over the land which is a kind of welfare system in itself.

Large ocean states are subject to a dual economy or divide between the traditional and the modern. All these states have cities where one can see the spread of western values permeating the culture. However, traditional society is alive although maybe not so well. Modern media reach is limited in most of these large island communities, but it has some impact. Nevertheless, many rural people do not have the means to have modern media in their homes so the idea of the western self-regulating market has less impact in rural areas. The real factor which defines these states is the degree to which land is bought and sold. Because land is not a commodity that can be bought and sold through the self-regulating market, communities still maintain a more traditional way of life. In both the Cook Islands and the Fiji Islands, for example, the sale of native land was prohibited by the British during colonization. This has led to a protective wall between the islanders and foreigners who might want to purchase land for their own economic gain. In Fiji, a small percentage of the land is free-hold and open for purchase through the self-regulating market system. Some land is "*crown land*" and controlled by the government. However, the majority of land is owned by the kin group. This is also true in many other parts of the South Pacific. Although this has prevented full degradation of the original inhabitants, it has caused problems to those who have migrated to the society and who remain landless. These individuals, often Chinese and Asian Indians, make their way using commerce through the modern or self-regulating market economy or market.

Polyani (1944) describes the development of the market economy. Laws passed in industrializing countries contribute to the development of a landless class who had no other option but to sell their labor to the market. The three tenets of the self-regulating economy are that labor should find a price on the market, that money should be supplied by a central authority, and that commodities should be free to move from country to country without concern for the consequences (Polyani, 1944).

The movement to a market economy leads to economic determinism with the economy a major determinant in creating social institutions rather than the economy being embedded in social institutions of kinship, religion, and polity. Humans in the market system support that system by teaching a managerial philosophy which is supportive of the self-regulating market. Yet, to what extent is the so called "*theory*" of marketing applicable to societies that reflect dualism or the great divide between the traditional and the modern?

It may be possible to develop a new way of looking at the economies where this great divide exists. To find a new approach, there are many questions to resolve. What are the norms, values, beliefs and behaviors of the traditional society under change? How deep is the layer of the modern society? How far does the modern reach into the traditional and how has this modern layer affected the traditional? What networks and links exist between the traditional and the modern layers of society?

It is necessary to analyze how the applicability of the substantive and formal definitions of economics to the South Pacific states helps to answer these questions. It is not possible to study these states by thinking of them as modern because they are not totally consumed by the self-regulating market. Traditional norms, values and beliefs continue to conflict with the modern and even educated people may not be desirous of self-interested gain.

It is hard to say what set of values will prevail in the South Pacific. People educated at the universities learn about a western way of thinking, including the value of free-markets. This thinking will not necessarily solve all the economic, political, and social problems of these societies. Individualism and laissez-faire are not necessarily the best values for every society. Conflict continues today in the South Pacific between the western and the traditional. The most obvious evidence of this was pointed out in *Tristes Tropiques*: "*Our Great Western Civilization, which has created the marvels we now enjoy, has only succeeded in producing them at the cost of corresponding ills*" (Levi-Strauss, 1955). Educators have a great responsibility to temper their economic and marketing exuberance to suit the existing cultural norms.

Theory, marketing practice, societal change, and prospects for the future

Theory and practice

The substantive vs. formalistic views of the world are reformulated into three different modules of human behavior and decision making (Wilk & Cliggett, 2007). The self-interested module is closest to the formalistic view with people making decisions based on mostly self-interest. This is the basis of western capitalism. The social model is closest to the substantive view. The moral module looks at what people think and believe about the world in order to understand individual actions. The social model proposes that individuals are driven by the norms and values of the group rather than individual self-interest driving behavior. This explains the importance of gifts in society as gifts cement relationships and social ties and reinforce group values. Cliggett's research on migration and gift exchange in Zambia shows that people who migrate but maintain relationships at home with their group through gifts and other means are allowed to come home and share in what the society has to offer (2003). Those who want to come back but have not maintained ties through gifts or interactions are not welcomed back and not allocated the use of land for subsistence. This is true in the South Pacific where the tradition of "*kerikeri*" still exists. Kerikeri means responsibility to kin and the extended group to provide what is needed and what one has the capability to provide.

In any culture, there may be elements of all three of these models. It is not an either/or scenario. We can place societies along coordinates with time on the vertical access and the social on the horizontal access (Wilk & Cliggett, 2007). Self-interested societies are at or near the (0, 0) location within this coordinate system. As one radiates out from the (0, 0) point, we see societies as more communal and interested in the group and behaving according to the values of the group. Motives are often rather messy and even within individualistic societies, some may have internal moral compasses which lead an individual to act altruistically. In addition, in communal societies, some can act in their own self-interest. In fact, as one student said about the chiefdom system in Fiji: not all chiefs are interested in advancing the village but more interested in advancing their own well-being by purchasing large SUVs. It is difficult to know if this self-interested behavior is simply personality aberration or the result of self-interested western thinking that now permeates Fijian society and easily learned through the education system, news, and advertising efforts. This way of conceptualizing the level of selfishness or altruism also recognizes the messiness that exists in society and the fact that values and norms are changing as a result of foreign thinking. In addition, people may have their own view of what is right or moral and these ideas may not fit exactly with the group view of what is right. However, the moral view is learned as one grows up in a culture and group such as a religious group. Thus, it is likely that the moral compass that influences decision making is part of the group or social model anyway.

It seems that governments and tertiary educational systems are poised to accept what the western world says about the value of capitalism and globalization. This is a move toward the self-interest module of decision making. The power of the chiefs in societies such as the South Pacific seems to be waning due to the efforts of governments to bring the societies closer to the capitalistic model. The move to the equal rent distribution policy is an example of a procedure by the iTaukei Land Trust Board of Fiji that may undermine the traditional system of redistribution. In Fiji, the people have little recourse to fight what the government puts into place even though the procedures and policies may undermine traditional society. For example, although the current leader was properly elected in 2014, he had been a dictator from 2006 until the September election in 2014. In some cases, it may be the intention of the government to undermine the traditional systems in place. The Great Council of Chiefs has lost outward influence due to decommission by the current leader of Fiji. However, it may maintain its informal power with traditional people. The new Rent Distribution law also undermines the traditional power structure by equal distribution of funds from economic use of village-owned land resources. These funds are moved quickly to the accounts of village families through the new electronic banking system bypassing the chiefs entirely. In the Cook Islands, the traditional roles of the chiefs are under attack as well. It appears that the traditional leaders of the Cook Islanders or maori (indigenous) people, called ariki (paramount chiefs), mataiapo (chiefs) and rangatira (sub-chiefs) have conflict over their roles and how to proceed in a society under the onslaught of western ideology (Rakanui, 2012).

The intake of western thinking can be seen in the marketing efforts of various commercial interests in the South Pacific. The commercials on television, over radio, and in print do not consider the communal nature of the society and the importance of family. Moreover, these commercials do not often reflect the importance of extended family or village relations and are more oriented to the nuclear family. Therefore, the ads in Fiji and the Cook Islands are more oriented to promoting self-interest. This might be viewed as another undermining feature of traditional values in these societies.

In essence, the traditional values of the South Pacific are under assault. Important systems of redistribution such as "*kerikeri*" in Fiji are seen as impediments to the movement of iTaukei (Melanesian Fijians) people into the modern economy. Those who say this are generally from other cultures that have come into the society from the outside or who have been brought up in a completely different system of values similar to western self-interested capitalism. Such values are not necessarily the best for the South Pacific. Many students at universities in the South Pacific promote the western marketing approach to encourage the sale of goods and services. Marketing itself is rarely questioned. Yet, from the macro-marketing perspective, it is certain that marketing changes the society. But are these changes for the better? Marketing is legitimized in higher education programs that offer courses in marketing and marketing management. However, there is no discussion of the effects of marketing on the quality of life and values of the South Pacific societies. The western marketing perspective is accepted as presented in the leading international textbooks used in these educational programs. In fact, there is no textbook that counters the information provided to students and no discussion of the effects of marketing on the quality of life and values of the South Pacific societies. Marketing is the outgrowth of western capitalism. Its culture-altering nature should be discussed and the effects of marking on the islands communities, both good and bad, should be addressed. It is limiting to think of marketing and capitalism in general as "*the*" economic way. Future leaders are being trained to accept the hegemony of this viewpoint without any thought about the effects on the traditional way of life. This hegemony does not take into account the traditional culture or the effects of this western approach on the traditional culture. It is almost as if the traditional culture is deemed bad or backward and anything western including marketing is good and progressive.

Problems and prospects

The so-called progressive economic thinking is not necessarily the cure for what ails non-western societies. In fact, there is a large body of writing that addresses just this issue. Not long ago there was a clear path to economic development, with economists advocating free markets, higher savings, and increased investment from local and outside sources. This thinking proposes that people are poor because their culture prevents them from applying free markets, hinders adequate savings and local investment, and is a barrier to outside investment or external aid. Perhaps the economic problems in the South Pacific can be placed at the door of conventional developmental economics and what these societies need is just more of the same western economic solutions. However, it is clear that in other parts of the world where this western economic thinking has occurred, there still is poverty and economic distress. This has been described as "*dualism*" which refers to a period where the old economy and the new economy exist together. Modernization, given the right amounts of investment, saving, and free markets, will eventually occur. However, it may be that this morphing into the modern may be illusionary. Andre Gunder Frank (1969) argues that the notion of this dualism eventually merging into modernization is an illusion. In fact, in Latin America, the countries that were poor became poorer because of the siphoning of their economic surplus by foreign capitalism. So, such economies remained dependent upon the largesse of western capitalism (Rodney, 1972; Amin, 1976). Although traditional society remains, it is not fully part of a capitalistic system. This poverty is not due to "*dead*" capital but the misuse of capital to enhance the welfare of the few and their western capitalist allies.

Capitalism is somewhat constrained in the South Pacific as a result of the traditional land norms which prevented alienation of the land from the village. The dual system that exists is partly the result of inalienable rights people must the ownership of land. This might be seen as a detriment to modernization but may also be seen as the reason why peasants have not ended up as in other countries, poor AND landless. The land is the person's fallback resource. This resource can be used to generate wealth for the village. It may or may not be "*dead*" capital (de Soto, 2000), depending on where the land resource is located and its ability to be used to increase wealth. South Pacific governments could be spending their time advocating for the conversion of "*dead*" capital to "*active*" capital, but they are still under the control of traditional landholders. Any move to dismantle the traditional landholding systems would place the people of the village in a situation similar to what has occurred in other parts of the world where wealth has been siphoned off by foreign interests or ended up in the hands of the few. Of course, the removal of surplus can only occur by force or as a result of corruption on the part of local leaders and politicians. So, part of the blame for the removal of economic surplus can be laid at the door of corrupt leaders who combine with rapacious or even enlightened foreign interests to remove wealth from the society.

Conclusions

What then are the prospects for South Pacific communities? Surely there must be a middle ground that takes the best from the West without losing the communal and traditional values of the society. It seems that the marketing examples show that western ideology is being taken on without any thought by anyone of the consequences. Marketing has a way of presenting the commercial options to those who see the marketing messages and this might be considered a positive function of marketing. However, if those options are beyond the reach of the average person, one wonders what the effect ultimately is. On the one hand, marketing can be used positively to convince people to eat better and refrain from bad habits. On the other, it can also be used to present marketing options that help the commercial interests more than the people as some of the consumer reward programs do in examples from Fiji. Marketing legitimizes western capitalism slowly but surely. The society needs to understand the underlying damage associated with marketing messages for a new shampoo, a new movie theater, a new movie, Skippy peanut butter, or any other product or service. It is the day by day and hour by hour contact with these messages that conveys the belief that these products and services are good things even though most of the advertising message legitimizes foreign imports.

Some might say that advertising messages only present what is available and that no one is forced to go and buy. But the constancy of the message is the problem. Marketing functions to enhance demand generation and consumerism. There is very little emphasis on the traditional parts of culture. When there is acknowledgement of culture, marketing is there only to better sell goods and services. There is NO analysis of the intended or unintended impacts of marketing on the society. There are no culture police, but perhaps there should be. Surely, someone must be interested in how marketing messages are changing society or reinforcing the capitalistic forces at work in the society either for the positive or for the negative. Everything capitalistic is not necessarily good. Neither is everything capitalistic bad. It is necessary to understand the cultural and economic effects of capitalism and marketing on society.

The problematic current economic situation facing the ocean states is difficult to change. Each of these countries has similar histories and face similar economic problems: a history of colonization, limited resources and capital ("*active*" or "*dead*"), large populations in relation to resources, largely agricultural exports, an agricultural subsistence-based economy, dependency on foreign aid and worker remittances, located in the middle of the Pacific Ocean which makes importing and exporting costly, dualism, and a small land mass. It does not seem that capitalism and its child, marketing, have done much to eliminate economic problems. The problems just mentioned still exist and do not seem to be going away. Accepting western economic thinking and western marketing theory is not a panacea for solving the economic difficulties.

Acknowledgements

Material in this paper is taken from a textbook currently under review for publication: *Marketing in the Large Ocean States: Theory, Practice, Problems and Prospects.*

References

Alderson, W. (1965). *Dynamic marketing behavior.* Homeward, Ill.: Richard D. Irwin, Inc.

Alderson, W. & Martin, M.W. (1965). Toward a formal theory of transactions and transvections. *Journal of Marketing Research,* 2, 117-127.

Amin, S. (1976). *Unequal development.* New York, NY: Monthly Review Press.

Aspinwall, L., (1958). The Characteristics of goods and parallel systems theories". In E.J. Kelly & W. Lazer (Eds.), *Managerial Marketing,* (pp. 434-450). Homewood, Ill.: Irwin, Inc.

Bagozzi, R. P. (1975). Marketing as exchange. *Journal of Marketing,* 39, 32-39.

Cliggett, L. (2003) Gift remitting and alliance building in Zambian modernity: old answers to modern problems. *American Anthropologist* 3, 543-553.

Copeland, M. T. (1923). *Principles of merchandising.* Chicago, Il.: A. W. Shaw.

Dalton, G. (1968). *Primitive archaic and modern economies essays of Karl Polyani.* Garden City, New Jersey: Double Day and Company.

De Soto, H. (2000). *The mystery of capital: why capitalism triumphs in the west and fails everywhere else.* New York, NY: Basic Books.

Enis, B. & Roering. K. J. (1980). Product classification taxonomies: synthesis and consumer implications. In *Theoretical developments in marketing* (pp. 186-189). Chicago: American Marketing Association..

Festinger, L. (1957). *A Theory of Cognitive Dissonance.* New York: Row, Peterson and Company.

Frank, A.G. (1969). *Capitalism and Underdevelopment in Latin America.* New York: Monthly Press Review.

Hirschman, E. C. (1983). "Religions Affiliation and Consumption Processes: An Initial Paradigm". In J. N. Sheth (Ed.) *Research in Marketing,* (pp.131-170). Greenwich, Conn.: JAI Press.

Holloway, R. J. & Hancock, R.S. (Eds.). (1964). *The Environment of Marketing Behavior: Selections from the Literature.* New York: John Wiley and Sons.

Holbrook, M. B. & Howard, J.A. (1977). Frequently purchased nondurable goods and services. In R. Farber (Ed.), *Selected aspects of consumer behavior: A summary from the perspective of different disciplines* (pp. 189-222). Washington, D.C.: National Science Foundation.

Howard, J.A. & Sheth, J.N. *The theory of buyer behavior.* New York: John Wiley and Sons.

Kassarjian, H. (1971). Personality and consumer behavior: a review. *Journal of Marketing Research,* 8, 409-418.

Katona, J.C. (1953). Rational behavior and economic behavior. *Psychological Review,* 60307-318.

Katz, D. & Kahn, R.L. (1966). *The social psychology of organizations.* New York: John Wiley, and Sons.

Katz, E, & Lazarsfeld, P.F. (1955). *Personal influence: the part played by people in the flow of mass communication.* New York: Free Press.

Kotler, P. (1986). Global standardization – courting danger. *The Journal of Consumer Marketing,* 3, 13-15.

Levy-Strauss, C. (1955). *Tristes tropiques.* New York: Penguin Classics.

Lewis, R.J. & Erickson, L.G. (1969). Marketing functions and marketing systems: a synthesis. *Journal of Marketing,* 33, 10-14.

McCarthy, E. J. (1960). *Basic marketing: a managerial approach.* Homewood: Richard. D. Irwin.

Polyani, K. (1957). The economy as instituted process. In C. Arensberg, C. & H. Pearsons (Eds.), *Trade and market in the early empires: economies in trade and history* (pp. 243-269). Glenco: Free Press.

Polyani, K. (1944). *The great transformation: the political and economic origins of our times.* New York: Farrar and Rinehart.

Rakanui, T. (2012). Comments in services marketing [personal communication]. Avarua, Cook Islands.

Rodgers, E.M. (1983). *Diffusing of innovation.* New York: Free Press.

Rodney, W. (1972). *How Europe underdeveloped Africa.* London: Bogle—L'Ouverture.

Sahlins, M. (1972). *Stone age economics.* New York: Aldine De Gruyter.

Sahlins, M. (2008). *The western illusion of human nature.* Chicago: Prickly Paradigm Press.

Sheth, J.N., Gardner, D.M., & Garrett, D.E. (1988). *Marketing theory evolution and evaluation.* New York: John Wiley and Sons.

Smith, W.R. (1956). Product differentiation and market segmentation as alternative marketing Strategies. *Journal of Marketing,* 21, 3-8.

Wilk, R. & Cliggett, L. (2007). *Economies and cultures: foundations of economic anthropology.* Boulder: Westview.

Chapter 13

Barbados at 50: Lessons for Other Small Developing Countries

Harold Codrington[28]

Abstract

During 1966, Barbados, Botswana, Guyana and Lesotho all transitioned to independent countries within the British Commonwealth. In this paper, a variety of indicators is used to measure the performance of each country over the last 50 years. These indicators speak to the quality of governance, as well as achievements in the areas of healthcare, education, information technology and infrastructure. Barbados, the smallest country (both in terms of population and area) and the one with the least physical endowments, is ranked first on all but one indicator. This shows that physical endowments are not the major driver of economic development. Instead, Barbados is the stellar performer because it excelled in the areas of external relations and macroeconomic policies, institutional building and governance.

Introduction

Barbados has been a sovereign nation for 50 years, having achieved independence from Britain in November 1966, after 300 years of colonial rule. During the last five decades, it has achieved much for a country of its size and physical endowments. It has a relatively high per capita income and ranks among the leading developing countries on the United Nation's Human Development Index which measures overall living standards among countries. It has gained a reputation for stability, democracy, and good governance. Guyana, Botswana, and Lesotho have all achieved independence in the same year as Barbados but have not developed quite as quickly, despite having more physical resources. This is an indication that physical endowments, though important, do not guarantee economic and/or social development. What are the factors that allow one developing country to

[28] E-mail: harev@hotmail.com

prosper more than its peers? This paper argues that while physical resources are certainly important considerations, the more critical attributes are the qualitative and intangible ones. In that regard, in the context of Barbados, the key features are stable government (including good governance) and strong institutions, pragmatic policies at home and abroad, and high levels of literacy and healthcare.

This paper will first provide some context to the achievement of the countries' independence. Then, it will use a number of macroeconomic indicators to show how the countries have fared between 1966 and 2016. In so doing, it will point out that those countries which deviated from sound principles of democracy and prudent social, economic, and financial policies did not develop as quickly as those that remained "*on track.*"

The colonial context

Many writers chronicled the negative impact of colonialism on the colonized territories and have highlighted the many ways in which this process played out. Economists long postulated that colonial rule is a constraint to faster economic development. Economic exploitation of the resources in the colonies had been a major driver of the growth of Western Europe. Dr. Eric Williams, historian, political scientist and first Prime Minister of Trinidad and Tobago, showed in *Capitalism and Slavery* how the triangular trade in slaves, sugar and merchandise created tremendous wealth for British interests. The money from the colonies went into shipping and ship-building, banking, heavy industry and insurance (1964). This policy of mercantilism was designed to strengthen the home economy at the expense of rivals. Therefore, the colonies were usually allowed to trade only with the "*mother*" country.

Apart from the economic dimension, colonial rule brought many other negatives. The colonizers sometimes used superior military might to enforce their rule and quell any opposition. Part of this process often involved the redefining of traditional borders. The ensuing conflicts resulted in much loss of life. Loss of life also came from the new diseases that were introduced by the Europeans which sometimes caused local epidemics of extraordinary virulence. For example, smallpox, measles, malaria, yellow fever, and others were unknown in pre-Columbian America. Another product of colonialism was cultural marginalization, whereby the indigenous customs, language, culture, history, religion, cuisine and general way of life were disparaged and sometimes obliterated.

It was into this fractured environment that the colonists imported their institutions and value system. In some cases, the transplant worked reasonably well, but in others, particularly those with large populations, it never took root or worked with limited success. Accordingly, after being under foreign rule for decades, some newly independent governments often lacked governmental institutions, good governance skills, and the governing experience needed to effectively rule their newly sovereign nations. In many cases, the transition from colonial status to independence was a violent and arduous journey (Marker, 2003).

Stylized facts

During the 1950s and 1960s, several former British colonies in Africa and the Caribbean gained independence. In 1966, this list included Barbados, Botswana, Guyana and Lesotho, meaning that in 2016, these countries celebrated 50 years of nationhood. During the last 50 years, these countries had very different experiences.

Barbados, Guyana and Lesotho are described by the World Bank as "*Small States*" since they all meet the criterion of having populations of 1.5 million or less. Botswana has a population of just over 2 million. These countries differ significantly in geography and demographics. Botswana and Guyana are all medium-sized continental territories while Barbados is a small island. Botswana and Lesotho are land-locked. Barbados is among the world's most densely populated countries while the others are sparsely populated. Barbados and Guyana are flat whereas Lesotho and Botswana are quite mountainous. Botswana also contains a large desert.

Of the four countries under consideration, Barbados was the least endowed in terms of natural resources. At the time of independence, sugar and its by-products were the mainstay of the economy, but by 2015, tourism became the major activity, supported by international financial services and light manufacturing. In Botswana, diamond mining fueled the economy and currently accounts for one quarter of GDP, approximately 85% of export earnings, and about one-third of the government's revenues. In addition, the country had access to copper, nickel, livestock and textiles.

Guyana is endowed with sugar, gold, bauxite, shrimp, timber, and rice. Much of Guyana's growth in recent years has come from a surge in gold production in response to higher global prices. Lesotho depends mainly on the exploitation of diamond and water resources. The South African Government pays royalties for water transferred to South Africa from a dam and reservoir system in Lesotho. Other earnings come from textile manufacturing, agriculture, remittances from migrants in South Africa and regional customs revenue.

The social and economic situation in 2015

Based on these economic bases, one would expect that Barbados should be the least likely to be the stellar performer in the group. However, judging from its performance on a range of yardsticks, Barbados has achieved far more than the others since independence. This is indicated by a variety of development indicators. The United Nations' Human Development Index (HDI) is an all-encompassing indicator of the standard of living. Since 1990, this index has ranked countries' social and economic development according to four criteria: life expectancy at birth, mean years of schooling, expected years of schooling and gross national income per capita. This paper also examines key components of the HDI, per capita GDP and life expectancy at birth. Transparency International is the global anti-corruption watchdog and provides a Corruption Index as an indicator of governance. On this index, a country's score indicates the perceived level of public sector corruption on a scale which ranges from 0 (highly corrupt) to 100 (very clean). A country's rank indicates its position relative to the other countries in the index (Corruption Perceptions Index).

Other important indicators of responsible use of government resources are represented by per capita spending on health and education. These are supplemented by figures on the level of literacy. To measure access to technology, the number of cellphones per 1000 inhabitants and the percentage of inhabitants with access to the internet are used. The percentage of roads that is paved is used as a proxy for the quality of the infrastructure.

Country performance on indicators

In fairness to the other countries, it would seem that Barbados was already ahead of the pack in 1966. Using per capita GDP as a proxy for the standard of living in 1966, its per capita GDP was US$ 524 followed by Guyana (US$ 348), Botswana (US$84), and Lesotho (US$ 60) *(World Bank estimates for1966)*

Since 2015, the HDI is considered a more reliable indicator of living standards/quality of life than per capita GDP. Barbados maintains its lead in overall living standards, but Botswana registers a significant increase (see Table 13.1).

Table 13.1: HDI Rank 2015

Country	Rank
Barbados	57
Botswana	106
Guyana	124
Lesotho	161

Source: ***UNDP***

On the 2015 HDI of 187 countries, Barbados comes in at No. 57, well in front of Botswana at 106, Guyana at 124, and Lesotho at 161. Strong economic activity in Botswana has significantly boosted its per capita income during the last decade or so. Buoyed by diamond mining, Botswana has now recorded one of the world's highest economic growth rates since independence. Table 2 shows how quickly the countries' per capita income grew between 1966 and 2015. Botswana's GDP per capita has risen by a factor of 73, most of it coming in the last half of the period; GDP per capita increases 30-fold in Barbados, 18-fold in Lesotho, and 11-fold in Guyana.

Table 13.2: GDP Per Capita in $ US

Country	1966	2015
Barbados	524	15912
Guyana	348	6160
Botswana	84	3993
Lesotho	60	1963

Source: ***UNDP***

As indicators of the health profile in 2015, this paper looks at figures for life expectancy and infant mortality (where the infant mortality rate is the number of infants dying before reaching one year of age, per 1,000 live births in a given year). Life expectancy is highest in Barbados at 78 years (ranked 38 of 194 countries). This is compared to 64 years in Botswana and Guyana (both ranked 147) and 50 years in Lesotho (ranked 193). On the infant mortality scale, on average out of 1000 births, there are 12 deaths of infants in Barbados, 32 in Guyana, 35 in Botswana and 69 in Lesotho.

Table 13.3: Life Expectancy and Infant Mortality

Country	Life Expectancy	Infant Mortality Out of 1000 Live Births
Barbados	78/38	12
Botswana	64/147	35
Guyana	64/147	32
Lesotho	50/193	69

Source: ***UNDP***

Next, this paper examines whether the government spends its resources wisely since the outcomes on other indicators may be linked to government policy. To do so, official spending on healthcare during a 13-year period is used as an available statistic. Per capita expenditure on healthcare in Barbados rises from US$ 521 in 2000 to US$ 1007 in 2013. Over the comparable period, spending on public health in the other countries is much lower and does not expand by quite as much, except in Lesotho where the figure almost trebled (see Table 13.4).

Table 13.4: Per Capita Spending on Healthcare in $ US

Country	2013	2000
Barbados	1007.0	521.0
Botswana	397.0	233.0
Guyana	150.0	199.0
Lesotho	123.0	45.0

Source: World Bank Open Data

With respect to levels of literacy, Barbados again tops the group, (with near universal literacy) although it was obvious that the other countries are making serious attempts to raise their levels.

Table 13.5: Level of Literacy

Country	%
Barbados	99
Botswana	88
Guyana	87
Lesotho	70

Source: UNESCO Institute for Statistics

This level of literacy may be a result of the spending on education. Barbados and Lesotho register the highest ratios with respect to expenditure on education (see Table 13.6).

Table 13.6: Spending on Education per Student/GDP per Capita

Country	%	Year
Barbados	22.5	2008
Botswana	10.3	2009
Guyana	7.8	2012
Lesotho	22.8	2008

Source: World Bank Open Data

As mentioned earlier, the quality of governance is measured by the level of corruption in the country. The year 2014 is the last one for which there is data for all four of the countries. Some 174 countries are surveyed and the rankings are shown below. Higher ranking indicates lower corruption. Barbados is the highest-ranked with Botswana, deemed the least corrupt country in Africa, not far behind.

Table 13.7: Corruption 2014

Country	Rank
Barbados	17
Botswana	21
Lesotho	55
Guyana	124

Source: Corruption Perception Index, 2014

On the two other indicators, the results are the same. With respect to access to technology, the study looks at the number of cellphones per 1000 inhabitants and the percentage of persons with access to the internet. Ownership of cellphones is highest in Barbados but also high in Botswana. This is evidence of the contention that African countries are using cellphone technology to bridge the so-called digital divide (see Table 13.8).

Table 13.8: Number of Cell Phones Per 1000 Inhabitants and Country Rank 2015

Country	No.	Rank
Barbados	840.9	67
Botswana	774.6	79
Guyana	365.1	134
Lesotho	214.3	169

Source: http://www.nationmaster.com/country-info/stats/Media/Telephones/Mobile-cellular/Per-capita

Access to the internet demonstrates a more substantial lead for Barbados. This perhaps reflects the fact that Barbados has higher levels of discretionary income.

Table 13.9: Internet Users Per 100 Inhabitants 2014

Country	Users
Barbados	76.7
Botswana	18.5
Guyana	37.4
Lesotho	11.0

Source: World Bank Open Data

The final comparison is made on the indicator of infrastructure – the percentage of paved roads. The available numbers may need some adjustments but, even then, Barbados would still retain the top spot. This is clearly facilitated by the small size of Barbados and its flat terrain. However, topography apart, it is also indicative of sensible spending by the government.

Table 13.10: Percentage of Paved Roads 2015

Country	%
Barbados	99.0
Botswana	35.3
Guyana	7.0
Lesotho	18.0

Source: http://chartsbin.com

Some explanations for performance

The statistics that are presented show that Barbados has the highest scores overall and that Barbados and Botswana perform much better on all indicators than Guyana and Lesotho. This section explores some reasons for the differences in the economic and social experiences of the four countries. Special conditions prevail on the experiences of each country. In Barbados, small size, a flat terrain and the absence of ethnic issues are positive influences. Botswana, Lesotho and Guyana are all hampered by ethnic diversity and a difficult topography. However, it is possible to identify a number of qualitative factors that influenced the relatively more successful experience of Barbados and Botswana. These are enabling institutions and stable government, pragmatic foreign policies, and (mostly) prudent macroeconomic policies.

Strong institutions and stable government

The colonial experience was not mutually beneficial. With respect to the creation of wealth, it undoubtedly worked to the benefit of the British. However, in order to maximize the extraction of wealth, the British had to transplant to the colonies the Westminster system of government and all of its associated institutions and practices. Over time, these included democratic elections every five years, a parliament, the rule of law, a well-organized civil service, and trade unions.

These practices and institutions underpin stable government and an impartial judiciary which are so crucial to implementing macroeconomic policies and achieving societal consensus. In such an environment, the administration is able to provide the populace with a wide range of services that increase prosperity and individual well-being. According to Burki et al. (1998), "*on average, higher scores in institutional development are associated with higher rates of growth.*" Briguglio et al. write that "*Recent research shows a strong link between improvements in the way states govern themselves and development results, whether in terms of income per capita, child mortality or literacy*" (2006). Efficient institutions are said to be good for economies because they provide clear, widely known, coherent, predictable, credible, and properly and evenly enforced rules. It is because of these benefits that senior government officials have highlighted governance as the most important determinant of development.

It is clear that since independence, Barbados and Botswana largely adopted these institutions and practices. In Barbados, free, regular, incident-free elections predated independence and were last held in February 2013. Botswana's most recent election, its eleventh, was held in October 2014. In Botswana and Barbados, the constitution served as the rule of law protecting the citizens and representing their rights. In both countries, the judiciary was set up as independent of the executive and the legislature. The politics of Barbados and Botswana took place in a framework of a monarchy and a representative democratic republic, respectively. Barbados also took steps to reduce mistrust between key economic agents. This was institutionalized in a social partnership agreement between government, the labor movement and the employers, resulting in a low number of days lost to work stoppage, when compared to regional peers.

The situation was quite different in Guyana and Lesotho, where political instability exerted major influence on the economies. Guyana came into independence with a history of political disturbances which had their origin in race or ethnicity. In 2016, the two major political parties remained divided along racial lines. There was no unquestioned acceptance of the Westminster model and since independence, there were attempted rebellions and violent riots during elections. There was widespread distrust of the electoral process and international observers were normally invited to monitor the national elections. In addition, trade unions were and continue to be very militant. This was an atmosphere characterized by distrust and uncertainty.

In Lesotho, the probability of strong institutions has been low from the start. A series of rebellions and military coups have been the defining feature of the post-independence period, with an aborted coup being staged as recently as 2014. These uprisings are accompanied by leadership disputes in the political parties and rejection of election results by the Opposition. The country's first peaceful elections have only taken place in 2002. To top it all, the country has been invaded by South Africa in 1999 and its main population centers destroyed. The legal system is based on a combination of English common law and Roman-Dutch law.

Pragmatic foreign policy

A country's relations with the international community have consequences for its development. Those that appear to be puppets of either the eastern bloc or western bloc countries are scorned by the opposing camp. The international lending agencies and the United Nations are controlled by the western democracies and therefore are prone to support countries that are of like mind. In the four countries under review, independence has brought responsibility for external affairs and the various governments set about forging relationships at the international level. However, the individual paths are quite different. A comparison between the different approaches adopted by Barbados and Guyana is instructive in this regard.

In its foreign relations, Barbados promotes a policy of "*friends of all, satellites of none.*" The phrase has been used by the first Prime Minister in his maiden address to the United Nations Assembly. Since then, successive administrations have continued to maintain a centrist, "*middle of the road*" approach to international affairs and political ideology. At the international level, this approach means that the country is virtually non-aligned and is therefore able to do business with all economic and political blocs. At the domestic level, it blunts the growth of the "*political tribalism*" which is so commonplace in many countries, and allows governments to get on with the country's business without being constrained by ideology.

Botswana since independence has also maintained a pragmatic approach to international relations. It has remained close to the major Western democracies, is a member of the economic and political integration movement in southern Africa, and has also cultivated diplomatic relations with the former Soviet Union and Russia.

On the other hand, ideology has been a dominant political influence in Guyana. One of the leading parties for many years has declared itself to be socialist in orientation with the party, espousing the doctrine of party paramountcy. This affects Guyana since it did not win Guyana the support of the leading Western powers or the multilateral financial institutions. Also, the attempts to build a socialist society alienate significant portions of the populace and cause a massive emigration of skilled workers contributing to a significant decline in the overall quality of life. Foreign relations, not dictated by ideology, have also influenced the Guyana economy. The most important of these is a long-standing border dispute with Venezuela that has negatively impacted Guyana's potential economic development. Consistency in foreign policy is also desirable for a small state. For example, Lesotho decides in 1990 to break relations with the People's Republic of China (the PRC or mainland

China) and re-establish relations with the Republic of China (commonly known as Taiwan), but later restores ties with the P.R.C.

Prudent economic policies

Another important ingredient of successful economies is prudent macroeconomic policies. These are crucial to providing the right signals to investors and consumers since the government is more often than not the largest consumer and investor in small developing states. The exchange rate and the debt situation are prime examples of variables that should be carefully managed.

The economic viability and international reputation of a country are heavily influenced by the stability of its exchange rate. A stable exchange rate provides a great degree of certainty for domestic economic agents and foreign investors. Domestic entities can make spending and investment decisions with confidence. Investors do not have to worry about the value of dividends, profits and other investment income which they may wish to transfer. The international rating agencies and the multilateral financial institutions advise countries to avoid exchange rate instability.

In Barbados, the anchor of the economy is a fixed exchange rate. The Barbados currency was fixed in 1975 at BD$2 to US$1 and has not been changed since then. So sacrosanct is the fixed exchange rate that it has universal political support. During the 1991-93 stabilization program with the International Monetary Fund, given a choice between devaluation and a very large cut in the fiscal deficit, the government has chosen the latter.

The situation in Guyana is completely different. Since independence, the Guyanese have experimented with many forms of exchange rate management. These include a fixed exchange rate, a "*crawling peg*", a "*currency basket*" mechanism, a "*managed float*" a "*secondary foreign exchange window*" and "*free floating.*" These all have failed to stabilize the value of the Guyana dollar. Between 1988 and 1991, the exchange rate has deteriorated at the rate of 250 percent annually. The Guyanese dollar has fallen from parity with the US dollar in 1986 to G$125 against the dollar in 1991 and G$140 in 1996. Into the new century, the slide has continued, with the rate deteriorating to G$184 in 2000, to G$ 204 in 2008 and G$ 206 in 2015.

Indebtedness can also be a big issue in some developing countries. Servicing of foreign debt, (which is payable in foreign currency), can become a problem since the available foreign exchange reserves have to go towards paying down the debt instead of providing housing, healthcare, education and infrastructure. With respect to external debt management, Barbados has had no problem for the vast majority of the time since independence in 1966.

Foreign borrowing has been modest and the level of amortization has never been so onerous that the country had to default on repayment. However, as the economic situation has deteriorated after the start of the recent financial crisis, there have been significant domestic and foreign borrowing. On the other hand, Guyana has been heavily indebted for many years. Reduction of the debt burden has been one of that country's top priorities. Guyana's extremely high debt burden to foreign creditors has meant limited availability of foreign exchange and reduced capacity to import necessary raw materials, spare parts, and equipment, thereby further reducing production and living standards.

Literacy

Literacy levels are simultaneously an indicator of development and a facilitator of development. A literate populace that understands the nexus between government revenue and the provision of services facilitates the collection of taxes, in particular income taxes (see Codrington, 1989). High rates of literacy make a workforce easily trainable and are an attraction to prospective investors. This environment also gives rise to a thriving middle class that can supply the resources for the national social safety net – unemployment benefits, welfare payments, subsidized bus fares, free healthcare. This in turn helps most of the working class to enjoy a reasonable standard of living, thereby reducing the probability of societal dislocation and unrest. Barbados has the highest level of literacy with near universal adult literacy. This has resulted in part from the early realization that, given the lack of physical endowments, people have to be placed at the center of the development thrust.

Conclusions

The four British colonies that gained independence in 1966 have had different experiences in the last 50 years. Barbados, the smallest and least physically-endowed has performed best, no matter what indicators are used. While it is clear that Barbados has obvious advantages – a head-start, a friendlier topography and a more homogeneous population – this paper shows that there are qualitative factors that led to the outcome.

The more successful countries – Barbados and Botswana – also have more stable governments and political environments, are less prone to be overly influenced by ideology, and generally practiced prudent economic policies, particularly with regard to exchange rate stability and debt management. These factors help to build confidence on the part of foreign investors and residents, thus creating incentives for private sector activity. They also remove uncertainties about, and garner support for, official policy-making, including on the part of the international community. Governments with good policies and institutions are known to be more likely to use development assistance effectively. This paper shows that scarcity of the traditional factors of production is not necessarily a constraint on growth and development in small states. Barbados relies on sound policies and strong institutions. Through fiscal discipline and sound management, Botswana has transformed itself from one of the poorest countries in the world to a middle-income country that is one of the wealthiest and most stable countries in Africa. There are lessons here for other small developing states.

References

Briguglio, L., Bishnodat, P. ,& Stern, R. (2006, September). *Toward an outward-oriented development strategy for small states: issues, opportunities and resilience building.* Paper presented at Small States Forum, Annual Meetings of the World Bank Group and the IMF, Singapore.

Burki, S. &Perry, G. (1998). *Beyond the Washington consensus: institutions matter,* (World Bank). Retrieved from World Bank web-site: http://documents.worldbank.org/curated/en/556471468265784712/Beyond-the-Washington-Consensus-institutions-matter.

Codrington, H. (1989). Country size and taxation in developing countries. *Journal of Development Studies,* 25 (4), 508-520.

Corruption Perceptions Index. (2014). Retrieved December 2016 from http://www.transparency.org/research/cpi/overview.

Marker, S. (2003, November "Effects of colonization." *Beyond Intractability.* [Conflict Information Consortium, University of Colorado, Boulder, Guy Burgess and Heidi Burgess, Eds.]. Retrieved from http://www.beyondintractability.org/essay/post-colonial.

Number of Cell Phones. Retrieved December 2016 from www.nationmaster.com/country-info/stats/media/telephones/mobile-cellular/per-capita.

Percentage of Paved Roads. Retrieved in December 2016 from http://chartsbin.com/.

UNESCO Institute for Statistics. Retrieved December 2016 from https://en.wikipedia.org/wiki/UNESCO_Institute_for_Statistics.

UNDP: United Nations Development Programme, Human Development Index, various editions. Retrieved December 2016 from http://hdr.undp.org/en/content/human-development-index-hdi.

Williams, E. (1964). *Capitalism and slavery.* London: Andre Deutsch.

World Bank Open Data. Retrieved December 2016 from http://data.worldbank.org/.

World Bank Estimates for 1966. Retrieved December 2016 from https://en.wikipedia.org/wiki/List_of_countries_by_past_and_projected_GDP_(nominal)_per_capita#World_Bank_estimates_between_1960_and_1969.

Chapter 14

Grass-Roots Initiatives Driving Economic Development in Rural Tanzania

Linda Winkler[29]

Abstract

Sub-Saharan Africa continues to have the largest percentage of poverty despite significant improvement in this century. Yet, Africa has been promoted as "the world's next major economic success story". Although economic growth is not uniform across the continent, the Gross Domestic Product (GDP) of Sub-Saharan Africa has consistently been stronger that the global GDP from 2013-2016 and it is projected to continue to be stronger through 2018. Outside investment plays a role in promoting economic development, but many of the success stories in Africa are local or regional, led by domestic Non-Governmental Organizations (NGOs), and enhanced by new technologies and newly available educational opportunities. This paper looks at three regional success stories in economic development in rural Tanzania using grassroots NGOs as examples. In addition, this paper outlines the role by which microfinance, cooperative groups, and local cultural entities have supported economic development. Local community-driven NGOs have served as a means of organizing efforts for economic improvement, including enhancing agricultural yield, increasing access to market, and improving investment. Whereas many of the grass-roots initiatives have started out small with limited focus, strong community involvement, consensual decision making, and strategic partnerships have led to a greatly expanded and sustainable presence in supporting change and development in multiple areas including infrastructure development and education. In addition, these organizations have formed important national and international partnerships which enhance funding and investment. Their development model is sustainable and can serve as a model for elsewhere.

---

[29]linda.winkler@wilkes.edu

Introduction

The Millennium Development Goals 2015 (MDGs) developed by the United Nations in 2000 have been instrumental in driving global development (United Nations Millennium Development Goals Report, 2015). As such, these goals are used to formulate policies and fund global organizations and national government initiatives around the world. The original MDGs have driven significant improvement in educational outcomes, poverty reduction, and global health outcomes since they were adopted over fifteen years ago. Although essentially a top-down approach, the linkage of policy to funding leads to substantial emphasis on development (as promoted by these MDGs) on the part of governments, researchers, and international, regional, and local agencies. Regional and local communities are often the place where the policy directives are operationalized either in response to national directives or as a result of the desire for funding.

The post-2015 Sustainable Development Goals have been recently approved at the United Nations and continue to focus on global development as well as on emphasizing the need for sustainability (see Sustainable Development Goals: Seventeen Goals to Transform Our World, 2015). These post-2015 goals embrace economic development and change as a means to combat extreme poverty worldwide. They include two goals, numbers eight and nine, which are directly linked to economic development. Goal Eight endeavors to "*promote inclusive and sustainable economic growth, employment and decent work for all.*" Goal Nine strives to "*build resilient infrastructure, promote sustainable industrialization and foster innovation*" (Sustainable Development..., 2015).

These two broad goals have many targets including a commitment to "promote development-oriented policies that support productive activities, decent job creation, entrepreneurship, creativity and innovation, and encourage formalization and growth of micro-, small-, and medium-sized enterprises" (ibid). Providing jobs or opportunities for youth is also highlighted. In addition, Goal Nine seeks to "develop quality, reliable, sustainable and resilient infrastructure, including regional... infrastructure..., increase the access of small-scale...enterprises, particularly in developing countries, to financial services including affordable credit and their integration into value chains and markets" and to "facilitate sustainable and resilient infrastructure development in developing countries through enhanced financial, technological, and technical support to African countries..." (ibid). These targeted development initiatives seek to "sustain per capita economic growth in accordance with national circumstances" and to increase the annual growth of real Gross Domestic Product (GDP) to at least

7% per annum in the least-developed countries "including much of Sub-Saharan Africa" (ibid). The commitment to build infrastructure in Sub-Saharan Africa reflects the fact that this region continues to have the largest percentage of people living in poverty despite significant improvement in this century. Africa is portrayed as "the world's next major economic success story" with Africa's GDP growing faster (5.6%) than the global average (4.2%) (Remarks by President Obama at Business Leaders Forum, 2013). The GDP of Sub-Saharan Africa is consistently stronger than the global GDP for the years 2013-2016 and is projected to continue so through 2018. In addition, within the Sub-Saharan region, East Africa has a 7% growth rate in 2015, higher than many other areas in the continent and the global GDP which was at 2.4% in 2015 (Global Economic Prospects Divergences and Risks, 2016). Policy guidelines such as the MDGs as well as outside investments play a role in promoting this economic development in East Africa (United Nations Millennial Development Goals Report 2015). Their strategic use helps promote change and program development. Building upon these successes, sustainability is seen as an important hallmark of success moving forward and meeting the benchmarks of the newly adopted Sustainable Development Goals.

Development done locally

Economic models of development consider multiple levels of policy involvement, governance, social structure, and the individual. Figure 14.1 demonstrates one model modified from Uphoff (1993) regarding development policy and economic development. Much of what is discussed about Africa and development in the media or in academic or policy publications involves initiatives at the top of this figure: regional or above. However, many of the success stories in Africa happen within regions, where policy is interpreted and implemented, led by local NGOs, and enhanced by new technologies and educational opportunities (Andrzejczak, 2015). In rural Sub-Saharan Africa, local community stakeholders continue to wield significant influence on development, the success of programs, and their sustainability. Grass-roots initiatives are primary drivers of local development and economic transformation within regions. Although regional policy and opportunity may be promoted through global and national policies and markets, it is the local entities of the household, local kin groups, and village or district entities which create the infrastructure and cultivate development. As such, policy and opportunity are reinterpreted in ways appropriate to local cultural norms and local communities.

Figure 14.1: Multiple Levels of Economic Development in Rural Sub-Saharan Africa

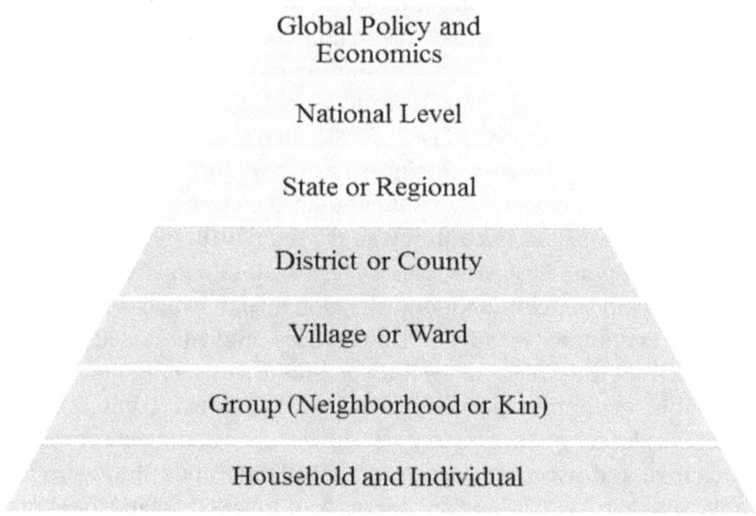

Source: Revised by author based on Uphoff (1993)

This paper looks at regional successes in economic development in rural Tanzania in the Karagwe and Kyerwa Districts (Kagera Region) using three grass-roots NGOs as examples: MAVUNO, the Women's Emancipation and Development Agency (WOMEDA), and the Family Alliance for Development and Cooperation (FADECO). Collectively, these NGOs serve in multiple roles including in microfinance, as cooperative groups, in education, by supporting underserved and vulnerable groups, and as local cultural entities in supporting economic development. These local community NGOs serve as a means of organizing efforts for economic improvement including enhancing agricultural yield, access to markets, and investment. Although all of these grassroots initiatives have started out small with limited focus, strong community involvement, consensual decision making, and strategic partnerships have led to a greatly expanded and sustainable presence for each. These NGOs support change and development in multiple areas including infrastructure development. In addition, some of these organizations form important national and international partnerships which enhance funding and investment. This paper compares their organizations, visions, partnerships, achievements, and discusses their sustainability.

The term "*societal entrepreneurship*" has been applied to grassroots initiatives which seek to link public and private sectors, often through the work of NGOs (Swart & Orsmond, 2011). They have become increasingly important as change agents. Such societal entrepreneurship utilizes local networks while simultaneously seeking to link global forces (policy, market opportunity) to local communities. They are important to development through innovation and their attempts to improve sustainability in multiple arenas including economic, cultural, and environmental (Gawell et al., 2009). Innovation can include new knowledge and technologies, cultural changes, changes related to creating new economic strategies, new organization pathways, or changes to infrastructure. It can involve entrepreneurs who enter a community from the outside, such as the leadership of WOMEDA, or it can come through entrepreneurial leadership from within the community as with MAVUNO. In all three cases discussed here, the leaders of the societal entrepreneurship seek to serve the community in a variety of ways and have had successes.

MAVUNO and FADECO both started as organizations to work with local farmers, offering support, new technologies, and other means to increase yield and access to markets. WOMEDA was established to offer legal support to women and children. All three either broadened their vision or in one case, shifted focus to seek funding since they began. All originate in the same area of northwestern Tanzania, the Karagwe district (Karagwe District Council, 2014). Beyond these similarities, these organizations evolve in substantially different ways (see Table 14.1). MAVUNO began as a local cooperative, started by farming families in the village of Ihanda in 1993. FADECO was started by entrepreneur Joseph Sekiku in the 1990s. He was raised outside of the area but settled in Karagwe and bought land there after living in Europe (Sekiku, 2007). WOMEDA was started by a group of Tanzanian lawyers and legal aid workers from outside of the area who moved to Karagwe to launch the NGO in 2003. MAVUNO started locally and remained local. The father of the current program manager was one of the founders.

Table 14.1: A Comparison of Key Components of Three NGOs.

NGO	FADECO	WOMEDA	MAVUNO
Year Began	1993	2002	1993
Leadership	Joseph Sekiku	Juma Masisi + legal team, Board Directors	Cooperative, Charles Bahati plus many others
Funding	Small Intl Funds, UNESCO, SIDA, Consulting, Self	Consulting & Grants, USAID, Amizade , Firelight Foundation	Coop Dues, Local funds, Partnership contributions
Projects	Agricultural development, Wind power, Fruit drying, IT, Radio	Legal support for women and children, Education	Agricultural development Seed security, Water supply, Conservation, Microfinance, Education, Needy children
Target	Kagera Region	Karagwe and Kyerwa Districts	Karagwe and Kyerwa Districts

The economic and development history of these NGOs is intertwined with local community involvement and dependent on local government infrastructure. Governance here begins with kinship groups (clans) which tend to live in the same locality or ward. Other governing structures are the local ward leadership (often kin-related) and the District Council (Karagwe District Council, 2014). Important decisions are made by these groups through discussion and consensus. Interactions between these NGOs and the broader community leadership are critically important to their success. Hiring local individuals to work with the NGOs and leadership living in the community are one means of building local support and networks into the district where kin-based clans shape local governance. Beyond the regional environment, these NGOs also need access to global partnerships, outside markets, and global policy agencies and funding sources. Therefore, global networks including social media and a web presence are also important to their success.

WOMEDA

The current mission statement of WOMEDA states that they promote the status of marginalized groups by creating and strengthening equal opportunities for women, men, and children through the provision of socioeconomic, legal, and human rights activities (WOMEDA Web-site, 2016). As societal entrepreneurs, this NGO's founding mission is that of a community change agent for vulnerable individuals (women and children primarily) by providing legal support to protect human rights and educating the community. Their name reflects this: Women's Emancipation and Development Agency. Their current vision broadens and to some degree redefines their mission from earlier years. They work closely with other NGOs, including one which provides human rights counseling and support to women and orphans affected by AIDS. International funding shifts several years ago have led to a change in focus with support ending for community partners such as the AIDS NGO. Since WOMEDA is partially dependent on grants and external funding to exist, the organization has broadened its mission by developing programs to support orphans in schools, for AIDS education, and to promote gender equality in order to continue to obtain funding. More recent activities focus on vulnerable children, children's rights, birth certificate registration workshops, and legal support of children. The birth certificate registration program is particularly important because it builds infrastructure for educational systems and economic interactions throughout East Africa. For example, birth certificates are required for school registration and many other government, economic, and employment interactions.

WOMEDA is quite successful in serving as an advocate for women and promoting human rights of women and children. This NGO has an executive director who has been with the group since it was founded in 2003. Local staff members are likewise instrumental in its success. It also has a board of directors which has been relatively consistent. One member of the board serves as a grant writer. The presence of a grant writer is critically important since grants remain a primary funding for this NGO. Although WOMEDA has international partners, the lack of a website, other than Facebook, and the lack of online social updates limit its communication with potential global partners. Its sustainability remains dependent on outside funding.

FADECO

As mentioned above, FADECO was started by a single individual, and he remains primarily responsible for its activities. This NGO is committed to promoting education of rural farmers, increasing their yield and enhancing their access to markets for their surplus crops. Initiatives include workshops on bee-keeping and drying fruits for market, promotion of sustainable organic farming, increasing tree planting, and creating a rural training center. More recently, this NGO focuses on information dissemination. The entrepreneurial activities are important in introducing and launching new technologies. It is instrumental in helping to initiate IT services in the area (Blayton, 2008) and in beginning a radio station (FADECO radio) in 2007.

The radio station is the most successful project of this NGO. Although other projects have some impact in the community, many such as the fruit drying (banana) initiative no longer appear viable. The radio station was started with a grant from United Nations Educational, Scientific, and Cultural Organization (UNESCO) and remains a UNESCO partner (UNESCO Empowering..., 2016). Although there is a public community radio station which also serves the area, FADECO radio remains active (FADECO website, 2016) and provides a wide variety of programming (Fadeco Community Radio–Karagwe Tanzania, 2012). Radio is very important in this rural area since literacy remains low among rural farmers and written materials for information dissemination are few. Battery operated radios are common and facilitate information flow.

The sustainability of FADECO's endeavors remains linked to the efforts of its founder. The ongoing activities of FADECO in Karagwe are at least partially supported by outside income (mostly consulting) of its founder, Joseph Sekiku

(Fadeco Community Radio–Karagwe Tanzania, 2012). Since much of his work is done elsewhere, he is often outside the area. This impacts his availability and interaction with the community. FADECO has a website, but it is unfinished, which limits its usefulness in global outreach.

MAVUNO

MAVUNO is a particularly interesting example since it started out as a local microfinance organization to support rural farmers in agricultural development in a single village. Today, it has multiple partnerships with European organizations, broad involvement in several villages, numerous projects in environmental sustainability and agriculture, water tank development programs, needy children programs, seed and food safety programs, and recently launched a cooperative secondary girls' school (MAVUNO Improvement for Community Relief and Services, 2015).

Funding for MAVUNO is substantially local with contributions from its 218 cooperative member families, local community contributions, and its microfinance program with supplementation by small outside grants. MAVUNO is involved in serving about 10,000 people today in several villages. This is quite an achievement given that the organization started with a small number of families and one village 30 years earlier. This NGO's accomplishments are ongoing and linked to the community, with cooperative members being closely involved in decision making and initiatives. Many of the cooperative communities are loosely structured through kinship ties since land historically was allocated through kin groups. Kin groups tend to make community decisions, and the cooperative structure of MAVUNO builds upon this underlying structure. Cooperative members pay dues and then participate in decision making on where to invest or loan these funds to others in their service area. Therefore, microfinance is closely interwoven with local community involvement. Traditionally, microfinance has funded agricultural initiatives, water tanks, or businesses. However, more recently, loans are given for educational expenses to help families pay school fees that are required for both public and private primary and secondary schools.

The development of a local secondary school for girls, which opened in 2016, is yet another example of community-based and -funded initiatives by this NGO. The school is seen as critically important in providing secondary education opportunities for young women. This type of investment has far reaching implications. Public secondary schools in Tanzania are generally some distance from home with crowded classrooms and far more males than females in attendance. Less than 20% of women attend secondary school and less than 5% finish it. (UNICEF, 2010; UNESCO, 2012). Many young women in rural areas report being harassed by males as they walk to school or are in classrooms with them, sexual harassment from male peers and teachers, and sexual involvement with male peers (Ngila et al., 2014; UNICEF, 2010). Girls-only boarding schools address these issues by creating an inclusive space, offering options for schooling in areas where public schools are limited, and by nurturing girls in a segregated educational space. The future payoffs of educating women improve their immediate futures and also the lives of their children (UNICEF 2010). Lower birth rates are also associated with higher education for women (Kravdal, 2012). Since population growth is one of the developmental pressures facing Sub-Saharan Africa, this inverse relationship is quite important. In addition, there may be community domino effects in areas where educated women influence their less well-educated peers to improve literacy and may lower birth rates through community interaction (Kravdal, 2012). Therefore, an investment by MAVUNO in education for women is quite strategic and important to the women, their children, and the broader community.

MAVUNO's development model is sustainable and can serve as a blueprint for implementation of sustainable development goals elsewhere. Major projects are funded through a combination of local donations and strategic international partnerships. This NGO is not dependent on major grants. The secondary school is one example. It has been built over a series of years as funding became available, much of it from the local community or small investors. Beyond serving as a school, the location is also planned to be an agricultural resource site with a storage facility for crop cooperative management prior to shipping to market and as a seed repository for local farmers. MAVUNO has several international partners, but much of their support remains logistical through volunteer activities or special projects such as solar panels for the school.

Lessons of leadership

Numerous factors play a role in the success of grassroots community-based organizations in rural areas in a less-developed country such as the three described above. Table 14.2 provides a list of key components integral to such initiatives and comparisons between these three NGOs. Many of these components are common to success across the globe whereas others such as consensual decision making are more often found in kin-based community governance structures.

Table 14.2: Comparison of Factors Important to Grass-Roots Leadership

	FADECO	WOMEDA	MAVUNO
Entrepreneurial Leadership	X	X	X
Customer Focus: Creating Value	X	X	X
Consensual Decision Making	?	X	X
Responsive to Market	X		X
Sustainable Business Plan Without Outside Funding	?		X
Access to Resources	X	X	X
Access to Education	X	X	X
Access to Market	X	X	X
IT Support and Marketing	X		X
Hire Local Leaders		X	X
Local Funding Source			X
Strategic Use of Partnerships in Building Capacity	X	X	X

The strong leadership demonstrated by these NGOs is partially responsible for their program successes. However, successful and sustainable development in areas such as Karagwe and other rural areas in Sub-Saharan Africa faces multiple challenges due to a lack of infrastructure, the lack of direct access to markets, the need for resources to build infrastructure, the need for skilled educated workers, a means to reach out to the community, much of whom may not be literate, a knowledge of cultural factors promoting consensual decision making, the understanding of kin-based land allotment, and a funding stream to support the programs. For example, most of Karagwe is without tarmac roads; rural areas are still without electricity; access to water remains challenging; internet service is very patchy and poor; secondary school completion remains very low; and most families rely on subsistence agriculture. Each of these NGOs has to not only create a vision and service plan and find funding, but also strategically determine how to attract clients, create a market or get goods to market, build infrastructure, and find committed educated staff.

These three NGOs have all made substantial contributions to their communities through their strong commitment to service to local people and grassroots development. All have built infrastructure as discussed. Two of the three (MAVUNO and FADECO) seek to link local economic potential including agricultural initiatives (farming, bee-keeping, and coffee) to national and global markets. These agricultural initiatives are fundamentally important to building infrastructure. Economic infrastructure investment in crop production and access to market helps to support broader development goals (Andrzejczak, 2015; Boateng, 2011). The post-2015 Sustainable Development Goals mentioned earlier specifically encourage the development of micro small scale enterprises which build infrastructure such as these (Sustainable Development…, 2015). WOMEDA has also successfully broadened infrastructure with its program supporting birth registration. Birth registration is necessary for school registration and for many types of employment. Having a birth certificate also allows citizens to apply for travel passes to cross borders in the East African Community for employment or business in member states, thereby linking local community with regional and international community.

WOMEDA works with other NGOs, the magistrates and justice system, village clan groups, and the schools to establish itself. Its willingness to assist other agencies in human rights support is important to its network building and success. FADECO has created a training center in a rural area for farmers but also uses the radio station to promote development. The radio station broadly disseminates information which facilitates rural training and awareness in an area where rural literacy remains low. MAVUNO achieves its successes in a variety of ways including: consensual decision making within its cooperative; a multilayered cooperative structure involving a substantial number of community members; community networks; building infrastructure such as underground water tanks within several villages; microfinance groups which invest in infrastructure development and education; strategic international partnerships of small investors who build water tanks or fund higher education for prospective staff members; and most recently, by building a girl's secondary boarding school.

MAVUNO's initiatives are community, and demand led. In addition, MAVUNO seeks to improve literacy and alleviate poverty. These are key components in local development (Boateng, 2011; Steel & Webster, 1992). It is the combination of the key components in Table 14.2 which underwrites the success and sustainability evident at MAVUNO. Its promotion of economic opportunity is very productive and supports other initiatives. For example, its members are working on improving local coffee yield in response to the greatly expanded marketing opportunities in the area over the last six years.

This facilitates cash flow for cooperative members and investment in other projects. MAVUNO also has the best internet access and website, which allows them to reach out to global partners. This success is noteworthy given that MAVUNO has been outside the electrical grid until recently (relying on solar panels) and is along a dirt road several kilometers from a nearby market town.

Successful societal entrepreneurship takes many forms as indicated here. Leaders and organizations serve as change agents to varying degrees. The range of their success is determined by multiple factors including the degree of community networks and support (economic and social) and the flexibility of leadership in responding to ongoing change and new possibilities. The ability to make and maintain global networks is likewise important in introducing innovation, providing ideas, and obtaining outside support. In the community environment in Karagwe, as described here, success is also driven by bottom-up involvement by the local community as demonstrated by the many successes of MAVUNO, a community cooperative. Since funding remains a limiting factor for community development NGOs, creating a local source of funding is the most sustainable option. Local funding streams can be quite successful, despite local poverty, as seen with MAVUNO's launch of the girls' secondary school. Similarly, the ability to overcome the limitations of infrastructure and to maintain a global presence via technology is also beneficial to sustainability.

Conclusions

This paper discusses three examples of grassroots organizations in rural Tanzania that serve as societal entrepreneurs. All are successful in development activities in the area as demonstrated by the community initiatives that they have implemented and sustained: an UNESCO affiliated radio station, water provision to over eight communities, legal education programs and birth registration in partnership with the schools and community throughout the district, ongoing microfinance support, and now a cooperative girls' school. All have been in existence for over ten years with stable leadership and ongoing activities. In addition, these organizations have many shared characteristics. These include entrepreneurial leadership, a mission which is service or customer focused, providing education to community groups through a variety of means, enhancing economic development through social justice initiatives, building community infrastructure, and strategic use of partnerships within the community or across the globe. However, funding remains an issue for two of the NGOs discussed here, since they remain somewhat dependent on outside funding or sources of support. The third NGO, MAVUNO, is largely self-supporting through its community-based cooperative model. MAVUNO demonstrates slow and steady growth throughout its twenty years. Its focus is local with strong community- based networks, continued sustainability and ongoing growth. Since these organizations grew out of local community initiatives, community members are invested and remain invested long- term. Additional long-term benefits for NGOs such as MAVUNO include an ongoing funding stream from community members due to their personal involvement and commitment and ongoing community investment through long-standing kinship and village networks. These community-roots initiatives are viable for organizations throughout the world. The model of MAVUNO may be particularly effective in communities where membership is based on real or fictive kin and social interactions and consensual decision making are valued.

Acknowledgements

I thank the marvelous leadership of MAVUNO, FADECO, and WOMEDA for sharing so much with me over the last 15 years. In particular, I am grateful for Charles Bahati, Juma Masisi, and Joseph Sekiku for their constant welcome and guidance.

References

Andrzejczak, K. (2015). Fighting alimentation problems with private sector development through business development services in Sub-Saharan Africa, in I. Gorges (Ed.), *Global Perspectives on Sustainable Regional Development* (pp. 267-288). Hamburg: Verlag Dr. Kovac.

Boateng, N. A. (2011). *Promoting rural enterprise growth and development from four projects in sub-Saharan Africa.* Retrieved from IFAD (International Fund for Agricultural Development): www.ifad.org/pub/pa/field/2.pdf.

Blayton, O. (2008, November). Fadeco: a model to follow. Retrieved from allafricanbazaar.blogspot.com/2008/11/fadeco-model-to-follow.html.

FADECO Web-site. (2016). Retrieved from www.fadeco.info/.

Fadeco Community Radio– Karagwe Tanzania. (2012). Retrieved from fadecofm.wordpress.com/2012/04/28/fadeco-community-radio-karagwe-tanzania/.

Gawell, M., Johanisson, B., & Lundqvist, L. (Eds.). (2009). *Entrepreneurship in the name of society: Reader's digest of a Swedish research anthology.* Stockholm: Knowledge Foundation.

Global economic prospects divergences and risks. (2016). Retrieved from The World Bank, Washington DC. (pubdocs.worldbank.org/en/842861463605615468/Global-Economic-Prospects-June-2016-Divergences-and-risks.pdf).

Karagwe District Council. (2014). Retrieved from karagwedc.go.tz/index.html).

Kravdal, Ø. (2012). Further evidence of community education effects on fertility in sub-Saharan Africa. *Demographic Research*, 27, 645-680. Retrieved from www.demographic-research.org/volumes/vol27/22/27-22.pdf).

MAVUNO Improvement for Community Relief and Services. (2015). Retrieved from www.mavunoproject.org/.

Ngila, W., Role, E., & Makewa, L. (2014). Safety, sexual harassment, sanitary facilities, and household chores as threats to girl child in mixed secondary schools. *Journal of International Forum of Researchers in Education*, 1, 36-53. Retrieved from www.ejournal.ifore.in.

Remarks by President Obama at business leaders' forum. (2013, July). *The White House Briefing Room.* Retrieved from www.whitehouse.gov/the-press-office/2013/07/01/remarks-president-obama-business-leaders-forum.

Sekiku, J. (2007). Retrieved from www.ashoka.org/fellow/joseph-sekiku.

Steel, W. and Webster, L. (1992). How small enterprises in Ghana have responded to adjustment. *World Economic Review*, 6(3), 423-438.

Sustainable Development Goals: Seventeen Goals to Transform Our World. (2015). Retrieved from www.un.org/sustainabledevelopment/.

United Nations Millennium Development Goals Report 2015. (2015). Retrieved from www.un.org/millenniumgoals/2015_MDG_Report/pdf/MDG%202015%20rev%20%28July%201%29.pdf.

UNESCO. (2016). *Empowering local radios with ICTS.* Retrieved from http://en.unesco.org/radioict/radios/fadeco-radio.

UNESCO (2012) *Global partnership for girls' and women's education one year on Tanzania.* Retrieved from www.unesco.org/eri/cp/factsheets_ed/TZ_EDFactSheet.pdf.

UNICEF (2010). *Children and women in Tanzania.* Retrieved from www.unicef.org/tanzania/SITAN_Mainland_report.pdf.

Uphoff, N. (1993). Grassroots organizations and NGOs in rural development: opportunities with diminishing states and expanding markets. *World Development,* 21(4), 607-622.

WOMEDA Web-site (2016). Retrieved from https://www.facebook.com/Womeda-285166848171570/info/?tab=page_info.

Index

A

B

C

D

E

F

G

H

Z

www.ingramcontent.com/pod-product-compliance
Lightning Source LLC
LaVergne TN
LVHW010721210926
848485LV00007B/1410/J